Dear Consumer,

The Montgomery Ward Microwave Oven which you have purchased combines the best in features and technology. Over two hundred engineers and quality control experts work constantly to maintain and improve the high performance of our microwave ovens. We are confident that their exceptionally high quality will provide you with years and years of excellent service.

Inside this cooking guide you will find more than 350 exciting recipes, from Appetizers to Sauces.

Microwave ovens present a new way of cooking for most people. As you adjust to new techniques and timings, you will find that it is really not all that different from conventional cooking. In fact, the biggest difference you will notice is the time you'll save waiting for food to finish cooking. The Gourmet Control feature (variable cooking power) will give you the flexibility to cook many different types of food with excellent results.

Please take the time to read the Operating Instructions that came with your Montgomery Ward Microwave Oven. We suggest keeping this instruction booklet in the pocket inside the front cover of this cooking guide for handy reference. Read the Introduction carefully before starting to cook. If you have any suggestions or ideas that you would like to share with us, please feel free to let us know. If you have a question, please include the model number of your microwave oven when you write.

Marti Murray

Marti Murray
National Home Economist

address all correspondence to:

Home Economist
Montgomery Ward Plaza
Merchandise Dept. 68, C-3
Chicago, Ill. 60671

Adventures in

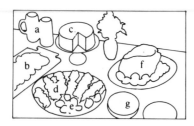

Microwave Cooking

Culinary Arts Institute®

Published Exclusively for Montgomery Ward

ADVENTURES IN MICROWAVE COOKING
**Marti Murray, Montgomery Ward Home Economist
and the Culinary Arts Institute Staff:**

Helen Geist: Director
Sherrill Weary: Editor
Donna Land: Associate Editor and Recipe Tester
Edward Finnegan: Executive Editor
Charles Bozett: Art Director
Malinda Miller: Copy Editor

PHOTO ACKNOWLEDGMENTS
American Dairy Association; American Egg Board;
Artichoke Advisory Board; Bob Scott Studios;
California Avocado Advisory Board; Culinary Arts Institute;
Diamond Walnut Growers, Inc.; Florida Department of Citrus;
Jell-o Gelatin; National Live Stock and Meat Board;
North American Halibut Association; Schieffelin and Company;
Spanish Green Olive Commission; Wheat Flour Institute;
Zdenek Pivecka

Contents

Precautions to Avoid Possible Exposure to Excessive Microwave Energy

(a) Do not attempt to operate this oven with the door open since open-door operation can result in harmful exposure to microwave energy. It is important not to defeat or tamper with the safety interlocks.

(b) Do not place any object between the oven front face and the door or allow soil or cleaner residue to accumulate on sealing surfaces.

(c) Do not operate the oven if it is damaged. It is particularly important that the oven door close properly and that there is no damage to the: (1) Door (bent), (2) Hinges and latches (broken or loosened), (3) Door seals and sealing surface.

(d) The oven should not be adjusted or repaired by anyone except properly qualified service personnel.

(e) Do not operate the oven with the temperature probe caught between the oven front face and the door.

Introduction

WHY COOK IN A MICROWAVE OVEN

Microwave cooking gives you the opportunity to show off your creative skills as a great cook without spending the entire day toiling over a hot stove. Microwave cooking is *fast;* many foods cook two to four times faster than when cooked conventionally; some are even faster than that! Microwave cooking is *cool cooking;* the microwave oven doesn't heat up your whole kitchen when you cook, only the food gets hot! Microwave cooking is *clean cooking;* foods don't burn on the dishes and spatters don't burn on the microwave oven walls, so cleaning is a breeze.

HOW MICROWAVES COOK

Microwave cooking is new to you, and like any new skill takes a little practice. You are accustomed to cooking with a conventional oven or range top using electricity or gas as a source of heat. The oven or cooktop on a conventional range becomes hot and the heat is transferred to the food through conduction or convection.

In a microwave oven foods are cooked by absorbing microwave energy. Microwaves are very short, high-frequency radio waves and are the same type of energy as AM, FM or CB radio, but the wave length is much shorter. The frequency assigned to the microwave oven is 2,450 MHZ (megahertz). The number indicates that the wave is vibrating 2,450 million times per second. The source or generator of the microwave in the microwave oven is the magnetron, which is a vacuum tube that operates as an oscillator (an electronic circuit producing an alternating current) to generate microwaves.

Microwaves travel directly to food without heating the air or the oven cavity. Microwaves are attracted to liquid, sugar, fat or moisture molecules, causing them to vibrate at extremely high speed. The vibrating molecules create friction, thereby creating heat. These vibrating molecules rub against others, starting them also to vibrate and cause heat. This process starts from the outside, where the microwaves first come in contact with the food, and moves toward the center of the food, with the heat from the friction cooking as it goes.

The combination of the microwaves' attraction to specific molecules and the high speed at which they vibrate results in the fantastic speed of microwave cooking. No time is lost in preheating the oven, as the microwaves immediately travel to the food.

Microwave energy is not absorbed by all materials or substances as it is by food. In fact, one of the unique characteristics of microwaves is that they can also be reflected or transmitted.

The metal walls of the microwave oven *reflect* the microwaves entering from the top, bouncing them all over the oven, and thus enabling them to penetrate the food from all sides. Metal pans, therefore, cannot be used in microwave cooking because the microwaves would bounce off the pans and never reach the food.

Paper, plastic and glass will *transmit* the microwaves. As the microwaves hit any of these substances, they pass through. Consequently, these materials are excellent for cooking utensils as the microwaves are neither absorbed nor reflected. For further details about microwave cookware, please refer to pages 14 and 15.

USES FOR THE MICROWAVE OVEN

The microwave oven has unlimited uses, and the secret of getting the most from your microwave oven is to "think microwave" every time you walk into the kitchen, whether you plan to do a quick snack or a gourmet dinner. Nearly all primary cooking can be done in the microwave oven. Exactly how much depends on you and your personal tastes. However, primary cooking is not the only use of the microwave oven. The microwave oven will defrost frozen food in minutes. It is no longer necessary to delay dinner or make a last-minute menu change because you forgot to defrost the meat or unexpected dinner guests arrived.

The microwave oven is also a natural companion for convenience foods, whether they are frozen foods, canned foods or dry mixes. Many convenience food packages have microwave directions.

The microwave oven can be used for heating. Many foods can be served warm in seconds. Gone are the days of cold sweet rolls, pastries, sandwiches, baby food and syrup for pancakes.

Also, reheating food can be done quickly and with excellent results in the microwave oven. Leftovers don't acquire that "warmed-over" flavor, and cleanup is extra easy because the food **won't burn in the dish. Meal planning is much** easier when everyone's dinner can be prepared at the same time, and latecomers can reheat their dinner in the microwave oven and still enjoy that fresh, just-cooked flavor. Or, when your schedule **is going to be extra busy, make your own conven-ience foods; food can be prepared ahead of time** and stored in the refrigerator or freezer to be reheated when needed.

The microwave oven can be used to reheat a cup of cold coffee, or food from a carry-out restaurant that has cooled before getting it home, and also to freshen bread, rolls and cake.

Not only can the microwave oven be used for primary cooking, defrosting, convenience foods, heating and reheating, but it is a great asset for food preparation in general. For example, you can melt chocolate, scald milk, dry bread crumbs or sauté onions in the microwave oven. You can also boil water or melt shortening right in a heat-resistant glass measuring cup. When you "think microwave" all the time, you will discover that much of your food preparation can be done in the microwave oven.

There is another whole area of microwave oven use, and that is combination cooking. There are times when the microwave oven is best used in combination with a conventional cooking appliance. For example, if you want to cook a large chicken on the outdoor grill, start it in the microwave oven before putting it on the grill, to prevent excess charring on the outside. Grill but undercook excess steaks and freeze for a later time; this way you only have to clean the grill **once. A double-crust pie can be baked in the** microwave oven and browned in a hot conventional oven. Cheese or chocolate fondue can be heated in the microwave oven and then transferred to the fondue pot.

Most of your favorite recipes can be converted to microwave cooking. Remember, microwave cooking is much faster than conventional cooking. Find a recipe in this cooking guide that is similar in ingredients and has approximately the same number of servings as your family favorite. Use the directions in the guide recipe for size of dish, cooking time and power level. Use the suggested time as a guide and check often so the food doesn't overcook. Make a notation on the recipe so the next time you want to make that food, you will have all the information you need. "Think

microwave" all the time, and you will be absolutely amazed at the many things your microwave oven is capable of doing.

MICROWAVE TERMS

Learning to use your microwave oven does not mean learning to cook all over again. However, some terms are different and need to be defined in "microwave language." Following is an alphabetical list of microwave terms. Read this list before you begin cooking, but don't feel you have to memorize it. You will probably find it helpful to refer to this section often.

Arcing. Arcing, or sparking, occurs in the microwave oven between separated particles of metal. It can happen between the ends of a metal twist tie, the metalic trim on a dish, or a metal utensil or a piece of aluminum foil that is almost touching the microwave oven wall. If you notice a spark in your microwave oven, remove whatever is causing the arcing, as prolonged arcing could damage your microwave oven.

Browning. You are accustomed to a brown appearance on many foods. Some foods do brown in the microwave oven. Large cuts of meat that require more than fifteen minutes cooking time will brown naturally without any browning aids. The fat in meats attracts microwaves. As the surface temperature increases, natural browning occurs. Smaller cuts of meat cook so quickly that browning does not occur. A browner appearance on steaks, chops and hamburgers can be achieved by using gravy browning sauce, soy sauce, onion soup mix, or dry gravy mix on the meat. The color of fish and poultry can be enhanced by sprinkling paprika on the food, or a coating mix can be used for both flavor and color. Cakes and breads cook very quickly, and since there is no drying heat in the microwave oven, the lack of browning may be disguised by using dark batters, topping with spices or spreading frosting on top. Casseroles can be topped with toasted bread crumbs.

The Browning Element that is part of some microwave ovens gives the eye appeal that you expect to many foods. It works particularly well on baked goods, and in browning the tops of casseroles and smaller cuts of meat. Remember to include browning time as part of the cooking time. Refer to the "Operating Instructions" for specific instructions.

If your microwave oven does not have a

Browning Element, you can obtain the same brown appearance by browning the food under a conventional broiler. Be sure to use a glass-ceramic utensil (i.e., Corningware® Cookware) if you plan to place the food under the broiler. Heat-resistant glass should not be used because the heat of the broiler can cause the glass to break. If you do not have a glass-ceramic utensil, transfer the food to a metal container before placing it under the broiler.

Browning can also be achieved in the microwave oven by using a Browner Grille®. The Browner Grille works like a hot fry-pan. The utensil has a special tin oxide coating on the bottom that must be preheated in the microwave oven. Be careful of where you place it; follow directions that come with the Browner Grille. Use it for sandwiches, steaks or eggs that you would normally fry on top of a conventional range.

Cooking Time. The cooking times given in this book are a guide. A number of factors can cause the time to vary, such as the starting temperature of the food, the quantity of food, type of cookware, and, of course, your personal preference. Check the food at the minimum time to see if it is cooked. If it is not finished cooking, add more time. An additional two or three minutes can overcook the food. If you find that the food is either dry or tough, it has been overcooked. Remember, standing time will finish the cooking; the food should be slightly undercooked when removed from the microwave oven. If it is not cooked enough for your taste, return to the microwave oven. Remember, you can continue cooking undercooked food, but you can't uncook overcooked food.

Even Cooking. Most conventional cooking requires stirring or turning to obtain the most even results, and this is also true with microwave cooking. Most food will require some attention during the cooking period. Even cooking is obtained by stirring, rotating the dish, turning the food over, or rearranging the food at least once during the cooking period.

Every microwave oven has its own particular cooking pattern. If you notice a "hot" or "cold" spot in your microwave oven where one part of the food is cooking at a different rate than the rest, merely stir or rotate the food to compensate.

Quantity (or Volume). Cooking time is determined by the quantity of food in the microwave oven. As you increase the amount of food to be cooked at one time, the cooking time will also increase. For example, one potato takes approximately six minutes to cook in the microwave oven, but two potatoes will take approximately seven to eight minutes. The number of microwaves in the microwave oven remains the same regardless of how much additional food you put in. If you double the quantity of food, the cooking time does not double but will increase by approximately two thirds.

Roast Rack. When you cook roasts in a conventional oven, you use a rack to hold the meat and poultry out of the cooking juices. Microwave cooking needs the same attention to prevent the food from stewing in the juices. There are a number of roast racks designed specifically for microwave cooking. They are made of microwave-safe materials, usually plastic or ceramic. Do not use a metal roast rack in the microwave oven. The roast rack should be placed in a two-quart glass baking dish so you can save the juices to make flavorful gravies. If you do not have a roast rack, an inverted saucer may be used as a substitute. Use the roast rack when cooking bacon for dry, crisp bacon.

The roast rack can also be used without the baking dish for heating sandwiches and breads. This will let the air circulate around the baked product so the excess moisture won't make the bottom of these foods soggy.

Shape of the Food. Microwaves penetrate the food from all directions. The best cooking pattern and least chance of overcooking come from cooking food that is evenly shaped. Whenever possible, the food should be uniform in size. For instance, in casseroles the food will cook more evenly if the ingredients are the same size and shape, and will cook faster if the pieces are smaller. Flat, thin pieces heat faster than large, chunky foods. When cooking a roast, buy one that is uniform in size and shape. A narrower end will cook faster than the rest and result in uneven cooking.

Foods cook better in a round shape; square shapes have corners that absorb more microwaves proportionately to the rest of the food mass. This could cause overcooked areas on the corners. If you notice overcooking, shield the corners with aluminum foil. Use round shapes whenever possible, such as round dishes for cakes or casseroles.

Some foods, like chicken pieces, are naturally uneven in shape. For even cooking, arrange the pieces in a circular pattern with thick portions toward the outside and thin areas toward the inside of the dish.

Shield. Aluminum foil reflects microwaves. There are times when shielding with foil is necessary for even cooking. For example, the leg tips and wing tips of chicken or turkey are very thin and would overcook by the time the remainder of the food was completely cooked. It is necessary to shield the thin areas for part of the cooking period. A small piece of foil can be placed neatly around a thin area during the first half of the cooking time. The foil is removed for the second half of the cooking period so that area of the food may cook. You can also use foil to shield areas that you notice are overcooking, for instance, corners of the food in square dishes or the breast of a large turkey.

Any time aluminum foil is used for shielding, the shielded area must be small in comparison to the whole food volume, otherwise the foil will interfere with the cooking. The foil should be tucked around the food and not stick out. It should never touch the microwave oven wall, another piece of foil or the Temperature Probe.

Starting Temperature of Food. The initial temperature of food will affect the cooking time. A lower temperature requires more microwave energy and time to cook. For example, frozen sweet rolls will take longer to heat than refrigerated sweet rolls, which in turn will take longer to heat than room-temperature rolls. Also, cold water will take longer to boil than warm or hot tap water. If you store your vegetables in the refrigerator, they will take longer to cook than vegetables kept at room temperature.

Temperature Probe. The Temperature Probe gives you truly carefree cooking by letting you know the internal temperature of the food. This is particularly important in meat and poultry cooking so you can cook to the exact degree of doneness you desire. Remember, the internal temperature will increase during the standing time, in large pieces of meat as much as 15 degrees. The Temperature Probe can also be utilized when heating beverages, soups, casseroles and leftovers.

Conventional metal and mercury thermometers cannot be used in the microwave oven during the cooking period. However, the food can be removed from the microwave oven after the minimum time has elapsed and the thermometer can be used to check the internal temperature. If the food is not done, remove the thermometer and return the food to the microwave oven for additional cooking.

Testing for Doneness. You can use most of the conventional tests to determine if the food is done. However, with microwave cooking you must allow for standing time. Therefore, food should be removed from the oven when it is slightly undercooked. A fork can be used to test for tenderness when cooking less-tender cuts of meat or vegetables. Meat and poultry can be checked for correct internal temperature with a Temperature Probe. A cake tester or wooden pick can be used for testing cakes, bar cookies and quick breads. The cake tester or wooden pick should be slightly moist, because the food will complete cooking during the standing time. The cake may also begin to pull away from the sides of the dish.

MICROWAVE TECHNIQUES

In this section, techniques for successful microwave cooking are explained. Many of these techniques are similar to those used in conventional cooking, but some pertain to microwave oven cooking only. All microwave ovens have a cooking pattern whereby some areas get more energy than other areas. It is important to move the food for even cooking. Conventional ovens also have a cooking pattern. The temperature will vary from one spot to another, but because the cooking is so much slower, it is not as obvious.

Arrange. When cooking two or more items in the microwave oven, it is important to place the food carefully so that all the food will cook evenly. Place the food in a circular, doughnut-shaped arrangement, leaving the center free of food. When cooking multiple items, like potatoes, leave at least a one-inch space between pieces so that the microwaves can penetrate the food from all sides and cook evenly. Place thick portions or shapes toward the outside when cooking food such as chicken pieces. If you are reheating food, follow this rule and place the thick food toward the outside of the plate. Food should be placed in a large enough dish so that the pieces are not stacked on top of one another.

Cover. A cover performs one of these functions: it holds in steam and speeds up the cooking, reduces spatters in the microwave oven and absorbs extra moisture.

Plastic wrap or an all-glass lid (without metal trim or metal screws) traps steam around the food that is being cooked. The steam increases the heat, and shortens the cooking time. Foods that need steam in their cooking include all vegetables, many meats, eggs and any dish that requires extra moisture. Fish that is covered with plastic wrap will have a poached flavor and texture. If you have a dish without an all-glass lid, an inverted plate makes a good substitute. When using plastic wrap as a tight-fitting cover, be sure to pierce or vent the plastic before removing it to allow excess steam to escape. Be careful when removing any cover; open it away from you to avoid painful steam burns.

Waxed paper makes an excellent cover to reduce spatters. It holds some heat around the food but does not give it a steamed flavor. Foods that have a dry topping should be covered with waxed paper.

Paper towels are an excellent cover for many baked goods, including sandwiches. The paper towel absorbs extra moisture that accumulates on the bottom of reheated bakery products. Use paper towels on top of cakes as they cook to give them a drier top and shorten the cooking time.

Rearrange. When cooking more than two items at a time, it is necessary to rearrange the foods halfway through the cooking period to allow more even cooking. Follow suggestions under **Arrange** for repositioning. Rearranging the food lets you move cooked peices around to let other pieces cook. It is especially helpful if you notice the food cooking unevenly. Potatoes, cupcakes and chicken pieces are a few foods that need to be rearranged halfway through the cooking time.

Rotate. Some foods cannot be stirred or rearranged as they cook. This pertains particularly to cakes, pies and casseroles that cannot be stirred. To obtain a more evenly cooked food, turn the dish in a clockwise rotation. Most recipes specify either a quarter or a half turn. The lower power settings have greatly reduced the need to rotate dishes. If you notice one side of the food cooking faster than the other or bubbling more, rotate a quarter turn as needed. When the recipe suggests rotating more than once, turn the dish at approximately even time intervals.

Stand. Food will continue to cook after being removed from an oven, whether it is conventional or microwave. However, this is more obvious in microwave cooking. When the microwave oven is turned off, microwave activity stops immediately. The water molecules which are vibrating at 2,450 million times per second can't stop that fast. Additional cooking will continue until they stop. That is why we have "standing time" in microwave cooking. Time must be allowed in the total cooking time to let the temperature in the food equalize. Slightly undercook food; during the standing time it will finish cooking. Remember, food won't look done when removed from the microwave oven.

Small foods (eggs, breads) need only two to five minutes standing time. Medium-size foods (vegetables, fish) need approximately five minutes standing time. Large items (roasts, casseroles) need ten to fifteen minutes standing time. Large turkeys and roasts will need twenty to thirty minutes standing time. Roast and turkey internal temperatures will rise 15 degrees during standing time. Plan to remove the food from the microwave oven when the internal temperature is below the desired degree of doneness. Use your Temperature Probe for best results and follow the charts for the temperature *before* standing time.

Stir. The microwaves heat and cook the food along the outside edges of the dish first. As in conventional cooking, it is necessary to stir to distribute the heat throughout. Gourmet Control reduces the amount of stirring that must be done, but most foods benefit from occasional stirring. In conventional cooking you move the cooked portions away from the bottom; in microwave cooking you move the cooked portions to the center and the cooler areas to the edge of the dish for even cooking. Many recipes suggest stirring a number of times. Stir at approximately even time intervals, or if you notice a food bubbling or starting to overcook, stir as needed. Many foods that need constant stirring when made on a conventional range top (puddings, candies, sauces) need only occasional stirring when cooked in the microwave oven. You can set the time for the total cooking time and interrupt the cooking cycle as needed. Some foods cannot be stirred for even distribution of heat; rearrange these or rotate as the recipe directs.

Turn. To assure even cooking in dense foods, it is advisable to turn the food over halfway through the cooking period. This is usually done for large foods, such as turkey, roasts, chicken. Some smaller foods, such as hamburgers, steaks and whole vegetables, also benefit from this attention, as they do when cooked conventionally.

Microwave-safe utensils

UTENSILS

Microwave cooking lets you use many utensils you already have in your kitchen cupboards; you won't need an entire set of new equipment. You'll also be able to use containers you never thought to cook in. If you are in doubt about whether a particular dish is microwave-safe or not, do this simple test. Put one cup of room-temperature water into a glass measuring cup. Place it in the microwave oven on top of or next to the dish. Microwave one minute at HIGH. If the water becomes hot, the dish is microwave-safe. If the dish is warm or hot, it is not microwave-safe and should not be used in the microwave oven.

Choose a dish large enough for food that is being cooked. A dish that is either too large or too small can affect the cooking time and alter the desired results. Consider the shape of the dish when cooking. A round dish as opposed to a square or rectangular dish will free you from worry about the corners overcooking.

Save on cleanup time by using the dish you prepare and cook in for a serving dish. A dish with handles is ideal. The handles will usually stay cool, but if they become hot, remember it is from the heat of the food, not the microwaves.

There are a number of new cooking utensils being introduced specifically for microwave cooking. They are designed with microwave cooking techniques in mind; for instance, cake dishes with higher sides, ring-shaped dishes, cupcake pans in a circular arrangement, etc. Some of these utensils can be used with both conventional and microwave cooking; refer to the manufacturer's instructions.

Glass, Glass-Ceramic or China. Ovenproof glass (Pyrex® by Corning and Fire King® by Anchor Hocking) is a natural for microwave cooking. It comes in many sizes and shapes which are perfect for many of the foods you cook. Much of the glassware available is also decorative and makes attractive serving pieces. It has the added advantage that you can see through the glass to check on the progress of the food as it cooks. Glass measuring cups are ideal as a measuring and cooking utensil and for easy pouring.

Glass baby bottles and ordinary glass jars can be used in the microwave oven for short heating times.

Glass-ceramic cookware (pyroceram, Corning Ware® by Corning) is ideal for the microwave oven because you can cook, store and serve all in the same container. Look for tags that say it is recommended for microwave cooking. Check to be sure there are no metal parts on the dish; for instance, screws on handles or lids or a metal trim. Remove these if possible. The Browner Grille® is a special pyroceram dish with a tin oxide coating on the bottom. The metal coating attracts microwaves while the dish is preheating in the microwave oven. It creates a very hot surface that sears the food and browns the surface when it is added. The Browner Grille is then returned to the microwave oven with the food to finish cooking.

Ceramic, china and earthenware can all be used for heating food in the microwave oven as long as they pass the dish test. Some dishes have metalic glazes, so be sure to check before using.

DO NOT USE:

- Centura® dinnerware by Corning and the closed-handled cup from Corelle® Livingware by Corning (all other Corelle® is acceptable). Because of the material composition of this dinnerware, it absorbs microwave energy.

- Glass utensils with metal screws, handles or bands.

- Dinnerware with gold or silver trim.

- Lead crystal.

Metal. In general, metal utensils should not be used in the microwave oven because they reflect microwaves away from the food. There are a few exceptions, however. Small pieces of aluminum foil can be used to shield areas that would overcook, such as leg tips and wing tips on chicken or turkey.

Metal skewers or poultry clamps are safe if there is a large quantity of food in proportion to the amount of metal. Do not let skewers touch the microwave oven walls or each other; arcing could occur.

The basic three-section TV dinner and foil trays less than 3/4 inch high can be cooked in the microwave oven, as long as the aluminum foil cover is removed. However, the food won't cook on the bottom. For faster cooking, transfer the food to a nonmetal container.

Temperature Probe and thermometers designed for microwave cooking are also acceptable because of their special design.

DO NOT USE:

- Foil plates or pans more than 3/4 inch high

- Metal cooking utensils, pots, pans, cookie sheets
- Silver or pewter dishes
- Conventional meat thermometers
- Sheets of aluminum foil

Paper. In conventional cooking you would never dream of using paper or paper products for cooking. Paper plates, cups, bowls are all used for cooking and heating food for short periods of time in the microwave oven; however, the paper could burn or the wax coating melt if allowed to heat too long. Plastic-coated paperboard trays can be used for cooking, much as you would use foil trays in conventional cooking.

Paper towels, napkins and waxed paper can all be used as a light cover over foods to prevent spattering. Paper towels and napkins can be used to wrap bread and sandwiches to absorb excess moisture as they are warmed or cooked. Line glass cake pans with paper towels cut to fit, to absorb moisture.

DO NOT USE:

- Paper bags to cook popcorn, as the paper could catch fire from the heat of the popcorn kernels
- Paper products of any kind under the Browning Element
- Paper towels made from recycled materials, as they may contain metal particles
- Foil-lined paper bags, boxes and baking trays, because the food will not be able to cook
- Fast-food cartons with metal handles, unless the handles are removed
- Newspaper, because some types of printer's ink absorb microwaves and could cause the paper to ignite

Plastic. Many plastic utensils work very well in the microwave oven. There are a number of plastics designed specifically for microwave cooking. Most can be used only in the microwave oven; however, a few can also be used in the conventional oven. Read the manufacturer's instructions before using plastic cake pans, roast racks, etc., in your conventional oven. Plastic spoons and spatulas can be left in the microwave oven when cooking sauces and foods that need to be stirred. If the spatula has a wood handle, use it for a short time only, because the wood becomes

hot. Plastic baby bottles can be warmed up in the microwave oven. Rigid, dishwasher-safe plastics can be used in the microwave oven for heating foods; however, the dishes may distort and melt if used to heat foods that get very hot because of their high fat content.

Foam cups and dishes can be used in the microwave oven; they are especially convenient when reheating single servings.

Plastic wrap is used to cover dishes when a tight-fitting lid is needed to hold in the steam. Be sure to pierce the plastic wrap or vent it before removing to allow steam to escape. Cooking bags and oven film can be used as long as the foil strip is removed. Do not use the metal twist to close the bag; tie the bag closed with string. When using cooking bags for meat, add one tablespoon flour to empty bag and shake, coating the bag; this will enable the meat juices to bubble smoothly while cooking.

Foods packaged in boilable plastic pouches are a natural for the microwave oven. Merely puncture the bag or cut an ''X'' in it to allow excess steam to escape.

DO NOT USE:

- Melamine plastic dishes, because the dishes will get hot in the microwave oven; the curing process lets the dishes absorb microwaves
- Freezer containers (such as Tupperware), because they distort easily from the heat of the food
- Lightweight plastic containers that are not dishwasher safe (such as margarine containers) because they can't withstand the heat of the food; they can melt and distort

Straw and Wood. Straw and wood bowls and baskets can be used for short heating periods, such as when warming rolls. Wood spoons can be left in the food as it cooks in the microwave oven; however, if it is a long cooking time the moisture in the wood will heat up, causing the handle of the spoon to become hot.

DO NOT USE:

- Wood cutting boards; the microwaves will dry the wood out and cause it to crack
- Baskets that have metal wires in them; they could cause a fire

Appetizers

Microwave cooking lets you mingle with your guests while you amaze them with the wide variety of tempting nibbles you have prepared with a minimum of last-minute fuss. Many of the appetizers can be prepared the night before and just popped into the microwave oven for last-minute heating as the guests arrive.

Choose appetizers that show off the versatility of microwave cooking. For instance, a very easy last-minute appetizer is cheese and crackers. Simply put a square of cheese on a cracker and heat in your microwave oven just until the cheese bubbles and starts to melt. Be careful not to overcook. Cheese melts rapidly and will become tough if cooked too long. Make use of cheeses that melt easily, like Swiss, Monterey Jack or process cheese spreads. You will find it helpful to use crackers that won't get soggy when a topping is heated on them. Melba toast, shredded wheat crackers and crispy rye crackers are a few that work outstandingly well. The crackers will also remain crisper if the topping is made up ahead of time, stored separately and then put on the cracker just as it is ready to be heated. Another trick for crispy crackers is to line the baking dish with paper towels. This will absorb the extra moisture. Guests may find it fun to make their own hot, tasty hors d'oeuvres from a selection of toppings that you have made before they arrived.

For greater convenience, heat the appetizers right on a microwave-safe serving plate. Remember to arrange individual appetizers in a circle for more even heating. If desired, place a bowl of cold snack food in the center of the serving plate. Or for a warm treat, heat a bowl of your favorite salted nuts for a few minutes for quick and easy munching.

Learn which types of appetizers work better than others in the microwave oven. Pastry hors d'oeuvres, for example, do not work well because there is no dry heat in the microwave oven to give them the needed crispy texture. If it is necessary to serve a large number of appetizers at exactly the same moment, you may find it more efficient and practical to use your conventional oven.

Another plus for microwaving appetizers is that they won't have the opportunity to burn, as can easily happen when heated under conventional broilers or in hot ovens.

For the following 3 recipes, leftover roast beef or cooked beef roast (See Meat Cooking Chart) may be used.

CUCUMBER BEEF ROLLS

2 **packages (3 ounces each) cream cheese**
½ **cup grated cucumber***
¼ **cup grated radishes**
2 **teaspoons onion salt**
18 **to 20 thin slices roasted beef round tip**

1. Soften cream cheese in a glass bowl in microwave oven (30 to 60 seconds at SIMMER).
2. Add cucumber, radishes and onion salt to cream cheese; mix well.
3. Spread mixture on slices of cold roast beef, allowing about 2 teaspoons for each slice; roll up slices, wrap and chill.
4. To serve, cut rolls in halves or thirds, depending upon length; secure each piece with a small wooden pick and arrange on platter.

3 to 4 dozen appetizers

*To grate cucumber, scoop out seedy center portion and grate remainder with skin on and press out liquid before measuring.

GUACAMOLE BEEF ROLLS

1 **medium avocado, peeled**
1 **tablespoon lime juice**
1 **tablespoon grated onion**
½ **teaspoon salt**
½ **teaspoon chili powder**
⅛ **teaspoon coriander**
4 **drops Tabasco**
¼ **cup chopped tomato**
18 **to 20 thin slices roasted beef round tip**

1. Mash avocado. Add lime juice, onion, salt, chili powder, coriander, Tabasco and tomato; combine thoroughly.
2. Spread on slices of cold roast beef, allowing about 2 teaspoons for each slice; roll slices; wrap and chill.
3. To serve, cut rolls in halves or thirds, depending upon length; secure each piece with a small wooden pick and arrange on platter.

3 to 4 dozen appetizers

EASY BEEF AND VEGETABLE APPETIZER

2 **pounds cooked roast beef, cut in ¾- to 1-inch cubes**
Celery sticks
Zucchini slices
Carrot sticks
Russian Dip (page 19)

1. Prepare beef cubes and vegetables, wrap separately and chill.
2. Serve the beef and vegetables with Russian Dip.

RUSSIAN DIP

½ **cup bottled Russian dressing**
1 **cup dairy sour cream**
½ **teaspoon Worcestershire sauce**
1 **tablespoon snipped parsley (optional)**

1. Thoroughly mix Russian dressing, sour cream and Worcestershire sauce. Chill 1 hour or more.
2. Before serving, stir in parsley, if desired, or garnish with parsley.

1½ cups

HOT TUNA CANAPÉS

1 **can (6½ or 7 ounces) tuna**
¼ **cup mayonnaise**
1 **tablespoon ketchup**
¼ **teaspoon salt**
   Few grains ground red pepper
2 **teaspoons finely chopped onion**
¼ **teaspoon Worcestershire sauce**
1 **cucumber**
   Paprika (optional)
48 **Melba toast rounds**
12 **pimento-stuffed olives, sliced**

1. Drain and flake tuna. Add mayonnaise, ketchup, salt, red pepper, onion and Worcestershire sauce.
2. Pare cucumber and slice paper-thin (if desired, sprinkle with paprika).
3. For each canapé, place cucumber slice on toast round, pile tuna mixture in center and top with olive slice.
4. Put 8 canapés in circle on 6 individual paper plates. For each plate, cook uncovered in microwave oven 30 to 60 seconds at HIGH.

HINTS: To add more zip to tuna filling, mix in **1 to 2 teaspoons horseradish** and ½ **teaspoon prepared mustard.**
•You can prepare the tuna filling ahead and refrigerate in a tightly covered container. Or you can prepare the canapés ahead, place on the paper plates and cover tightly with plastic wrap. Just before serving, remove plastic wrap and heat the individual plates 1 to 1¼ minutes at HIGH.

CHEESE AND MUSHROOM CANAPÉS

1 **tablespoon butter**
1 **drop Tabasco**
1 **tablespoon flour**
2 **tablespoons cream**
1 **can (3 ounces) chopped mushrooms, drained; reserve broth**
1 **cup shredded sharp Cheddar cheese**
48 **Melba toast rounds or crackers**
1 **tablespoon chopped parsley**
1 **small jar pimentos, drained and thinly sliced**

1. Melt butter with Tabasco in a 1-quart glass casserole in microwave oven (15 seconds at HIGH).
2. Stir flour into melted butter. Blend in cream and mushroom broth.
3. Add cheese to sauce and cook uncovered in microwave oven 1 minute at HIGH.
4. Stir chopped mushrooms into cheese sauce.
5. Spread mixture on toast rounds or crackers and garnish with parsley and pimento.
6. Put 6 canapés in a circle on 8 individual paper plates. For each plate, cook uncovered in microwave oven 30 seconds at HIGH, or until hot.

PIZZA HORS D'OEUVRES

2 **English muffins**
⅓ **cup tomato paste**
½ **teaspoon oregano**
Dash garlic powder
½ **cup shredded mozzarella**

Optional ingredients:
Chopped onion
Chopped green pepper
Pepperoni
Italian sausage, cooked
Anchovies
Chopped ripe olives
**Pimento-stuffed green
olives, sliced**
Mushrooms
Cooked shrimp
Grated Parmesan cheese

1. Split English muffins in half and toast in toaster.
2. Mix tomato paste, oregano and garlic powder. Spread on toasted muffin halves. Sprinkle with shredded cheese.
3. Top with desired optional ingredients.
4. Cut each muffin half into 4 pieces. Place 8 pieces in a circle on 2 individual paper plates. For each plate, cook uncovered in microwave oven 1 minute at HIGH; or until cheese is melted.

16 appetizers

BEEF BALLS ROSÉ

3 **envelopes beef-flavored
instant broth and
seasoning**
¼ **cup hot water**
2 **pounds ground beef**
1 **egg, beaten**
½ **cup hot water**
¼ **cup (½ stick) butter**
¼ **cup flour**
1 **cup rosé wine**
2 **sprigs parsley**
2 **tablespoons ketchup**
¼ **teaspoon thyme**
1 **clove garlic, crushed**
2 **tablespoons snipped
parsley**

1. Add 1 envelope beef-flavored seasoning to ¼ cup hot water and combine with ground beef and egg. Shape mixture into balls (1 tablespoon each) and put into two 2-quart glass baking dishes, leaving the center open. Cover with waxed paper and cook, one dish at a time, in microwave oven 3 minutes at HIGH; rotate dish one-half turn once. Turn meatballs over and continue cooking 1 minute at HIGH. Pour off liquid. Continue cooking 30 seconds at HIGH. Put meatballs into 1 dish; cover.
2. Stir ½ cup hot water with 2 envelopes seasoning mix until dissolved.
3. Melt butter in a 1½-quart glass bowl in microwave oven (30 seconds at HIGH).
4. Stir flour into butter; add broth and wine gradually, stirring well. Add parsley sprigs, ketchup, thyme and garlic. Cook uncovered in microwave oven 4 minutes at BAKE, or until thickened; stir frequently. Remove parsley.
5. Pour sauce over beef balls. Heat uncovered in microwave oven to serving temperature (2 to 3 minutes at HIGH). Sprinkle with snipped parsley.

About 4 dozen balls

PARTY MEATBALLS

1 **pound ground beef**
1 **tablespoon each finely chopped onion and parsley**
½ **cup soft bread crumbs**
1 **egg, slightly beaten**
2 **tablespoons milk**
1 **teaspoon salt**
¼ **teaspoon garlic salt**
⅛ **teaspoon each allspice and cloves**

1. Combine all ingredients.
2. Form into 40 balls (about 1 inch in diameter). Place 8 balls in a circle on 5 individual paper plates and cover with waxed paper. For each plate, cook in microwave oven 1½ minutes at HIGH.
3. Serve meatballs with fancy picks.

About 40

HINT: Meatballs may be prepared ahead, frozen or refrigerated and cooked at serving time. If frozen, cooking time will be 2½ to 3 minutes at HIGH; if refrigerated, 1½ to 2 minutes at HIGH.

STUFFED MUSHROOMS

32 **fresh mushrooms**
1 **cup fine soft bread crumbs**
1 **cup finely chopped pecans**
2 **tablespoons chili sauce**
2 **tablespoons lemon juice**
1 **teaspoon salt**
⅛ **teaspoon pepper**
1½ **tablespoons chopped parsley**
2 **tablespoons butter**
⅓ **cup finely diced onion**

1. Clean mushrooms; remove stems.*
2. Combine bread crumbs, nuts, chili sauce, lemon juice, salt, pepper and parsley in a bowl.
3. Put butter and onion into an 8-inch glass pie plate. Cook uncovered in microwave oven 3 minutes at HIGH; stir after 1 minute.
4. Add butter and onion to ingredients in bowl; mix.
5. Stuff the mushroom caps generously.
6. Put 8 mushrooms in a circle on 4 individual paper plates and cover with waxed paper. For each plate, cook in microwave oven 1 minute at BAKE; rotate plate one-half turn and continue cooking 1 minute at BAKE, or until hot.

*Mushroom stems can be chopped and mixed with stuffing or saved and used in soup or vegetable recipes.

HINT: Stuffed Mushrooms can be prepared ahead and refrigerated. At serving time, follow above cooking instructions, but increase cooking time.

RUMAKI

½ **pound chicken livers**
1½ **tablespoons honey**
1 **tablespoon soy sauce**
2 **tablespoons vegetable oil**
½ **clove garlic, crushed in a garlic press**
Bacon slices, cut in halves
1 **can (5 ounces) water chestnuts, drained**

1. Rinse chicken livers under running cold water and drain on paper toweling; cut into halves and put into a bowl.
2. Pour a mixture of honey, soy sauce, oil and garlic over the liver pieces; cover. Let stand about 30 minutes, turning pieces occasionally. Remove from marinade and set on paper toweling.
3. Wrap a piece of bacon around a twosome of liver and water chestnut, securing with a wooden pick.
4. Put 6 appetizers in a circle on individual paper plates lined with a triple thickness of paper towels. For each plate, cover with a double thickness of paper towels and cook in microwave oven about 5 minutes at HIGH, or until bacon is done; rotate plate one-half turn after 2½ minutes.
5. Serve hot.

About 18 appetizers

ANGELS ON HORSEBACK

12 **oysters in shells**
   Freshly ground pepper
12 **slices bacon**
 1 **lemon, thinly sliced**

1. To open oysters, place 6 oysters in a round glass cake dish. Heat uncovered in microwave oven 45 seconds to 1 minute at HIGH (time depends on size of oysters), or just until shells open slightly; do not cook oysters.
2. Remove oysters from shells; discard shells. Season oysters with pepper.
3. Arrange 6 slices bacon on a roast rack set in a 2-quart glass baking dish. Cover with a paper towel. Partially cook bacon in microwave oven 2 minutes at HIGH; rearrange bacon as necessary. Repeat with remaining bacon.
4. Wrap a slice of bacon around each oyster; secure with a wooden pick. Arrange on rack. Cover with a paper towel.
5. Cook in microwave oven 3 to 3½ minutes at HIGH (time depends on size of oysters), or until oysters are cooked; rotate dish one-half turn halfway through cooking period.
6. Serve with lemon slices.

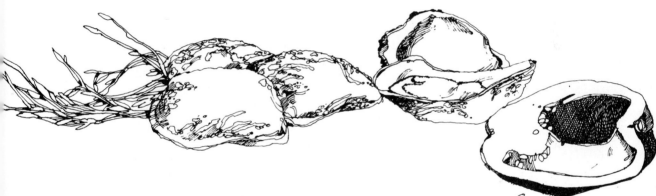

BEEF TERIYAKI KABOBS

 2 **pounds beef loin sirloin**
   steak, cut ¾ inch thick
 ¼ **cup bottled Italian salad**
   dressing
 ½ **cup soy sauce**
 ¼ **cup white wine**
 2 **tablespoons honey**
 ½ **teaspoon ground ginger**
 1 **can (13¼ ounces)**
   pineapple chunks,
   drained
 8 **preserved kumquats,**
   halved
 8 **fresh mushrooms, halved**
 8 **canned water chestnuts,**
   halved

1. Cut steak into ¾-inch cubes and put into a bowl.
2. Combine Italian dressing, soy sauce, wine, honey and ginger in a 1½-pint glass bowl. Heat uncovered in microwave oven to boiling (about 2½ minutes at HIGH).
3. Cool marinade. Pour over beef cubes, cover bowl and marinate in refrigerator at least 1 hour.
4. Remove beef cubes from marinade and thread on bamboo skewers, alternating each cube with a piece of pineapple, kumquat, mushroom or water chestnut.
5. Place kabobs in a large baking dish or on the microwave oven cooking tray. Cover with waxed paper. Cook in microwave oven 2½ minutes at HIGH. Turn each kabob over and rearrange; continue cooking 2½ minutes at HIGH, or until done as desired. Serve hot.

About 15 kabobs

HINT: Kabobs can be done in 2 batches. For each batch cook 1½ minutes at HIGH. Turn kabobs over and continue cooking 1 to 1½ minutes at HIGH, or until done.

FRUIT SHRIMP KABOBS

1 can (8 ounces)
  unsweetened pineapple
  chunks
1 firm ripe small
  cantaloupe
2 oranges
16 cooked shrimp
¼ cup firmly packed brown
  sugar
2 tablespoons cider vinegar

1. Drain pineapple; reserve pineapple juice.
2. Cut cantaloupe into quarters lengthwise, remove rind and cut cantaloupe into chunks.
3. Peel and section oranges.
4. Alternate fruits and shrimp on bamboo skewers, beginning and ending with cantaloupe. Put 4 kabobs into a 2-quart glass baking dish.
5. Mix reserved pineapple juice, brown sugar and vinegar; pour half of liquid over kabobs. Heat uncovered in microwave oven 3 to 4 minutes at BAKE; turn and rearrange kabobs after 1½ minutes.
6. Repeat procedure for remaining kabobs.

8 kabobs

BARBECUED FRANKFURTERS

½ cup ketchup
¼ cup chili sauce
¼ cup water
1 tablespoon
  Worcestershire sauce
1 teaspoon salad oil
1 teaspoon sugar
½ teaspoon salt
  Tabasco (several drops)
4 frankfurters, quartered,
  or 16 cocktail franks

1. Combine all ingredients except franks in an 8-inch round glass cake dish.
2. Add franks to sauce in dish and stir to coat with sauce. Cover with waxed paper. Heat in microwave oven 4 minutes at HIGH; stir after each minute.

HINT: Sauce can be used for additional franks. Heat 1 to 2 minutes at HIGH, or until franks are hot.

CHEESE AND CLAM SPREAD

⅓ cup butter
1 small onion, finely
  chopped
½ small red or green
  pepper, finely chopped
1 can (8½ ounces) minced
  clams, drained
1 pound pasteurized
  process American cheese,
  diced
½ cup ketchup
1 tablespoon
  Worcestershire sauce
1 tablespoon sherry
¼ teaspoon ground red
  pepper

1. Put butter, onion and pepper into a 1½-quart glass casserole. Cook uncovered in microwave oven 3 to 4 minutes at HIGH; stir after 1 minute.
2. Add drained minced clams and remaining ingredients. Mix well and cook uncovered in microwave oven 4 to 5 minutes at HIGH, or until cheese melts; stir mixture often.
3. Serve on **crackers, chips** or **Melba toast rounds**.

About 3 cups

HINT: Spread may be prepared ahead and refrigerated. At serving time, reheat in microwave oven and, if desired, serve from a chafing dish. Mixture must be hot for serving.

CREAMY CORN DIP

Thin slices of rye bread (about 2 inches in diameter) buttered and crisply toasted, or crusty French-bread cubes make perfect "dippers." If using bread cubes, spear with a fork, dunk and twirl in the dip.

> 2 tablespoons butter or margarine
> 2 tablespoons finely chopped green pepper
> ¼ cup flour
> ¼ teaspoon salt
> ⅛ teaspoon ground red pepper
> 1½ cups chicken broth
> 1 cup shredded Swiss cheese
> 1 cup (8-ounce can) cream-style corn
> 4 drops Tabasco

1. Put butter and green pepper into a 1½-quart glass bowl. Cook uncovered in microwave oven 1 minute at HIGH.
2. Add flour, salt and red pepper to mixture in bowl; stir. Blend chicken broth into flour mixture. Cook uncovered in microwave oven 4½ to 6½ minutes at HIGH, or until thickened; stir occasionally.
3. Add cheese to sauce and stir until melted. Stir in corn and Tabasco. Heat uncovered in microwave oven to serving temperature (1½ to 2 minutes at HIGH).

HINT: Dip may be prepared ahead and refrigerated. At serving time, reheat in microwave oven and, if desired, serve from a chafing dish.

TOASTY PUMPKIN SEEDS

> 1 cup pumpkin seeds*
> Salt

1. Rinse seeds, removing fibers.
2. Sprinkle salt lightly over bottom of a large shallow glass baking dish. Arrange moist seeds in a single layer on the salt. Cook uncovered in microwave oven 6 to 7 minutes at HIGH, or until seeds are crisp to the bite; stir after each minute.
3. Remove excess salt before serving.

*Butternut squash seeds or sunflower seeds may be substituted. If using sunflower seeds, cook uncovered 5 minutes at HIGH, or until crisp.

CRISPY NIBBLERS

> 1½ cups stick pretzels
> 1 cup *each* ready-to-eat crisp corn cereal, oat cereal, bite-size shredded wheat biscuits and salted or dry-roasted peanuts
> ¼ cup (½ stick) butter or margarine
> 1 tablespoon Worcestershire sauce
> ¼ teaspoon *each* celery salt, onion salt and garlic salt

1. Combine pretzels, cereal and peanuts in a large glass bowl.
2. Melt butter in a 1-cup glass measuring cup in microwave oven (30 seconds at HIGH).
3. Add seasonings to melted butter and pour over cereal mixture while tossing. Heat uncovered in microwave oven 5 to 6 minutes at HIGH; stir well after each 2 minutes.
4. Serve warm or at room temperature.

Beverages

One of the most convenient daily uses of your microwave oven is for making and reheating beverages. The day of the cold cup of coffee is gone! In a matter of seconds you can reheat the cooled beverage to that piping hot temperature it had been before you were interrupted by an untimely phone call. No need to keep a pot of coffee plugged in all day. The coffee will stay as fresh as when it was perked without getting a bitter taste. Each cup of coffee or tea can be reheated as it is needed, right in the serving cup (microwave-safe, of course!)

A neat trick of microwave cooking is preparing beverages right in the serving cup, and that includes stemmed glassware. Festive punches can be made in the heat-resistant glass punch bowl you use for serving. While some punches may take almost as long to heat as when made on the conventional range, the added convenience of heating in the serving bowl makes it worthwhile. The Temperature Probe can also be effectively used for worry-free heating. What could be easier!

Hot, nutritious milk-based beverages are easy to prepare in the microwave oven. They should be heated in an extra-large container because they can easily boil over; watch them closely and stir often while they are heating. Cooking times for beverages will vary a great deal, depending on the starting temperature of the ingredients. For example, warm tap water will heat much faster than cold water.

If you wish to take the chill off a refrigerated glass of milk, heat at HIGH for a few seconds and stir before serving.

Remember to stir all beverages before serving, to evenly distribute the heat in the container.

INSTANT COFFEE
(Individual Serving)

Water*
Instant coffee

1. Pour water into a microwave-safe serving cup. Add desired amount of instant coffee. Heat in microwave oven to serving temperature (about 1½ to 2 minutes at HIGH).
2. Stir before serving.
*For quick heating, use hot tap water.

HINTS: Additional cups (no more than 4) can be heated at the same time; add 1 to 1¼ minutes per cup to the heating time.
•Cooled coffee can be reheated quickly to serving temperature in about 45 seconds.

INSTANT TEA
(Individual Serving)

Water*
Instant tea or tea bag

1. Pour water into a microwave-safe serving cup. Heat in microwave oven to boiling (about 2 minutes at HIGH).
2. Remove from oven. Add desired amount of instant tea or a tea bag.
3. Stir before serving.
*For quick heating, use hot tap water.

SPICED CITRUS TEA MIX

**1 cup orange-flavored
  breakfast drink mix**
**1 package (about 3 ounces)
  sugar-sweetened
  lemonade mix**
¼ cup instant tea
¼ teaspoon cinnamon
¼ teaspoon cloves

1. Combine all ingredients, mixing thoroughly.
2. To serve, pour water into a microwave-safe serving cup. Add 1½ teaspoons mix or more to taste; stir. Heat uncovered in micro-wave oven to serving temperature (1½ to 2 minutes at HIGH).
3. Stir well before serving.

About 1½ cups mix

HINT: Additional cups (no more than 4) can be heated at the same time; add 1 to 1¼ minutes per cup to the heating time.

HOT CHOCOLATE

**2 ounces (2 squares)
  unsweetened chocolate**
1 cup water
**3 to 4 tablespoons sugar
  Dash salt**
**3 cups milk
  Marshmallows**

1. Put chocolate and water into a 2-quart glass casserole and heat uncovered in microwave oven 4 to 5 minutes at HIGH, or until chocolate melts.
2. Stir chocolate mixture; add sugar and salt. Stir in milk gradually and heat uncovered in microwave oven to boiling (4 to 6 minutes at HIGH); stir occasionally.
3. Beat hot chocolate with rotary beater. Pour over marshmallows in mugs.

4 to 6 servings

FRENCH CHOCOLATE

½ **cup water**
2½ **ounces (2½ squares)**
  unsweetened chocolate
⅔ **cup sugar**
½ **teaspoon salt**
½ **cup whipped cream**
  Hot milk

1. Put water and chocolate into a 1-quart glass measuring cup or 1-quart glass casserole. Heat uncovered in microwave oven 3 to 4 minutes at HIGH, or until the chocolate melts; stir occasionally during heating and stir well at end of heating.
2. Blend sugar and salt into melted chocolate. Heat uncovered in microwave oven 1½ minutes at HIGH.
3. Cool to room temperature. Fold in whipped cream. Store in refrigerator.
4. To serve, place 1 heaping tablespoonful of chocolate mixture in each cup and fill with hot milk. Stir well.

8 to 10 servings

HOT MOCHA DELIGHT

2 **cups water**
2 **ounces (2 squares)**
  semisweet chocolate, cut
  in pieces
1 **cinnamon stick**
  (about 3 inches)
2 **tablespoons sugar**
2 **tablespoons instant coffee**
  (regular or espresso)
½ **cup whipping cream**
  Ground cinnamon

1. Combine water, chocolate, cinnamon stick and sugar in a 1-quart glass measuring cup. Heat uncovered in microwave oven about 5 minutes at HIGH, or until chocolate is melted; stir occasionally.
2. Stir coffee into chocolate mixture. Discard cinnamon stick.
3. Whip the cream. Pour hot mixture into demitasse cups, top with whipped cream and sprinkle with cinnamon.

8 demitasse servings

COCOA

(Individual Serving)

1 **tablespoon unsweetened**
  cocoa
1 **tablespoon sugar**
  Few grains salt
¼ **cup water**
½ **cup milk**
⅛ **teaspoon vanilla extract**

1. Combine cocoa, sugar and salt in a microwave-safe serving cup. Mix in water. Heat uncovered in microwave oven 30 seconds at HIGH.
2. Stir milk and vanilla extract into cocoa mixture. Heat uncovered in microwave oven to serving temperature (about 1 minute at HIGH).
3. Stir before serving.

BUTTERSCOTCH BENCHWARMER

4 cups milk
½ cup butterscotch-flavored pieces
Miniature marshmallows

1. Combine milk and butterscotch pieces in a 4-quart glass bowl. Heat uncovered in microwave oven (about 7 minutes at HIGH), or until butterscotch pieces are melted; stir occasionally.
2. Stir beverage. Pour into glasses or mugs and top with marshmallows.

About 1 quart

CHEERLEADERS' CHOICE

½ cup water
¼ cup red cinnamon candies
¼ cup sugar
2 tablespoons whole cloves
⅛ teaspoon salt
4 cups milk
Cinnamon sticks

1. Combine water, candies, sugar, cloves and salt in a 4-quart glass bowl. Heat uncovered in microwave oven to simmering (about 5 minutes at HIGH); stir after each minute.
2. Strain mixture and return liquid to bowl. Add milk. Heat uncovered in microwave oven to serving temperature (6 to 8 minutes at HIGH, or if using Temperature Probe, set at 160°F and at HIGH); stir occasionally.
3. Stir beverage and pour into glasses or mugs. Serve with cinnamon sticks.

About 1 quart

ORANGE HONEY HERO

4 cups milk
½ cup instant vanilla pudding mix
6 tablespoons thawed frozen orange juice concentrate
1 tablespoon honey
Orange slices (optional)

1. Combine all ingredients in a 4-quart glass bowl. Heat uncovered in microwave oven to serving temperature (about 10 minutes at HIGH, or if using Temperature Probe, set at 160°F and at HIGH); stir occasionally.
2. Stir beverage and pour into glasses or mugs. Garnish with orange slices, if desired.

About 5 cups

GRAPEFRUIT SPRITZER

1 can (6 ounces) frozen grapefruit juice concentrate
2½ to 3 cups chilled club soda

1. Put frozen grapefruit juice concentrate into a pitcher and heat in microwave oven 1 to 2 minutes at HIGH, or until just thawed.
2. Slowly add club soda to pitcher; mix well.

About 4 servings

BUTTERED RUM TODDY
(Individual Serving)

2 ounces rum
1½ teaspoons butter
2 ounces water
Grated nutmeg

1. Put rum and butter into a mug or old-fashioned glass.
2. Measure water in a glass measuring cup. Heat in microwave oven to boiling (about 1 minute at HIGH).
3. Add boiling water to rum and butter; stir well.

HINT: For additional servings, measure rum and butter accordingly. Heat water at HIGH in glass measuring cup as follows: 1½ minutes for 4 ounces water, 2 minutes for 6 ounces and 2½ minutes for 8 ounces.

TOM AND JERRY TODDY
(Individual Serving)

2 teaspoons confectioners' sugar
1 egg, well beaten
2 ounces rum
2 to 4 ounces water
Grated nutmeg

1. Combine sugar, egg and rum in an old-fashioned glass or mug.
2. Measure water in a glass measuring cup. Heat uncovered in microwave oven to boiling (1 to 1½ minutes at HIGH).
3. Fill glass with boiling water; stir. Top with nutmeg.

HINT: For additional servings, combine ingredients in glasses. Heat water at HIGH in glass measuring cup as follows: 2 minutes for 6 ounces and 2½ minutes for 8 ounces.

OLD ENGLISH WASSAIL

3 bottles (12 ounces each) ale
¾ to 1 cup sugar
10 thin strips lemon peel
3 whole cloves
3 whole allspice
1 small cinnamon stick
1 small whole nutmeg, cracked (optional)
1½ cups dry sherry

1. Pour 1 bottle of ale into a heat-resistant glass punch bowl. Add sugar, lemon peel and spices. Heat uncovered in microwave oven to simmering (3 minutes at HIGH).
2. Add sherry and remaining ale. Heat uncovered in microwave oven just to simmering (10 minutes at HIGH), or if using Temperature Probe, set at 160°F and at HIGH.
3. Stir wassail. Remove spices and peel. If desired, float small baked apples or lemon slices in wassail. Serve in heat-resistant punch cups.

About 1½ quarts

HOT SPICED APPLE CIDER

2 quarts sweet apple cider
1 teaspoon whole cloves
1 teaspoon whole allspice
2 cinnamon sticks
(about 3 inches each)
½ cup firmly packed light
brown sugar
Few grains salt
Red apple slices

1. Combine apple cider, cloves, allspice, cinnamon sticks, brown sugar and salt in a heat-resistant glass punch bowl. Heat uncovered in microwave oven to boiling (15 to 20 minutes at HIGH); or if using Temperature Probe, set at 170°F and at HIGH.
2. Stir cider. Remove spices. Serve hot, garnished with apple slices.

About 2 quarts

Breads and Sandwiches

Homemade breads are an exciting addition to any meal. Almost everyone can conjure up memories of Grandmother making bread, and of the wonderful aroma filling the kitchen. But best of all is the memory of the taste of bread fresh from the oven! Many also remember the long hours it took to make those delectable products. The microwave oven can be used to effectively speed up the process.

Breads are generally divided into two groups, quick breads and yeast breads.

Quick breads are even "quicker" to make with the help of your microwave oven. Now you can have a batch of muffins full of plump blueberries for the early risers without having to forfeit your own sleep. But because the cooking time is so fast, quick breads won't have time to brown. This need not be a problem if dark batters are used, or if a topping such as cinnamon and sugar is sprinkled on top. For some breads you might want to use combination cooking: cook until almost done in the microwave oven and then transfer to a preheated conventional oven to finish cooking and browning.

Quick breads, like cakes, have an even texture and a greater volume when made in the microwave oven. Remember to fill baking dishes and muffins pans only half full with batter. To test for doneness, use your conventional test: when a wooden pick is inserted into the center of the bread, it should come out slightly moist but clean. The cooked quick bread will have moist edges when it is removed from the oven. During the standing time, the bread will finish cooking. Covering the bread with a paper towel while it is cooking will help absorb some of the moisture that collects on top of the loaf. You will notice that the term "quick breads" refers not only to the method of preparation, but also to how quickly they'll disappear.

Your microwave oven can also save you time in the preparation of yeast breads. It can be used to defrost, proof and partially bake the bread. The time spent waiting for yeast breads to rise can be cut down dramatically. And even more time can be saved by using prepared frozen breads.

Yeast bread doughs can be completely baked in the microwave oven; however, the appearance of the resulting product will be unlike breads baked conventionally. As there is no hot air in the microwave oven to dry out the surface, a crust will not form. The soft crust will probably be a treat for children who don't like to eat hard crusts. We recommend using the conventional oven to finish baking yeast breads for brown, dry crusts.

Defrosting bread and bakery goods is accomplished quickly and easily in your microwave oven, too! The fast defrosting will keep breads fresh-tasting and tender. When defrosting these products, it is important to remember to open their wrappers to let excess moisture escape. This will help keep the bread from getting soggy. Be sure to remove metal twist ties from the wrapper, since under some conditions the package and twist tie could catch fire. Heating rolls and freshening day-old bread takes only a few seconds. Place the rolls on a paper towel to absorb extra moisture. Heat just until the surface of the bread is warm to the touch. Be careful not to heat these products too long, or they will become tough and dry.

Leftover bread can be turned into croutons for salads and soups. Cut the bread into cubes and season as you like: plain, herb, cheese. Heat in a glass baking dish until dry and crisp. Sealed tightly in a jar, your croutons will keep for weeks.

Tired of the same old lunch-meat sandwich? With microwave cooking, cold sandwiches can be transformed into piping-hot, tasty treats. The addition of a bowl of soup or salad can create a whole meal. When making sandwiches, follow the same tips as for reheating bread; do not overheat. Place sandwiches on paper towels or a roast rack to prevent the bottom of the bread from getting wet and soggy.

Have fun and experiment, the days of the cold sandwiches are gone!

BANANA BREAD

¼ **cup shortening**
1¾ **cups all-purpose flour**
2½ **teaspoons baking powder**
½ **teaspoon salt**
⅔ **cup sugar**
2 **eggs**
1 **cup mashed banana**
   (2 to 3 bananas)

1. Melt shortening in a glass measuring cup in microwave oven (about 1 minute at HIGH). Set aside to cool.
2. Sift flour, baking powder, salt and sugar together into a bowl.
3. In a separate bowl beat the eggs.
4. Add the beaten egg, mashed banana and cooled shortening to dry ingredients. Mix quickly and lightly until dry ingredients are moistened.
5. Line a 1½-quart (8½x4½x2½-inch) glass loaf dish with a paper towel. Turn mixture into dish. Cover with paper towel. Cook in microwave oven 7 to 9 minutes at BAKE, or until done (see page 75); rotate dish one-quarter turn twice during the cooking period.

1 loaf bread

PACKAGED QUICK BREAD

1 **package quick bread mix**
   (such as banana, nut,
   date)

1. Prepare quick bread mix following directions on package. Turn mixture into a 2-quart (9x5x3-inch) glass loaf dish. Cover with a paper towel.
2. Preheat conventional oven to 425°F.
3. Put filled dish into microwave oven. Cook 7 to 10 minutes at BAKE, or until nearly done (insert wooden pick; pick should be slightly moist); rotate dish one-quarter turn twice.
4. Place bread in preheated oven 8 minutes, or until browned.

1 loaf bread

HINT: For a party, bread can be spread with cream cheese and cut into finger sandwiches. Or bread can be cut into shapes with a cookie cutter and spread with **marmalade.**

SOUR CREAM COFFEE CAKE

1 **cup all-purpose flour**
1 **teaspoon baking powder**
½ **teaspoon baking soda**
¼ **teaspoon salt**
¼ **cup (½ stick) butter**
1 **teaspoon vanilla extract**
½ **cup sugar**
1 **egg**
½ **cup dairy sour cream**
½ **cup finely chopped**
   walnuts
2 **tablespoons sugar**
1 **teaspoon cinnamon**

1. Sift flour, baking powder, baking soda and salt together.
2. Cream butter, vanilla extract and ½ cup sugar thoroughly in a bowl. Add egg and beat well. Alternately add dry ingredients and sour cream to creamed mixture, beating until blended after each addition.
3. Spoon half of batter into a greased 8-inch round glass cake dish.
4. Mix walnuts, remaining sugar and cinnamon. Spoon half of nut mixture over batter in dish. Spoon remaining batter into dish and top evenly with remaining nut mixture.
5. Cook uncovered in microwave oven 7 minutes at SIMMER; rotate dish one-half turn after 4 minutes.
6. Cover with plastic wrap and allow to stand 10 minutes in dish. Serve warm.

One 8-inch coffee cake

Packaged Quick Bread

BLUEBERRY MUFFINS

2 cups all-purpose flour
⅓ cup sugar
1 tablespoon baking powder
½ teaspoon salt
1 egg
1 cup milk
¼ cup oil
1 cup frozen whole blueberries
½ teaspoon cinnamon
1 tablespoon sugar

1. Sift flour, ⅓ cup sugar, baking powder and salt together into a bowl.
2. Beat egg slightly in a bowl and blend in milk and oil. Add egg mixture to dry ingredients; mix quickly and lightly just until dry ingredients are moistened. Mix in frozen blueberries.
3. Line microwave-safe muffin-pan wells with 2 paper baking cups each. Fill each well half full with batter, using about ¼ cup batter for each.
4. Sprinkle tops of muffins with a mixture of cinnamon and 1 tablespoon sugar.
5. Cook uncovered in microwave oven 4 to 5 minutes at BAKE; rotate pan one-quarter turn halfway through cooking period.
6. Immediately remove muffins from muffin pan, discard extra baking cups and allow muffins to cool on a rack.
7. Repeat steps 3 through 5, using remaining batter.

About 18 muffins

HINT: Six-ounce glass custard cups can be used in place of the muffin pan. Line with paper baking cups, fill as directed and rearrange once during cooking.

DUMPLINGS

2½ cups beef or chicken broth (canned or made from bouillon cubes)
1 cup sifted all-purpose flour
2 teaspoons baking powder
½ teaspoon salt
½ cup milk
2 tablespoons vegetable oil

1. Pour broth into a 3-quart glass casserole. Cover with an all-glass lid or plastic wrap. Heat in microwave oven to boiling (about 5 minutes at HIGH).
2. Meanwhile, sift flour, baking powder and salt together into a bowl. Combine milk and oil; add to dry ingredients and stir with a fork just until moistened.
3. Drop dumpling mixture by tablespoonfuls onto boiling broth. Cook covered in microwave oven 5½ minutes at HIGH.
4. Allow to stand covered 5 minutes before serving.

4 to 6 servings

QUICK DUMPLINGS

2½ cups beef or chicken broth (canned or made from bouillon cubes)
2 cups all-purpose biscuit mix
¾ cup milk

1. Pour broth into a 3-quart glass casserole. Cover with an all-glass lid or plastic wrap. Heat in microwave oven to boiling (about 5 minutes at HIGH).
2. Meanwhile, combine biscuit mix and milk in a bowl; stir just until dry ingredients are moistened.
3. Drop dumpling mixture by tablespoonfuls onto boiling broth. Cook covered in microwave oven 6 minutes at HIGH.
4. Allow to stand covered 5 minutes before serving.

4 to 6 servings

HERB BREAD

½ **cup (1 stick) soft butter**
2 **teaspoons chopped parsley**
½ **teaspoon salt**
½ **teaspoon basil**
¼ **teaspoon paprika**
1 **loaf French or Vienna bread**

1. Cream butter with parsley, salt, basil and paprika.
2. Cut bread diagonally, almost through to bottom crust, in 12 equal slices. Spread herb butter between slices and over top of loaf. Place bread on paper toweling and heat in microwave oven 1 minute at BAKE.

Onion Bread: Follow recipe for Herb Bread; omit paprika and herbs and add **3 tablespoons minced onion** to butter.

GARLIC BREAD

1 **loaf Vienna bread**
⅓ **cup melted butter**
½ **teaspoon garlic salt**
1 **tablespoon Parmesan cheese**

1. Cut bread, almost through to bottom crust, in ½-inch slices.
2. Combine melted butter, garlic salt and Parmesan cheese. Spread mixture on each slice of bread and brush over top of loaf. Place on paper toweling and heat in microwave oven 45 seconds to 1 minute at BAKE.

HOT DOG/HAMBURGER BUNS

4 **hot dog or hamburger buns**

Place buns in a paper bag; close bag. Heat in microwave oven 20 to 25 seconds at HIGH, or until buns are warm.

BAKED BREAD

(Frozen Dough)

1 **loaf frozen bread dough**

1. Put greased frozen bread dough into a well-greased glass loaf dish (follow directions on package for size of dish). Cover with plastic wrap. Heat in microwave oven 4 to 5 minutes at DEFROST, or until defrosted at edges; turn loaf over each minute. Dough will still be frozen in center. Remove from oven and allow to stand covered.
2. Meanwhile, put 3 cups water into a 1½-quart glass baking dish. Heat uncovered in microwave oven 6 minutes at HIGH, or until very hot. Set a roast rack crosswise on baking dish and place filled loaf dish on it (loaf dish should be above the water and not in it). Allow to stand uncovered in microwave oven 30 minutes.
3. Remove rack and dish of water. Cook bread dough uncovered in microwave oven 5 minutes at KEEP WARM; rotate dish one-quarter turn each minute. Allow to stand in microwave oven 45 minutes, or until dough rises above dish.
4. Preheat conventional oven to 325°F.
5. To partially bake bread, cook uncovered in microwave oven 4 minutes at SIMMER; rotate dish one-quarter turn once.
6. Bake bread in conventional oven 15 to 20 minutes. Remove from dish to rack and cool before slicing.

1 loaf

COTTAGE CHEESE ROLLS

1 teaspoon grated orange peel
¼ cup orange juice
1 package active dry yeast
1 cup (8 ounces) creamed cottage cheese
2 teaspoons caraway seed
1 tablespoon sugar
1 teaspoon salt
¼ teaspoon baking soda
1 egg, slightly beaten
2⅓ cups all-purpose flour

1. Set orange peel aside. Put orange juice into a large glass bowl. Heat uncovered in microwave oven to lukewarm (105° to 115°F), about 15 seconds at HIGH.
2. Sprinkle yeast over orange juice and stir until yeast is dissolved.
3. Heat cottage cheese uncovered in a small glass bowl in microwave oven just to lukewarm (30 to 45 seconds at HIGH). Stir into yeast mixture, then stir in all remaining ingredients, except flour; mix well.
4. Beat in flour gradually, scraping down sides of bowl as necessary, until completely blended; beat vigorously about 20 strokes (dough will be sticky and heavy).
5. Cover with a clean towel; let rise in a warm, draft-free place 1 hour, or until double in bulk.
6. Stir dough down, divide evenly into 12 buttered wells of muffin pans safe for use in microwave and conventional ovens. Cover with a towel, let rise in a warm place 45 minutes, or until double in bulk.
7. Meanwhile, preheat conventional oven to 400°F.
8. Cook uncovered 6 rolls at a time in microwave oven 3 to 5 minutes at SIMMER, or until hollow-sounding when tapped. Rotate pan one-quarter turn during cooking period.
9. Immediately transfer rolls to preheated oven and bake 10 minutes, or until golden brown.
10. Serve while hot.

12 rolls

HINT: Twelve buttered 6-ounce glass custard cups may be used in place of the muffin pans. Rearrange rolls once during microwave cooking time.

DRY BREAD CRUMBS

2 slices white bread

1. Place bread on the microwave oven tray and heat uncovered 1 to 2 minutes at HIGH, or until nearly dry; turn bread over and rearrange once.
2. Let stand 5 minutes. During standing time bread will completely dry. Break bread into pieces and place in an electric blender to crumb.

½ cup

HINT: For additional dry bread crumbs, follow above procedure. Heat only 2 slices of bread at a time in the oven.

CANADIAN MUSHROOM SANDWICHES

6 **kaiser rolls**
Butter or margarine,
softened
1 **tablespoon chopped**
uncooked bacon
2 **tablespoons chopped**
onion
1 **jar (2 ounces) sliced**
mushrooms, drained
1 **teaspoon snipped parsley**
18 **slices (about 1 pound)**
smoked pork loin
Canadian-style bacon, cut
⅛ inch thick
6 **slices (1 ounce each)**
Swiss cheese
6 **thin green pepper rings**
Paprika

1. Split rolls; if desired, reserve tops to accompany open-faced sandwiches. Spread roll bottoms with butter.

2. Combine bacon, onion, mushrooms and parsley in a 2-cup glass measuring cup. Cook uncovered in microwave oven about 2 minutes at HIGH, or until onion is tender; stir once.

3. Arrange 3 slices Canadian bacon on each buttered roll and top with mushroom mixture and 1 slice cheese. Place 1 green pepper ring on each cheese slice; sprinkle paprika inside ring.

4. Place sandwiches on paper towels or roast rack. Heat uncovered in microwave oven 4 to 6 minutes at BAKE, or until cheese is bubbly and meat is hot.

5. If using roll tops, heat uncovered in microwave oven 45 seconds at BAKE.

6. Serve sandwiches garnished with a **cherry tomato** and a **pimento-stuffed olive** on each skewer.

6 open-faced sandwiches

HOT DOGS

Hot dog buns
Hot dogs

Spread bun with **mustard, chili sauce, etc.** Place hot dog in bun and wrap in a paper napkin. The following are suggested cooking times:

1 hot dog—30 to 45 seconds at HIGH
2 hot dogs—45 seconds to 1 minute at HIGH
4 hot dogs—1½ minutes at HIGH

HAM 'N' SWISS CHEESE SANDWICH

½ **cup soft butter**
¼ **cup grated onion**
¼ **cup prepared mustard**
6 **large buns**
6 **slices cooked ham**
6 **slices Swiss cheese**

1. Cream butter with onion and mustard.
2. Spread butter mixture on cut sides of buns. Put ham on bottom halves of buns, cover with cheese, and top with bun halves.
3. Place sandwiches on a paper towel or roast rack. Heat 3 sandwiches at a time in microwave oven 1 to 2 minutes at BAKE, or until cheese is melted.

6 sandwiches

CHEESE 'N' TUNA SALAD SANDWICHES

1 **cup diced or shredded Cheddar cheese**
3 **hard-cooked eggs, chopped**
1 **can (6½ or 7 ounces) tuna, drained and flaked**
1 **teaspoon lemon juice**
2 **tablespoons chopped green pepper**
2 **tablespoons chopped onion**
2 **tablespoons chopped pimento-stuffed olives**
2 **tablespoons chopped sweet pickle**
½ **cup mayonnaise**
8 **buns, split and toasted**

1. Combine all ingredients for filling and mix lightly.
2. Fill buns. Wrap each sandwich in waxed paper. Heat 4 at a time in microwave oven 3½ to 4½ minutes at BAKE.

8 sandwiches

BACON CHEESE-MELT SANDWICHES

6 **slices bacon, halved**
4 **slices bread**
Butter
4 **large tomato slices**
4 **pasteurized process American cheese slices**

1. Arrange bacon on a roast rack set in a 2-quart glass baking dish. Cover with a paper towel. Cook in microwave oven 5 minutes at HIGH.
2. Meanwhile, toast bread and lightly spread with butter.
3. Put toast on roast rack and top with bacon pieces. Put a tomato slice on each toast slice, and then a slice of cheese. Heat uncovered in microwave oven 2 minutes at SIMMER, or until cheese melts. Serve immediately.

4 sandwiches

CORNED BEEF AND SLAW ON RYE

3½ **cups shredded cabbage**
½ **cup white vinegar**
1 **teaspoon caraway seed**
⅓ **cup chopped onion**
½ **teaspoon salt**
 Few grains pepper
12 **to 16 thin slices cooked corned beef**
4 **slices dark rye bread**

Horseradish Sauce:
1 **cup dairy sour cream**
1 **tablespoon prepared horseradish**
 Dash Worcestershire sauce
 Few grains salt

1. Put cabbage, vinegar, caraway, onion, salt and pepper into a 1½-quart glass casserole. Cover with an all-glass lid or plastic wrap. Cook in microwave oven 9 minutes at HIGH; stir once.
2. Put corned beef slices into a shallow glass baking dish. Cover dish with waxed paper. Heat in microwave oven 7 to 8 minutes at BAKE, or until warm.
3. Put 3 or 4 slices corned beef on each rye bread slice. Top each with hot slaw.
4. Combine ingredients for sauce. Serve sauce with sandwiches.

4 sandwiches

SAUCY BEEF 'N' BUNS

2 **tablespoons butter**
½ **cup chopped onion**
1 **pound ground beef**
1 **teaspoon salt**
¼ **teaspoon black pepper**
¾ **cup chopped celery**
¾ **cup chopped green pepper**
1 **cup chili sauce**
1 **cup ketchup**

1. Put butter and onion into a 2-quart glass baking dish. Cook uncovered in microwave oven 4 minutes at HIGH, or until onion is soft; stir after 1 minute.
2. Add meat and cook uncovered in microwave oven 5 minutes at HIGH, or until meat is no longer pink; stir occasionally and separate meat into small pieces. Drain off fat.
3. Blend in remaining ingredients. Cover with waxed paper. Cook in microwave oven 8 to 10 minutes at HIGH; stir occasionally.
4. Serve on buttered toasted **hamburger buns**. (Toast hamburger buns under conventional broiler.)

About 6 servings

SLOPPY JOES

¾ **pound ground beef**
⅓ **cup chopped onion**
⅓ **cup chopped green pepper**
¾ **cup thick tomato sauce**
2 **teaspoons brown sugar**
1 **teaspoon salt**
¼ **teaspoon paprika**
 Few grains pepper
4 **buns**

1. Combine meat, onion and green pepper in an 8-inch round glass cake dish. Cover with waxed paper. Cook in microwave oven 4 minutes at HIGH; stir once.
2. Add tomato sauce and seasonings to meat mixture; stir. Cover and cook in microwave oven 5 to 7 minutes at HIGH; stir occasionally.
3. Split buns; spoon meat mixture onto bottom halves and cover with top halves. Place sandwiches on paper towels or roast rack. Heat uncovered in microwave oven 1 minute at HIGH.

4 sandwiches

Cereal, Rice and Pasta

The great advantage of cooking cereals in your microwave oven is that individual servings can be cooked right in their cereal bowls, eliminating the cooking pan that all too often results in cereal scorched on the bottom. Even children can make their own hot breakfasts using instant cereals, without their parents worrying about burned little fingers.

When cooking cereal in your microwave oven, use a dish larger than normal. Cereals, particularly those made with milk, have a tendency to boil over. Standing time is important to finish the cooking; follow the guidelines in the recipes as to the cooking and standing times. Use a cover to keep the steam trapped around the food and help shorten the cooking time.

Rice is a versatile and exciting dish. Use rice as a pleasant accompaniment to many main courses, or try a rice ring for a elegant buffet. Rice, with the exception of brown rice, takes almost as long to cook in a microwave oven as it does on top of a range because the dried rice grains must be rehydrated. Rice has a more distinctive shape and texture when cooked in a microwave oven than when prepared on a conventional range.

As the rice cooks it will expand, so use a dish two to three times larger than you would ordinarily use. This will also allow the water to boil vigorously. Be sure to cover the container with a glass lid or plastic wrap to hold in the steam necessary to cook the rice. A teaspoon of butter added to the cooking water will prevent the individual grains from sticking to each other. The butter will also prevent boiling over. Note that the standing time is important to finish cooking. Try not to stir or toss the rice while it cooks. This will result in broken, mushy rice.

A real advantage of cooking rice in the microwave oven is that at the end of the set time, the microwave oven automatically turns off. It's not necessary for you to dash back to the kitchen to prevent the rice from overcooking. Rice that is reheated in the microwave oven stays fluffy and moist. Conventionally, it is necessary to add additional water so the rice won't stick to the pan. But with your microwave oven, you can merely cover the dish and the moisture in the rice will create enough steam to gently warm but not overcook the rice. Stir the rice carefully once while it is reheating for an even temperature. This is particularly important if the rice is at refrigerator temperature.

Pasta comes in hundreds of different sizes and shapes. Whether topped with a sauce, stuffed with a filling or buttered and served as a side dish, pasta remains a favorite with everyone. Pasta can be cooked in your microwave oven, but be sure to use a container large enough for the boiling water. Always cover pasta with water to prevent the strands from drying out. Use the suggested time as a guide, but test to see if the pasta is as tender as desired, then drain the liquid and rinse under hot tap water. There is no standing time, so when the pasta is cooked enough for your taste, drain it.

You will find that very little time is saved by cooking pasta in your microwave oven; like rice, pasta needs to be rehydrated. You may find it more advantageous to cook the pasta on the conventional range top and prepare the main dish or sauce in the microwave oven.

CREAM OF WHEAT

2½ **cups water or 3 cups milk**
½ **teaspoon salt**
½ **cup quick-cooking cream of wheat**

1. Combine water, salt and cream of wheat in a 1-quart glass casserole. Cover with an all-glass lid or plastic wrap. Cook in microwave oven 5 to 6 minutes at HIGH; stir after 3 minutes.
2. Allow to stand covered 5 minutes before serving.

About 4 servings

CREAM OF WHEAT

(Individual Serving)

¾ **cup water or milk**
Dash salt
2½ **tablespoons quick-cooking cream of wheat**

1. Combine water, salt and cream of wheat in a microwave-safe serving dish. Cover with plastic wrap. Cook in microwave oven 1½ minutes at HIGH; stir after 1 minute.
2. Allow to stand covered 2 to 3 minutes before serving.

QUICK-COOKING OATMEAL

3 **cups water**
¾ **teaspoon salt**
1½ **cups quick-cooking oats**

1. Combine water, salt and oats in a 1½-quart glass casserole. Cover with an all-glass lid or plastic wrap. Cook in microwave oven 5 to 7 minutes at HIGH; stir after 3 minutes.
2. Allow to stand covered 5 minutes before serving.

4 to 6 servings

HINT: If using old-fashioned oats, increase cooking time to 9 minutes.

QUICK-COOKING OATMEAL

(Individual Serving)

¾ **cup water**
Dash salt
¼ **cup quick-cooking oats**

1. Combine water, salt and oats in a microwave-safe serving dish. Cover with plastic wrap. Cook in microwave oven 1½ minutes at HIGH.
2. Stir, cover and allow to stand 3 minutes before serving.

QUICK-COOKING GRITS

4 cups water
1 cup quick-cooking white hominy grits
1 teaspoon salt

1. Heat water in a 2-quart glass casserole in microwave oven to boiling (about 6 minutes at HIGH).
2. Add grits and salt to boiling water; stir. Cook uncovered in microwave oven 5 minutes at HIGH; stir once during cooking.
3. Cover; allow to stand 5 minutes before serving.

About 6 servings

CORNMEAL

3 cups water
1 teaspoon salt
1 cup cornmeal

1. Combine water, salt and cornmeal in a 1½-quart glass casserole. Cover with an all-glass lid or plastic wrap. Cook in microwave oven 9 minutes at HIGH; stir after 5 minutes.
2. Allow to stand covered 5 minutes before serving.

HONEY GRANOLA

2 cups uncooked old-fashioned oats
¾ cup toasted wheat germ
½ cup chopped almonds or filberts
¼ cup sesame seed
¼ cup oil
⅓ cup honey

1. Combine oats, wheat germ, nuts and sesame seed in a 2-quart glass casserole. Pour oil and honey over mixture; stir to coat. Heat uncovered in microwave oven 5 minutes at HIGH; stir every minute.
2. Turn mixture into a storage container; cool, stirring occasionally. Store covered.
3. If desired, serve granola topped with raisins or snipped dried apricots.

About 3 cups

WILD RICE

2½ cups water
1 teaspoon salt
2 teaspoons butter
1 cup wild rice

1. Combine water, salt and butter in a 2-quart glass casserole. Cover with an all-glass lid or plastic wrap. Heat in microwave oven to boiling (about 5 minutes at HIGH).
2. Add wild rice to casserole; stir to combine. Cover and cook in microwave oven 18 to 22 minutes at SIMMER.
3. Allow to stand covered 5 minutes before serving.

About 4 servings

LONG GRAIN RICE

2 cups water
1 teaspoon salt
1 teaspoon butter
1 cup long grain rice

1. Combine water, salt and butter in a 2-quart glass casserole. Cover with an all-glass lid or plastic wrap. Heat in microwave oven to boiling (about 5 minutes at HIGH).
2. Add rice to casserole; stir to combine. Cover and cook in microwave oven 10 to 14 minutes at SIMMER.
3. Allow to stand covered 5 minutes before serving.

About 4 servings

QUICK-COOKING RICE

1½ cups water
1 teaspoon salt
1½ cups packaged precooked rice

1. Combine water, salt and rice in a 2-quart glass casserole. Cover with an all-glass lid or plastic wrap. Cook in microwave oven 2 to 4 minutes at HIGH.
2. Allow to stand covered 10 minutes before serving.

4 to 6 servings

PACKAGED RICE MIX

1 package (6 ounces) seasoned rice mix
1¾ cups hot water
2 teaspoons butter

1. Combine rice, water and butter in a 3-quart glass casserole. Cover with an all-glass lid or plastic wrap. Cook in microwave oven 5 minutes at HIGH.
2. Continue to cook in microwave oven 12 to 15 minutes at SIMMER.
3. Allow to stand covered 5 minutes before serving.

About 4 servings

CONFETTI RICE RING

4½ cups cooked rice
6 tablespoons butter or margarine
¾ cup snipped parsley
3 canned whole pimentos, drained and chopped

1. Prepare rice. While hot, stir in butter, parsley and pimento.
2. Pack rice mixture into a buttered 5-cup glass ring mold. Cover with plastic wrap.
3. Heat thoroughly in microwave oven (5 to 6 minutes at BAKE). Uncover and allow to stand 3 minutes.
4. Unmold on a warm serving plate. Fill ring as desired.

BROWN RICE

3 cups water
1 teaspoon salt
1 cup brown rice

1. Combine water and salt in a 2-quart glass casserole. Cover with an all-glass lid or plastic wrap. Heat in microwave oven to boiling (about 5 minutes at HIGH).
2. Add brown rice to water; mix. Cover and cook in microwave oven 15 to 17 minutes at HIGH.
3. Allow to stand covered 10 minutes before serving.

About 4 servings

COOKED PASTA

1 quart hot water
1 teaspoon salt
8 ounces macaroni, spaghetti or noodles

1. Combine water and salt in a 3-quart glass casserole. Cover with an all-glass lid or plastic wrap. Heat in microwave oven to boiling (8 to 9 minutes at HIGH).
2. Add pasta and stir through water. Cover and cook in microwave oven 6 to 10 minutes at SIMMER, or until tender; stir once.
3. Drain and rinse with warm water.

4 to 5 cups cooked pasta

FETTUCCINE

8 ounces fine egg noodles
3 tablespoons butter
¼ cup grated Parmesan or Romano cheese

1. Cook noodles following recipe for Cooked Pasta.
2. Return drained noodles to the casserole, add butter and cheese and toss lightly until butter is melted. Serve hot.

About 6 servings

Cheese and Eggs

Many years ago (before microwave ovens were even invented), cooks everywhere knew of the delicate flavor of cheese, and the many uses of eggs. One day, a creative cook mixed these two ingredients with delicious results. The flavor and texture of cheese and eggs complement one another. This partnership has given us many culinary classics: the quiche and the soufflé, to name two. Individually they stand on their own; as a pair they create a taste sensation. The Gourmet Control low-power settings on your microwave oven make it possible to cook some of the most delicate foods with excellent results.

Cheese, a very flavorful food, is often a featured ingredient in recipes. Both natural and process cheeses heat easily because the high fat content attracts microwaves. Natural cheese melts rapidly, but can quickly become stringy if overcooked. Care and attention are needed when cooking with natural cheeses; use process cheese for more foolproof results. The flavors of process cheeses are not as strong as those of natural cheeses, but their smooth texture and ease in cooking may make up for the loss in flavor. Cheese, whether cooked in a microwave oven or conventionally, turns tough and stringy when overcooked. Use the low-power settings for dishes that have cheese as a major ingredient to prevent the cheese mixture from curdling or overcooking.

Cheese is a delicate food. When preparing dishes that require a small amount of cheese as a topping—for instance, casseroles or vegetables—sprinkle the cheese on after the food has finished cooking. The heat of the food during the standing time will melt the cheese on top. Cover with a glass lid or plastic wrap to hold in steam and hasten melting. This method eliminates the chance of overcooking. In recipes that call for cheese slices—for example, sandwiches—layer the cheese slices between the ingredients so the other foods will absorb some microwaves, preventing overcooking of the cheese.

Eggs are a versatile food that can be cooked in many exciting ways. Of course, we all think of eggs as the mainstay for a nutritious breakfast, but egg dishes are equally delicious with other meals. When cooked in a microwave oven, eggs cook quickly and don't scorch in the dish. Egg yolks, like cheese, cook quickly because of the high fat content. If you are making poached or baked eggs, remove the egg from the microwave oven before the white is completely set. Standing time is essential to finish cooking. A cover on the dish will hold in the steam and also speed up cooking.

Poached eggs can be cooked to each person's liking by placing each egg in an individual dish.

Egg recipes that mix the white and yolk cook evenly with excellent results in the microwave oven. Scrambled eggs are light and fluffy and need only a minimum amount of stirring. Omelets are easy to make and can be finished with a variety of fillings. Try an omelet filled with seafood for a change of pace in dinnertime foods.

Use the low-power settings for most egg dishes to let them cook gently and evenly. The exception is scrambled eggs, which can be cooked at HIGH because they are stirred during cooking. Soufflés use both DEFROST and SIMMER to slowly cook the delicate egg-foam structure. Overcooked eggs will be tough and rubbery. Remember standing time will finish the cooking.

For added convenience, omelets and scrambled eggs can be prepared ahead of time and quickly reheated right on the serving plate; no need for the sleepyheads in your family to have cold eggs.

When cooking poached eggs, carefully prick the yolk membrane before cooking to allow built-up steam to escape. Failure to pierce the egg may cause the yolk to burst.

DO NOT COOK EGGS IN THE SHELL IN THE MICROWAVE OVEN. As the egg cooks, steam builds up inside the egg. The only way for the steam to escape is by breaking through the shell. It is impossible to put enough holes in the eggshell to let out the steam. If you need hard-cooked eggs, cook them on top of your conventional range. A word of caution though: do not try to reheat hard-cooked eggs in your microwave oven. The pressure build-up while heating could cause the eggshell to burst.

Welsh Rabbit

WELSH RABBIT

1½ teaspoons butter
2 cups shredded pasteurized process sharp Cheddar cheese
¼ teaspoon Worcestershire sauce
¼ teaspoon dry mustard
  Few grains ground red pepper
⅓ cup milk
  Toast

1. Melt butter in a 1-quart glass casserole in microwave oven (about 15 seconds at HIGH). Add cheese and heat uncovered in microwave oven about 1 minute at HIGH, or until cheese begins to melt; stir after 30 seconds.
2. Add Worcestershire sauce, dry mustard and red pepper to cheese. Add milk gradually, stirring constantly. Heat uncovered in microwave oven to serving temperature (1½ to 2½ minutes at BAKE); stir occasionally.
3. Serve immediately on hot toast.

4 to 6 servings

HINT: Crisp **chopped bacon, tomatoes** or **fresh basil** may be added as garnish.

CHEESE SOUFFLÉ

¼ **cup all-purpose flour**
½ **teaspoon dry mustard**
¾ **teaspoon salt**
⅛ **teaspoon paprika**
¼ **teaspoon Tabasco**
1 **can (13 fluid ounces) evaporated milk**
2 **cups shredded sharp Cheddar cheese**
6 **eggs, separated**
1 **teaspoon cream of tartar**

1. Tie a waxed paper collar around an ungreased 2-quart glass soufflé dish. Set aside.
2. Mix flour, dry mustard, salt and paprika in a 1-quart glass measuring cup. Add Tabasco and then evaporated milk gradually, stirring until smooth.
3. Cook uncovered in microwave oven 3 to 4 minutes at HIGH, or until sauce thickens; stir after 2 minutes, then every 30 seconds. Add cheese and stir until melted. Set aside.
4. Beat egg whites and cream of tartar in a large bowl until stiff, not dry, peaks form.
5. Beat egg yolks in a medium bowl until thick and lemon colored. Gradually add cheese sauce to egg yolks until thoroughly blended. Carefully fold sauce into beaten egg whites.
6. Turn mixture into prepared soufflé dish.
7. Cook uncovered in microwave oven 15 to 18 minutes at SIMMER, or until set at edges; rotate dish one-quarter turn twice. Cook uncovered 10 to 15 minutes at DEFROST, or until top is no longer moist; rotate dish one-quarter turn every 5 minutes.

6 to 8 servings

CHEESE FONDUE

1 **clove garlic, split in half**
¾ **pound natural Swiss cheese, shredded**
⅛ **teaspoon nutmeg Few grains pepper**
1 **to 1½ cups dry white wine**
3 **tablespoons cornstarch**
3 **tablespoons water**
¼ **teaspoon brandy extract Toasted French or Italian bread cubes**

1. Rub garlic on inside of a 2-quart glass casserole. Add cheese, nutmeg, pepper and enough wine to almost cover this mixture. Cook uncovered in microwave oven 4 to 5½ minutes at ROAST, or until the cheese melts; stir occasionally. (The cheese and wine will not be blended.)
2. Make a smooth paste of the cornstarch, water and brandy extract. Add to the cheese mixture and mix well. Cook uncovered in microwave oven 3 minutes at ROAST; stir every 30 seconds until the mixture starts to thicken. (Be careful not to overcook.)
3. Remove from oven and stir until well blended.
4. Serve in a chafing dish or fondue pot. Accompany with toasted bread cubes.

About 3 cups

CHEESE "CROUTONS"

3 **tablespoons butter or margarine**
1½ **cups bite-size shredded wheat biscuits**
½ **cup grated Parmesan cheese**

1. Melt butter in a 1½-quart glass casserole in microwave oven (15 seconds at HIGH).
2. Add shredded wheat biscuits and heat uncovered in microwave oven 1½ minutes at HIGH; stir every 30 seconds.
3. Add cheese and toss lightly to coat biscuits.
4. Serve warm or cool. Store in a tightly covered jar in refrigerator.

1½ cups

CHEESE CREOLE

3 tablespoons butter
¾ cup minced onion
¾ cup chopped green
  pepper
½ cup chopped celery
½ cup milk
¾ cup condensed tomato
  soup
3 cups shredded process
  cheese spread with
  pimento or process
  American cheese spread
3 egg yolks, beaten
12 slices toast

1. Put butter, onion, green pepper and celery into a 2-quart glass casserole. Cook uncovered in microwave oven 5 minutes at HIGH; stir every minute.
2. Add milk and soup to onion mixture; mix well. Continue cooking uncovered 2 minutes at HIGH.
3. Add cheese, stir well and continue cooking uncovered 3½ minutes at ROAST; stir after 2 minutes.
4. Blend some of the hot mixture with egg yolks, then blend into remaining hot mixture. Cook uncovered in microwave oven 2½ to 3 minutes at ROAST; stir once.
5. Serve over toast slices.

About 6 servings

QUICHE LORRAINE

Baked Pastry Shell I or II
  (page 85)
6 slices bacon, cooked
  (page 137) and crumbled
2 cups shredded Swiss
  cheese
3 green onions, thinly
  sliced
3 eggs, slightly beaten
1 cup half-and-half
½ teaspoon salt
⅛ teaspoon pepper
¼ teaspoon nutmeg

1. Prepare pastry shell; set aside.
2. Sprinkle bacon, cheese and onion over bottom of baked pastry shell.
3. Mix eggs, half-and-half, salt, pepper and nutmeg. Pour over ingredients in the pastry shell. Cook uncovered in microwave oven 9½ to 11 minutes at SIMMER, or until center is set; rotate the pie plate one-quarter turn once.
4. Allow to stand 5 minutes before serving.

About 6 servings

POACHED EGGS

2 cups hot water (or
  enough to cover eggs)
4 eggs

1. Put water into a deep 1½-quart glass casserole. Cover with an all-glass lid or plastic wrap. Heat in microwave oven to boiling (4 to 5 minutes at HIGH).
2. Break eggs, one at a time, into a saucer or small dish. Slip each egg into hot water. Cover and cook in microwave oven 1½ to 2 minutes at SIMMER.

Cottage Cheese Rolls, 40; Grapefruit Spritzer, 32;
Eggs Florentine à l'Orange, 56

EGGS FLORENTINE À L'ORANGE

1 package (10 ounces) frozen chopped spinach
1 tablespoon butter
½ cup chopped onion
4 ounces mushrooms, cleaned and sliced
1 teaspoon salt
⅛ teaspoon pepper
1 cup orange sections, cut in half
2 teaspoons butter
4 eggs
   Salt and pepper

1. Put spinach into a glass dish, cover with a paper towel and heat in microwave oven until thawed (about 5 minutes at DEFROST), separating spinach as it thaws. Drain.
2. Put 1 tablespoon butter, onion and mushrooms into a 1½-quart glass baking dish. Cook uncovered in microwave oven 3 to 3½ minutes at HIGH, or until onion and mushrooms are soft; stir twice.
3. Add spinach, 1 teaspoon salt, ⅛ teaspoon pepper and orange pieces to dish; mix well. Divide mixture equally in 4 ramekins or shallow baking dishes. Make a depression in each. Set aside.
4. Put ½ teaspoon butter into each of four 6-ounce glass custard cups; heat in microwave oven until butter is melted (about 15 seconds at HIGH).
5. Slip an egg into each cup and pierce egg yolk. Cover with plastic wrap. Cook in microwave oven 4½ to 5½ minutes at SIMMER, or until nearly set; rotate custard cups once during cooking period.
6. Remove eggs from oven and set aside.
7. Heat ramekins uncovered in microwave oven 2 minutes at HIGH, or until spinach is hot.
8. Slip an egg into depression in each dish and continue heating uncovered 30 seconds at HIGH.

4 servings

FRENCH OMELET

4 eggs
¼ cup milk or water
½ teaspoon salt
⅛ teaspoon pepper
2 tablespoons butter or margarine

1. Beat eggs, milk, salt and pepper together until blended.
2. Melt butter in a 9-inch glass pie plate in microwave oven (about 15 seconds at HIGH).
3. Pour egg mixture into pie plate. Cover with plastic wrap. Cook in microwave oven 4 to 5 minutes at ROAST. As edges of omelet begin to thicken, draw cooked portions toward the center with a spoon or fork to allow uncooked mixture to flow to bottom; tilt pie plate as necessary, but do not stir.
4. Remove omelet from the oven before it is completely set. Fold in half. Allow to stand covered a few minutes before serving.

2 or 3 servings

COTTAGE CHEESE OMELET

4 eggs
¼ cup water or milk
½ teaspoon salt
⅛ teaspoon pepper
⅔ cup creamed cottage cheese
1½ tablespoons finely chopped pimento
2 teaspoons minced chives
2 tablespoons butter or margarine

1. Beat eggs, water, salt and pepper together until blended.
2. Mix cottage cheese, pimento and chives thoroughly and blend into egg mixture.
3. Melt butter in a 9-inch glass pie plate in microwave oven (about 15 seconds at HIGH).
4. Pour cheese-egg mixture into pie plate. Cover with plastic wrap. Cook in microwave oven 4 to 5 minutes at ROAST. As edges of omelet begin to thicken, draw cooked portions toward the center with a spoon or fork to allow uncooked mixture to flow to bottom; tilt pie plate as necessary, but do not stir.
5. Remove omelet from oven before it is completely set. Fold in half. Allow to stand covered a few minutes before serving.

About 3 servings

DENVER OMELET

2 **tablespoons butter**
3 **tablespoons chopped green pepper**
3 **tablespoons chopped green onion**
4 **eggs**
⅛ **teaspoon salt**
⅛ **teaspoon pepper**
3 **tablespoons chopped pimento**
½ **cup finely diced ham**

1. Put butter, green pepper and green onion into a 9-inch glass pie plate. Cook uncovered in microwave oven 3 minutes at HIGH, or until green pepper is soft; stir after 1 minute.
2. Beat eggs slightly in a bowl and mix in salt, pepper, pimento and ham. Pour into pie plate. Cover with plastic wrap.
3. Cook in microwave oven 4 to 5 minutes at ROAST, or until almost set. Draw cooked portions toward the center with a spoon or fork to allow uncooked mixture to flow to bottom; tilt pie plate as necessary, but do not stir.
4. Remove omelet from oven and fold in half. Allow to stand covered a few minutes before serving.

3 servings

HINT: Prepare ahead, if desired, and refrigerate; cover with plastic wrap and heat 45 to 60 seconds at HIGH.

CRAB MEAT OMELET

1 **tablespoon butter or margarine**
1 **package (6 ounces) frozen crab meat, thawed, drained and flaked**
2 **teaspoons finely chopped onion**
2 **teaspoons dried parsley**
¼ **cup dairy sour cream**
1 **tablespoon dry sherry**
8 **eggs**
¼ **cup water**
1 **teaspoon salt**
¼ **teaspoon pepper**
2 **tablespoons butter**

1. For filling, melt 1 tablespoon butter in a small glass dish in microwave oven (15 seconds at HIGH). Add crab meat, onion and parsley; mix well. Cover with plastic wrap. Cook 1½ to 2 minutes at HIGH.
2. Add sour cream and sherry to crab mixture; mix well. Set aside.
3. For omelets, beat eggs slightly in a bowl. Add water, salt and pepper; beat.
4. Melt 1 tablespoon butter in a 9-inch glass pie plate in microwave oven (30 seconds at HIGH). Pour half the beaten eggs into pie plate. Cover with plastic wrap. Cook 4 minutes at BAKE. As edges of omelet begin to thicken, draw cooked portions toward the center with a fork to allow uncooked mixture to flow to bottom; tilt pie plate as necessary, but do not stir. Remove omelet from oven before it is completely set. Allow to stand covered a few minutes.
5. Place half the crab filling in the middle of omelet. Fold omelet in thirds to enclose filling.
6. Repeat procedure for making omelet, using the remaining butter, beaten eggs and crab meat filling. Garnish with **parsley**. Serve hot.

4 servings

EGGS BENEDICT

2 **English muffins, split**
4 **(¼-inch) slices smoked pork loin Canadian-style bacon**
4 **Poached Eggs (page 54)**
Hollandaise Sauce (page 177)

1. Toast muffins in toaster; keep warm.
2. Put Canadian bacon in a glass pie plate. Cover with waxed paper. Heat in microwave oven 2 to 3 minutes at HIGH.
3. Put muffin halves on individual serving plates; top with bacon slices, poached eggs and Hollandaise Sauce. Serve immediately.

4 servings

COUNTRY-STYLE EGGS

4 slices bacon
2 tablespoons butter
2 cups shredded cooked
  potatoes, or 6 ounces
  packaged frozen hash
  brown potatoes, cooked
¼ cup chopped onion
¼ cup chopped green
  pepper
6 eggs
¼ cup milk
½ teaspoon salt
  Dash pepper
1 cup shredded mild
  Cheddar cheese

1. Arrange bacon on roast rack set in a 2-quart glass baking dish. Cover with a paper towel. Cook in microwave oven 4 to 6 minutes at HIGH, or until done. Crumble bacon and set aside.
2. Put butter, potato, onion and green pepper into a 2½-quart 10-inch shallow glass casserole. Cook uncovered in microwave oven 12 minutes at HIGH, or until vegetables are tender; stir after 1 minute, then stir once halfway through cooking period.
3. Mix eggs, milk, salt and pepper. Flatten potato mixture and pour egg mixture over top. Cover with an all-glass lid or plastic wrap. Cook in microwave oven 5 to 6 minutes at ROAST, or until egg mixture is almost set; rotate casserole one-quarter turn once.
4. Sprinkle bacon and cheese over top of egg mixture. Heat uncovered in microwave oven 45 seconds at ROAST, or until cheese just starts to melt.
5. Remove from oven and allow to stand covered 5 minutes.
6. Cut into wedges to serve.

4 to 6 servings

CREAMED EGGS

6 eggs
2 cups Medium White
  Sauce (page 176)
  Salt and pepper
  (optional)
  Toast

1. Hard-cook eggs on a conventional range.
2. Dice eggs into ½-inch pieces and put into a 1-quart glass casserole. Add white sauce and seasoning, if desired; mix. Cover with an all-glass lid or plastic wrap. Heat in microwave oven to serving temperature (2½ to 3 minutes at BAKE).
3. Serve creamed eggs on toast.

6 servings

CREAMED EGGS AND MUSHROOMS

1 small can (⅔ cup)
  evaporated milk
½ pound pasteurized
  process American cheese,
  shredded
4 hard-cooked eggs,
  quartered
½ cup drained canned
  broiled-in-butter
  mushrooms
  Salt and pepper
  Toast

1. Heat milk in a 1½-quart glass casserole in microwave oven 1½ minutes at HIGH.
2. Add cheese, eggs and mushrooms to milk. Heat uncovered in microwave oven to serving temperature (3 to 5½ minutes at ROAST); stir occasionally.
3. Season to taste with salt and pepper and serve over toast.

HINT: Do *not* hard-cook eggs in microwave oven; cook conventionally.

Variations: **Cooked asparagus, green beans** or **ham** may be added.

Scrambled Eggs

SCRAMBLED EGGS

4 eggs
¼ cup milk or cream
Salt
1 tablespoon butter

1. Beat eggs; add milk and salt to taste.
2. Melt butter in an 8-inch round glass cake dish in microwave oven (about 15 seconds at HIGH). Pour egg mixture into dish. Cook uncovered 3 minutes at HIGH, or until nearly set; stir after 2 minutes.
3. Remove from oven; stir and allow to stand covered a few minutes before serving.

2 servings

BAKED EGGS IN SOUR CREAM

1 tablespoon butter
1 teaspoon flour
1 cup dairy sour cream
4 eggs
Salt and pepper

1. Melt butter in a 1½-quart glass casserole in microwave oven (about 15 seconds at HIGH). Blend in flour, then sour cream. Cook uncovered in microwave oven 1 to 2 minutes at HIGH, or until hot and bubbly; stir occasionally.
2. Break eggs, one at a time, into a custard cup and carefully slip egg into the hot sour cream. Cover with an all-glass lid or plastic wrap. Cook in microwave oven 5 to 6 minutes at ROAST, or until whites are nearly set.
3. Remove from oven and allow to stand covered a few minutes before serving. Sprinkle with salt and pepper.

4 servings

AMERICAN SCRAMBLED EGGS

4 **eggs**
¼ **teaspoon salt**
Few grains pepper
¼ **cup finely shredded
American cheese**
1½ **tablespoons butter**

1. Beat eggs, salt, pepper and cheese with a fork until just blended.
2. Melt butter in a 1-quart glass casserole in microwave oven (15 seconds at HIGH). Pour egg mixture into casserole. Cook uncovered 3 to 4 minutes at HIGH, or until eggs are almost set; stir twice during cooking.
3. Remove from oven; stir and allow to stand covered a few minutes before serving.

2 servings

Scrambled Eggs with Tomato: Follow recipe for American Scrambled Eggs; add to the beaten egg mixture ¼ **teaspoon Worcestershire sauce** and ⅓ **cup chopped peeled tomato**. Top with **herb croutons** before serving.

BACON AND CREAM CHEESE SCRAMBLED EGGS

¼ **cup milk or cream**
2 **ounces cream cheese**
3 **tablespoons butter or
margarine**
4 **eggs**
¼ **teaspoon salt**
⅛ **teaspoon pepper**
½ **cup cooked diced bacon**

1. Put milk, cream cheese and butter into a 1-quart glass casserole. Heat uncovered in microwave oven 15 to 30 seconds at HIGH, or until cream cheese is softened; stir to blend.
2. Beat eggs, salt and pepper until blended. Add egg mixture and bacon to cheese mixture. Cook uncovered in microwave oven 2½ to 3 minutes at HIGH, or until eggs are almost set; stir after 2 minutes.
3. Remove from oven; stir and allow to stand covered a few minutes before serving.

2 servings

ORIENTAL SCRAMBLED EGGS

2 .**tablespoons butter**
1 **jar (2½ ounces) sliced
mushrooms, drained**
¾ **cup finely chopped celery**
2 **green onions with some
green tops, sliced**
4 **eggs, slightly beaten**
¼ **teaspoon salt**
⅛ **teaspoon pepper**
½ **cup well-drained bean
sprouts**
¾ **cup chopped cooked
chicken**

1. Put butter, mushrooms, celery and onion into an 8-inch round glass cake dish. Cook uncovered in microwave oven 2 minutes at HIGH; stir after 1 minute.
2. Combine eggs, salt, pepper, bean sprouts and chicken; add to vegetables and mix. Cover with plastic wrap and continue cooking about 4 minutes at HIGH; stir every 30 seconds.
3. Remove from oven; stir and allow to stand covered a few minutes before serving.

About 4 servings

EGG FOO YUNG

2 teaspoons butter or
  margarine
⅓ cup chopped onion
4 eggs
½ teaspoon salt
  Few grains pepper
1 cup drained bean sprouts
2 teaspoons butter or
  margarine
  Soy sauce

1. Put 2 teaspoons butter and onion into a glass pie plate. Cook uncovered in microwave oven 4 minutes at HIGH; stir twice.
2. Beat eggs, salt and pepper together until well blended but not foamy. Mix in bean sprouts and cooked onion.
3. Put ½ teaspoon butter into each of four 10-ounce glass casseroles. Heat in microwave oven until butter is melted (about 15 seconds at HIGH).
4. Divide egg mixture evenly in the dishes. Cover with plastic wrap and cook in microwave oven 5½ minutes at ROAST. Stir; rearrange the casseroles. Continue to cook 3 to 4½ minutes at ROAST, or until almost set.
5. Remove from oven and let stand covered several minutes. Loosen around edges and invert onto plates. Serve with soy sauce.

4 servings

CORNED BEEF HASH AND EGGS

1 can (15½ ounces) corned
  beef hash
½ teaspoon Worcestershire
  sauce
4 eggs
  Salt and pepper

1. Combine corned beef hash and Worcestershire sauce. Divide the mixture evenly into four 10-ounce glass casseroles. Make a well with back of spoon in each portion of hash. Break eggs, one at a time, and slip into wells. Sprinkle eggs with salt and pepper. Pierce egg yolks. Cover with all-glass lids or plastic wrap.
2. Cook in microwave oven 6 to 8 minutes at SIMMER, or until nearly set; rotate casseroles one-quarter turn twice.
3. Remove from oven and allow to stand covered about 1 minute before serving.

4 servings

MACARONI AND CHEESE

3 cups cooked elbow
  macaroni (page 49)
3 tablespoons butter or
  margarine
3 tablespoons flour
½ teaspoon salt
  Dash pepper
2 cups milk
2 cups shredded pasteurized
  process sharp Cheddar
  cheese
  Paprika (optional)

1. Prepare macaroni and set aside.
2. Melt butter in a 2-quart glass casserole in microwave oven (about 30 seconds at HIGH). Blend in flour, salt and pepper. Add milk gradually, stirring constantly. Cook uncovered in microwave oven 8 minutes at HIGH; stir often.
3. Add cheese to sauce; stir. Cook uncovered in microwave oven 1 minute at HIGH.
4. Add cooked macaroni to cheese sauce; mix. Cook uncovered in microwave oven 8½ to 10 minutes at BAKE; stir halfway through cooking period.
5. Sprinkle with paprika, if desired.

6 servings

DINNER IN FREEZER

HEAT IN MICROWAVE

MOM

Convenience Foods

Convenience foods and microwave ovens are natural partners. The time-saving advantages of both make them an integral part of a busy household. Many convenience foods now list microwave directions. Follow the directions on the packages as a guide to check for doneness after the minimum time has elapsed. The food industry every day introduces new foods specifically designed for microwave ovens.

In general, when cooking convenience foods, cover to shorten the cooking time and prevent spatters in the microwave oven. Use covered casseroles or dishes or cover with plastic wrap. Be careful when removing covers not to get a steam burn.

Frozen foods, especially precooked meals, adapt well to the microwave. TV dinners have been the mainstay of many people when they have a hectic schedule. The basic three-section TV dinner can be cooked in the foil tray in the microwave oven; however, it will cook much faster if the frozen food is popped out of the foil tray and put on a microwave-safe plate. Cook one dinner at a time. When heating the food directly in the foil tray, remove the foil cover, then cover with waxed paper or return to its original box to hold the moisture around the food. It you notice any rough edges on the foil tray, turn them down to prevent arcing. If bread or dessert is included with the dinner, remove from the tray and heat separately.

The more sections there are in the foil tray, the longer it will take for the food to cook in the microwave oven. If the dinner consists of more than three sections it will be best to remove the contents to a glass casserole for heating.

Family-size main dishes frequently are packaged in aluminum foil trays. If the tray is more than 3/4 inch high, remove the food to a glass casserole for cooking, because the height of the tray will not let microwaves penetrate the food from the sides or bottom. The only area that can absorb microwaves is the top, and that would overcook before the food is heated throughout.

When cooking frozen food in plastic pouches, be sure to puncture the pouch before cooking to let steam escape. For serving ease, cut an "X" in the pouch and place the pouch "X" side down in a glass casserole or dish. Do not add water. When cooking is completed, grasp the top of the pouch and the food will pour out into your serving dish.

Canned foods of a wide variety, from soups to vegetables to main dishes, are convenience foods that have become a standard in most households. To heat canned foods, remove the contents from the can and place in a glass casserole or serving dish. These foods will heat quickly to serving temperature. Stir halfway through the cooking period for even distribution of heat. Some canned foods, for instance canned soups, can be heated using the Temperature Probe to the exact serving temperature you desire.

There are a great number of dry mixes available to save you time in the kitchen. Some of these foods have microwave cooking directions. If not, follow package instructions but cook in the microwave oven in microwave-safe dish. Dry mixes that are dehydrated will need time to absorb water. They will take almost as long to prepare in the microwave oven as when done conventionally.

Some foods can be heated directly in a glass jar. But a word of caution; if the jar has a small, restricted neck in comparison to the rest of the shape, remove the contents from the jar and heat in a separate container. It is possible for enough pressure to build up inside the jar to break it. Baby food should be removed from the jar to a small glass dish for heating.

Many food companies are working to design convenience foods exclusively for microwave ovens. Many foods have both microwave and conventional cooking directions on the package. A third group prints an address to contact for microwave directions for the food products. There are many exciting new food products coming, so keep a watchful eye in your supermarket for the newest in convenience foods.

Convenience foods prepared

CONVENIENCE FOODS

FROZEN FOODS

Food	Quantity	Cooking Time	Procedure
Beef stew	10-oz. pouch	7-8 minutes at HIGH	Cut an "X" in the pouch and place pouch "X" side down in a glass casserole. Cook 5 minutes. Remove pouch, cover and continue cooking. Stir once.
Breakfast in aluminum tray	4½ oz.	2-3 minutes at HIGH	Remove aluminum foil top and cover with waxed paper or plastic wrap.
Cabbage rolls, stuffed	14 oz.	7-9 minutes at HIGH	Place cabbage rolls in a 1½-qt. glass casserole and cover. Turn cabbage rolls over once during the cooking period.
Chicken à la king	5 oz.	3-5 minutes at HIGH	Cut an "X" in the pouch and place pouch "X" side down in a glass casserole.
Chicken, batter fried	16 oz.	8-10 minutes at HIGH	Place chicken in a glass baking dish with thin portion of chicken pieces toward the center. Do *not* pile chicken.
Chicken, creamed	6½ oz.	5-6 minutes at HIGH	Place creamed chicken in a 1-qt. glass casserole. Cover. Stir once.
Fish sticks, breaded	4 fish sticks	1½-2½ minutes at HIGH	Arrange fish sticks in a circle on a paper plate. Cook uncovered until fish flakes easily.
Lasagna	21 oz.	19-24 minutes at BAKE	Place lasagna in a glass baking dish. Cover with plastic wrap and heat for 10 minutes. Rotate the dish one-half turn. Continue to heat 9-14 minutes, or until heated through.
Macaroni, beef and tomatoes	11½ oz.	7-8 minutes at HIGH	Place macaroni casserole in 1½-qt. glass casserole. Cover. Stir once.
Macaroni and cheese	12 oz.	8½-11 minutes at BAKE	Place macaroni and cheese in 1½-qt. glass casserole. Cover. Stir once.
Peppers, stuffed	2 servings	8-10 minutes at HIGH	Place peppers in glass casserole and cover. Stir sauce once.
Potatoes, baked, stuffed	2	5-7 minutes at HIGH	Place potatoes in a glass baking dish; cover with waxed paper.
Potatoes, Tater Tots	16 oz.	4-6 minutes at HIGH	Spread potato pieces on a paper plate.
Pot pie	8 oz.	8-10 minutes at HIGH	Remove pot pie from aluminum foil container and place in glass casserole. If additional browning is desired, place in conventional oven at 425°F for an additional 15 minutes, or brown top under microwave browning element for 7 minutes.

Assortment of frozen foods includes products that are being test marketed at this time and are only in limited distribution

Food	Quantity	Cooking Time	Procedure
Rice, frozen cooked	10-oz. pouch	5 minutes at HIGH	Cut an "X" in the pouch and place pouch "X" side down in a glass casserole.
Salisbury steak with gravy	14 oz.	8-10 minutes at HIGH	Place steaks in a glass baking dish and cover with plastic wrap. After 5 minutes separate steaks and turn over.
Sauce, frozen	8 oz.	2½-3 minutes at HIGH	Place sauce in a 2-cup glass measuring cup; stir once.
Scallops or shrimp, breaded	7 oz.	1-2 minutes at HIGH	Arrange fish in a circle on a paper plate and cook uncovered.
Spaghetti and sauce	14-oz. pouch	5-7 minutes at HIGH	Cut an "X" in the pouch and place pouch "X" side down in a glass casserole.
Swiss fondue	10-oz. pouch	5½-7 minutes at ROAST	Cut an "X" in the pouch and place pouch "X" side down in a glass casserole. Stir well before serving.

Convenience Foods (cont.)

Food	Quantity	Cooking Time	Procedure
TV DINNERS			
Meat and potato entrée	9-10 oz.	6-7 minutes at HIGH	Remove aluminum foil cover and cover with waxed paper or plastic wrap. Or, food can be transferred to a nonmetal cooking utensil or plate; reduce cooking time 1 minute.
Meat and two vegetables	16 oz.	7-8 minutes at HIGH	Same as above.
Complete dinner: soup, meat, vegetable and dessert	16 oz.	2 minutes at HIGH	Heat soup first in separate container, 2 minutes.
		7 minutes at HIGH	Place remaining food in a nonmetal cooking utensil or plate, cover with waxed paper and heat 7 minutes.
Tuna-noodle casserole	11½ oz.	6-7 minutes at HIGH	Transfer contents of package to a 1½-qt. glass casserole. Cover. Stir once.
Welsh rarebit	10 oz.	5-6 minutes at HIGH	Place welsh rarebit in 1-qt. glass casserole. Cook covered. Stir after the first 2 minutes, then at the end of each minute.
CANNED FOODS			
Baked beans	21 oz.	5-7 minutes at HIGH	Empty beans into 1½-qt. glass casserole; cover. Stir once during cooking period and before serving.
Beef gravy	10½ oz.	3-4 minutes at HIGH	Empty gravy into 2-cup glass measuring cup. Stir once during heating period and before serving.
Beef stew	24 oz.	7-9 minutes at HIGH	Empty stew into 2-qt. glass casserole; cover. Stir twice during cooking period and before serving.
Potato salad, German style	15 oz.	5-6 minutes at HIGH	Empty potato salad into 1½-qt. glass casserole; cover. Stir once during cooking period and before serving.
Sauce	8 oz.	1½-2 minutes at HIGH	Empty sauce into 2-cup glass measuring cup. Stir once during cooking period and before serving.
Soup	10¾ oz.	3-4 minutes at HIGH	Add milk or water to soup in 2-qt. glass casserole; cover. Stir once or twice during cooking period and before serving.
Spaghetti with meat balls	15 oz.	5-6 minutes at HIGH	Empty spaghetti into 1½-qt. glass casserole; cover. Stir once during cooking period and before serving.

Food	Quantity	Cooking Time	Procedure
Vegetables	8 oz.	1½-2 minutes at HIGH	Empty vegetables into 1-qt. glass casserole; cover. Stir once during cooking period and before serving.
	12 oz.	2-2½ minutes at HIGH	Same as above.
	16 oz.	2½-3½ minutes at HIGH	Empty vegetables into 1½-qt. glass casserole; cover. Stir once during cooking period and before serving.

DRY MIXES

Food	Quantity	Cooking Time	Procedure
Dehydrated soup mix	2½-oz. pkgs. with 4 cups water	6-8 minutes at HIGH to heat water; 4-5 minutes at HIGH to heat soup	Pour water into 2-qt. glass casserole and heat to boiling. Add soup mix. Stir once.
Hamburger Helper	1 pkg.	5 minutes at HIGH to cook meat; 18-22 minutes at HIGH	Cook meat first in 3-qt. glass casserole. Add mix and water according to package directions. Cover and cook 18-22 minutes. Stir occasionally.
Hash brown potatoes	6 oz.	12 minutes at HIGH	Follow instructions for rehydrating. Stir once.
Instant mashed potatoes	3-4 servings	2-3 minutes at HIGH	Heat water, butter and salt in microwave oven.
Noodles Romanoff mix	6¼ oz.	10 minutes at HIGH	Add 1½ cups water and ½ cup milk to mix in a 2-qt. glass casserole. Cover and cook. Stir occasionally.
Scalloped potatoes mix	5⅛ oz.	15-18 minutes at HIGH	Follow package instructions and place all ingredients in a 3-qt. glass casserole. Cover and cook until potatoes are tender. Stir occasionally.
Skillet casserole mixes	12-18 oz.	5 minutes at HIGH to cook meat; 7 minutes at HIGH to cook casserole	Cook meat first in a 2-qt. glass casserole. Add remaining ingredients, reducing liquid by ¼ cup. Cover and cook. Stir occasionally.
Tuna Helper	1 pkg.	18-22 minutes at HIGH	Place tuna in a 3-qt. glass casserole. Add mix and water according to package directions. Cover and cook 18-22 minutes. Stir occasionally.

Defrosting and Reheating

It's been one of those days: when you get home, you discover you forgot to defrost the meat for dinner. Don't panic! You can defrost and cook the whole meal in your microwave oven. Dinner won't be hours later than you planned, nor will you have to change your menu.

Defrosting was the first major benefit of microwave ovens. Technology has given us the special defrost setting that eliminates much of the attention necessary to prevent food from cooking while defrosting. Successful results can be achieved by following the times given in the charts in this chapter; standing time will let the temperature equalize. If you notice that the food is defrosting unevenly and starting to cook, just rotate the food in the oven.

When defrosting, leave the food wrapped in the original freezer wrapping paper, unless it is wrapped in aluminum foil. Foods like frozen fish can be defrosted right in the package. Some foods, particularly bakery products, are packaged in plastic bags with a metal twist tie. It is imperative to remove the twist tie, because it could ignite in the microwave oven.

Foods that are frozen in a block but have many pieces will defrost more evenly and quickly if the pieces are separated after half of the defrosting time.

Hot dogs and other foods with a tight skin need to have the skin pierced before defrosting so the steam can escape. This rule also applies to plastic pouches.

Being able to defrost meats in your microwave oven can save you many anxious moments and is easy to do. In general, meat can be defrosted in its freezer wrappings. Roasts sometimes require a little special attention. Cover the roast with waxed paper while it is defrosting to hold the warmth around the food, and rotate for even defrosting. If corners get warm or start to cook, shield with aluminum foil.

Ground meat needs attention. As the edges defrost, remove the thawed portions to prevent the meat from cooking.

Defrost a turkey in its original plastic package. As the turkey defrosts, pour off the liquid that accumulates. Leave the metal clamp that holds the legs together in the turkey, but don't let it touch the oven walls.

Frozen fruit will taste garden fresh if you let a few ice crystals remain. Flex plastic pouches to break the pieces and aid in even defrosting. Orange juice can be defrosted in its cardboard container as long as the metal top is removed and the container is not foil-lined. Breads and cakes defrost quickly; watch carefully to avoid defrosting too long.

Your freezer and microwave oven are natural partners. Leftovers or large quantities of food can be frozen for quick meals at a later date. Remember to follow good home freezing techniques. Be sure to blanch fresh vegetables first (see Preserving chapter) before freezing.

When packaging food for freezing, wrap in materials that go directly from freezer to microwave oven. If possible, freeze the food in the dish that will be used for reheating. Make your own TV dinners by using sectional paper plates.

You can also use your microwave oven to reheat foods without loss of quality or texture; they will taste freshly cooked. Foods don't burn or scorch in the pan, so cleanup is easy.

Reheating dinner for one or two people is very easy. Place the desired quantity on a microwave-safe dinner plate, cover with waxed paper to hold in the heat and moisture and heat in the microwave oven. As a general rule, the food will be hot when the center of the plate feels hot on the bottom.

When reheating, be careful not to cook the food further, merely heat it. Add gravy to keep the meat from drying out. Use caution when reheating rare meat so that it doesn't become well done. A paper towel under bread and baked products will keep the bottom from getting soggy.

Quick defrosting and reheating of foods

DEFROSTING

The automatic defrost control automatically cycles the microwave energy on and off for defrosting. Some foods will require additional attention during the defrost cycle to prevent cooking on the outside. Refer to the chart for direction.

Set oven control at DEFROST for all foods in this chart, unless otherwise designated. At the end of the defrost cycle, some ice crystals should remain in the center of the food. The food will finish thawing during the standing time. If corners begin to cook, protect those areas with small pieces of foil.

Most foods can be defrosted in their original package, as long as there is no metal. **Be sure to remove metal twist ties from any paper or plastic wrappers. Food in metal containers more than ¾ inch high should be transferred to a glass container for thawing.**

Food	*Quantity*	*Procedure and Time*
MEAT		
Bacon	1 lb.	Defrost 3 minutes—turn package over. Defrost 2 minutes, or until bacon strips can be separated.
Chops	1 lb.	Defrost 4 minutes—separate and turn meat over. Defrost 2 minutes—stand 5 minutes.
	2 lbs.	Defrost 6 minutes—separate and turn meat over. Defrost 4 minutes—stand 5 minutes. Defrost 2 minutes—stand 5 minutes.
Ground meat, beef or pork	1 lb.	Defrost 3 minutes—remove thawed portion. Defrost 2 minutes—remove thawed portion. Defrost 1 minute—stand 5 minutes.
	2 lbs.	Defrost 5 minutes—remove thawed portion. Defrost 3 minutes—remove thawed portion. Defrost 2 minutes—remove thawed portion. Defrost 1 minute—stand 5 minutes.
	4 patties	Defrost 3 minutes—stand 5 minutes.
Hot dogs	1 lb.	Defrost 4 minutes—stand 3 minutes or until hot dogs can be separated.
Roast	2 lbs.	Defrost 8 minutes—turn meat over—stand 10 minutes, shield warm areas with foil. Defrost 4 minutes—stand 10 minutes.
	3 lbs.	Defrost 10 minutes—turn meat over—stand 10 minutes, shield warm areas with foil. Defrost 6 minutes—stand 10 minutes.
Sausage, pork, bulk	1 lb.	Defrost 4 minutes—separate sausage. Defrost 2 minutes—stand 3 minutes.
Spareribs, pork	3 lbs.	Defrost 6 minutes—separate and turn meat over. Defrost 4 minutes—stand 10 minutes.
Steak (sirloin or round)	1-1½ lbs.	Defrost 5 minutes—turn meat over. Defrost 2 minutes—stand 10 minutes.
Stew meat	1½ lbs.	Defrost 5 minutes—separate meat. Defrost 3 minutes—stand 5 minutes.

Food	*Quantity*	*Procedure and Time*
POULTRY		
Chicken pieces	2½-3¼ lbs.	Defrost 8 minutes—separate chicken pieces. Defrost 3 minutes—remove wings. Defrost 2 minutes—stand 10 minutes.
Chicken, whole	2 lbs.	Defrost 6 minutes—turn chicken over, shield warm areas with foil. Defrost 4 minutes—stand 10 minutes.*
	3 lbs.	Defrost 8 minutes—turn chicken over, shield warm areas with foil. Defrost 4 minutes—stand 10 minutes. Defrost 4 minutes—stand 10 minutes.*
		*If chicken is not thawed enough to remove giblets, run under cold water.
Cornish hen	1-lb. hen	Defrost 5 minutes—turn hen over. Defrost 3 minutes—stand 5-10 minutes.
	2 1-lb. hens	Defrost 8 minutes—turn hens over. Defrost 6 minutes—stand 10 minutes.
Duckling	4-5 lbs.	Defrost 10 minutes—stand 10 minutes, shield warm areas with foil. Defrost 8 minutes—stand in cold water 30 minutes.
Turkey breast	5 lbs.	Defrost 10 minutes—stand 10 minutes. Defrost 8 minutes—stand 10 minutes.
leg	2 (10 oz. each)	Defrost 5 minutes—stand 5 minutes.
roast	2½-3 lbs.	Defrost 8 minutes—stand 10 minutes. Defrost 6 minutes—stand 10 minutes.
whole	12 lbs.	Defrost 20 minutes—turn turkey over; stand 10 minutes, shield warm areas with foil. Defrost 15 minutes—stand in cold water 1 hour or until thawed, remove giblets.
SEAFOOD		
Crab (pouch)	6 oz.	Defrost 2 minutes—separate pieces.
Fish fillets	1 lb.	Defrost 2 minutes—turn fish over. Defrost 2 minutes—stand 5 minutes.
Fish, whole	12 oz.	Defrost 4 minutes—turn fish over. Defrost 4 minutes—rinse cavity in cold water until thawed.
Lobster tail	8 oz.	Defrost 3 minutes—stand 5 minutes.
Shrimp	1 lb.	Defrost 1 minute—separate shrimp. Defrost 1 minute—stand 5 minutes.
BREAD		
Loaf, small*	1 lb.	Defrost 1½-2 minutes at HIGH—stand 5 minutes.
Dinner rolls*	12	Defrost 1-2 minutes at HIGH—stand 5 minutes.

*Remove any metal twist ties before defrosting.

Defrosting (cont.)

Food	Quantity	Procedure and Time
DESSERTS		
Brownies	13 oz.	Defrost 1-1½ minutes at HIGH—stand 10 minutes.
Cake	17-20 oz.	Defrost 1-2 minutes at HIGH—stand 10 minutes.
Cheesecake	19 oz.	Defrost 3-4 minutes—cut into pieces and stand 15 minutes.
Fruit	10 oz.	Defrost 1-2 minutes at HIGH—stand 5 minutes.
Non-dairy whipped topping	4½ oz.	Defrost 30-45 seconds at HIGH—stir well.
	9 oz.	Defrost 45-60 seconds at HIGH—stir well.
MISCELLANEOUS		
Egg substitute*	8 oz.	Defrost 2½-3½ minutes—shake well and stand 10 minutes.
Frozen orange juice	6 oz.	Defrost 1½-2½ minutes at HIGH—stand 3 minutes. (Remove metal lid from one end to defrost.)
Hash brown potatoes	12 oz.	Defrost 5 minutes—stir halfway through and stand 5 minutes.
Pancake batter*	7 oz.	Defrost 2-3 minutes—shake well and stand 10 minutes.

*Open carton to defrost.

REHEATING

The following is a basic chart for foods frequently reheated in the microwave oven. The times are based on 1 serving. For each additional serving, increase the time by ⅔ of the original time. For example, if one serving takes 45 seconds to reheat, 2 servings will take 1 minute 15 seconds and 3 servings will take 1 minute 45 seconds.

A rule of thumb for reheating foods that are not on the chart is 1½ minutes per cup measure or 1½ minutes per 8 ounces of weight.

To keep the food from drying out, cover with an all-glass lid, plastic wrap or waxed paper, unless otherwise indicated.

FOR UNITS WITH "REHEAT" SETTING: IF REHEATING TIME IS MORE THAN 30 SECONDS, USE "REHEAT" SETTING. IF REHEATING TIME IS LESS THAN 30 SECONDS, USE "HIGH" SETTING.

FOR UNITS WITHOUT "REHEAT" SETTING: USE "HIGH" SETTING AND MINIMUM TIMES, AS SHOWN ON TIME CHART.

Food	Time*	Special Instructions
MEAT AND EGGS		
Bacon (3 slices)	20-30 seconds	Place bacon on paper plate or paper towel. Cover with a paper towel.
Casserole (1 serving)	45 sec.-1½ min.	Cover and stir once during the heating period. Additional servings may require additional stirring.
Chicken (6-8 oz.)	45 sec.-1¼ min.	Place chicken on plate or glass utensil and cover with waxed paper.

Food	*Time**	*Special Instructions*
Fish (3-4 oz.)	30-45 seconds	Place fish on plate or in glass utensil and cover with waxed paper.
Hamburger (4 oz.)	45 sec.-1½ min.	Place hamburger on plate or in glass utensil and cover.
Omelet	45-60 seconds	Heat covered on microwave-safe serving plate.
Roast beef (1 slice)	30-45 seconds	Place beef on plate or in glass utensil and cover with plastic wrap.
Steaks and chops (1)	45 sec.-1½ min.	Place meat on a plate or in a glass utensil and cover.
Scrambled eggs (1 serving)	20-30 seconds	Cover and stir once during the heating period.
VEGETABLES		
Vegetables (4 oz.)	30-45 seconds	Cover and stir once during the heating period. Additional servings may require additional stirring.
Mashed potatoes (1 serving)	45 sec.-1 min.	Cover and stir once during the heating period. Additional servings may require additional stirring.
BREADS		
Bread slice (1)	10-15 seconds	Place bread on a paper towel.
Pastries (1 serving) includes pie and cake	15-30 seconds	Place pastries on paper towel.
Roll (1)	10-15 seconds	Place roll on paper towel.
Sandwich (1)	20-45 seconds	Wrap sandwich in waxed paper or a paper napkin.
Sweet roll (1)	15-30 seconds	Place roll on paper towel.

*These times are a guide and may vary depending on quantity and temperature of food to be reheated. Check after minimum time has elapsed. Overheating will result in a tough, dried-out product.

Desserts

A homemade dessert makes any meal a festive occasion. Satisfy your family's or your guests' sweet tooth by serving a flaming fruit dessert or a luscious pie to complete a lovely dinner. Candy or bar cookies will be appreciated for a midafternoon or late night snack. The microwave oven makes preparation of these treats quick and easy. Many desserts can be cooked right in a glass or ceramic serving dish.

Cakes made in the microwave oven are moist, airy and fluffy. They have a greater volume than conventionally baked cakes because there is no dry heat in the microwave oven to form a crust. A round glass or plastic cake dish will give the best results; no need to worry about corners overcooking. Line the cake dish with two layers of paper toweling; this will absorb extra moisture and make it easy to remove the cake when it is finished cooking. If you plan to serve the cake directly from the dish, lightly grease but do not flour. Cover the cake with a paper towel while it is cooking to absorb the extra moisture on top.

As in conventional baking, the cake is cooked when the top springs back or a wooden pick inserted in the center comes out clean. You will notice moist spots on top of the cake; the moisture will evaporate during the standing time. Microwave cakes are moist! If your cake is dry, it is overcooked. A more even top will be obtained by rotating the cake dish. Fill the cake dish only half full and refrigerate the leftover batter to make fresh cupcakes for tomorrow's lunch. Cakes are one item that won't brown in a microwave oven, but by using either dark batters or a frosting this will not be ovbious. Angel food and chiffon cakes don't bake successfully because they need dry heat to form the cake structure.

Bar-type cookies turn out exceptionally well when cooked in the microwave oven. However, like cakes, they won't turn brown because of the short cooking time. Dark batters or spices, as well as frosting, help make a pleasing appearance. Use conventional cake-testing techniques for doneness.

An elegant finale to any dinner is a homemade pie. Crumb crusts can be made quickly and easily in a microwave oven. The only dish you need is the glass pie plate for mixing and cooking. A one-crust pastry shell can be completely cooked in the microwave oven for a tender, flaky crust. Use a clear glass pie plate and check at the end of the cooking time for raw spots. A brown appearance can be obtained by brushing with vanilla extract, adding yellow food coloring to the dough, using the browning element in the microwave oven or browning in a hot conventional oven. Making a two-crust pie in your microwave oven is best accomplished by using combination cooking. Cook the filled pie in the microwave oven and brown in a preheated conventional oven.

You can make delicious candy with only occasional stirring because the microwaves are absorbed from all surfaces—top, bottom and sides. Sugar syrups need containers two to three times greater than the ingredient volume to avoid boiling over. The sugar syrup gets very hot; use a container that can withstand the high temperatures without breaking. Be careful when moving the container that it doesn't spill. The hot candy could cause serious burns. Refer to the Syrup and Candies Chart for candy tests.

Fruit desserts cooked in the microwave oven retain their refreshing flavor and color because of the short cooking time. Most fruits need little or no water. Cook fruit desserts until the fruit is fork tender. Remember to allow about five minutes standing time to complete the cooking, to assure soft and tender desserts.

Raisins plump quickly by heating with one tablespoon water for thirty seconds; other dried fruits need to be covered with water and heated for six minutes at HIGH.

Custards and puddings are microwave specialities. The Gourmet Control lets you cook them gently and without constant stirring. For ease of preparation and clean-up, they can be prepared right in the glass measuring cup. Plan to use a glass dish that is twice as large as the food volume to prevent spillovers. Standing time will finish the cooking. Be careful not to overcook. Overcooked custards will curdle and separate.

YELLOW CAKE

½ cup shortening
1 teaspoon vanilla extract
1 cup sugar
2 eggs
2 cups plus 2 tablespoons sifted cake flour
2 teaspoons baking powder
½ teaspoon salt
¾ cup milk

1. Line two 8-inch round glass cake dishes with 2 layers of paper towels cut to fit. Set aside.
2. Cream shortening, vanilla extract and sugar thoroughly in a large bowl. Add eggs, one at a time, and beat thoroughly after each.
3. Sift flour, baking powder and salt together. Alternately add flour mixture and milk to creamed mixture, beating until blended after each addition.
4. Divide batter evenly in the lined cake dishes. Tap the bottom of each dish to remove large air bubbles. Cover each with a paper towel. Cook one layer at a time in microwave oven 4 to 5 minutes at BAKE, or until done (see page 75); rotate dish one-quarter turn twice.
5. Cool on a rack 5 minutes before removing cake from dish.
6. Run a knife around edge of each dish, invert on rack, remove dish and peel off paper.

Two 8-inch round cake layers

OLD-FASHIONED FUDGE CAKE

4 ounces (4 squares) unsweetened chocolate
⅔ cup butter
1 teaspoon vanilla extract
1¾ cups sugar
2 eggs
2½ cups sifted cake flour
1¼ teaspoons baking soda
½ teaspoon salt
1¼ cups ice water

1. Line two 8-inch round glass cake dishes with 2 layers of paper towels cut to fit. Set aside.
2. Melt chocolate in a glass custard cup in microwave oven (1½ to 2 minutes at HIGH). Cool.
3. Cream butter, vanilla extract and sugar thoroughly. Add eggs, one at a time, beating well after each addition. Beat in melted chocolate.
4. Sift flour, baking soda and salt together. Alternately add flour mixture and ice water to creamed mixture, beating until blended after each addition.
5. Divide batter evenly in the lined cake dishes. Tap the bottom of the dish to remove large air bubbles. Cover with a paper towel. Cook one layer at a time in microwave oven 7 to 8½ minutes at BAKE, or until done (see page 75); rotate dish one-quarter turn once.
6. Cool on rack 5 minutes, then remove cake from dish and peel off paper.

Two 8-inch cake layers

CUPCAKE COOKING CHART

Prepare cake mix according to package directions. Put 2 paper baking cups into each well of a microwave-safe muffin pan. Fill cups half full with batter and cook in microwave oven at BAKE.

Cook as follows:

Number	Minutes
2	1
4	1½
6	2

(rotate pan after 1 minute)

Cupcakes will be moist at edges. Remove from pan and discard outer paper cup. Allow to cool on rack before frosting as desired.

APPLESAUCE CAKE

1½ **cups sifted cake flour**
½ **teaspoon baking soda**
½ **teaspoon salt**
1 **teaspoon cinnamon**
½ **teaspoon each cloves,
  nutmeg and allspice**
½ **cup shortening**
1 **cup packed brown sugar**
1 **egg**
½ **cup raisins**
½ **cup chopped walnuts**
1¼ **cups unsweetened
  applesauce**

1. Line a 1½-quart glass baking dish with 2 layers of paper towels cut to fit. Set aside.
2. Sift flour, baking soda, salt and spices together.
3. Cream shortening and brown sugar. Add egg and beat thoroughly.
4. Add raisins and walnuts to applesauce; mix. Alternately add dry ingredients and applesauce to creamed mixture, mixing well after each addition.
5. Pour batter into the paper-lined dish. Cover with a paper towel. Cook in microwave oven 11 to 13 minutes at BAKE, or until done (see page 75); rotate dish one-quarter turn once.
6. Cool on rack 5 minutes, then remove cake from dish and peel off paper.

HINT: If the corners of cake are baking too fast, cover each corner with a *small* piece of aluminum foil.

PREPARED CAKE MIX—SHEET CAKE

1 **package prepared cake
  mix**

1. Line a 2-quart glass baking dish with 2 layers of paper towels cut to fit. Set aside.
2. Prepare cake mix as directed on the package.
3. Pour batter into the lined dish. Tap the bottom of dish to remove large air bubbles. Cover with a paper towel. Cook in microwave oven 12 to 14 minutes at BAKE, or until done (see page 75); rotate dish one-half turn twice.
4. Cool on rack 5 minutes, then remove cake from dish and peel off paper.

HINTS: If the corners are cooking too fast, cover each corner with a *small* piece of aluminum foil.
•Fill baking dish only half full. Any remaining batter can be used for cupcakes.

PREPARED CAKE MIX—LAYER CAKE

1 **package prepared cake
  mix**

1. Line two 8-inch round glass cake dishes with 2 layers of paper towels cut to fit. Set aside.
2. Prepare cake mix as directed on the package.
3. Fill each of the lined cake dishes half full with batter. (Use any remaining batter for cupcakes.) Tap the bottom of the dish to remove large air bubbles. Cover with a paper towel. Cook one layer at a time in microwave oven 6 to 7 minutes at BAKE, or until done (see page 75); rotate dish one-quarter turn twice.
4. Cool on rack 5 minutes, then remove cake from dish and peel off paper.

Two 8-inch cake layers

PINEAPPLE UPSIDE-DOWN CAKE

2 tablespoons butter
½ cup packed brown sugar
6 slices pineapple
6 maraschino cherries
½ package yellow cake mix
⅓ cup pineapple juice
Water

1. Melt butter in an 8-inch round glass cake dish in microwave oven (30 seconds at HIGH).
2. Mix brown sugar into melted butter. Cook uncovered in microwave oven until brown sugar melts (about 2 minutes at HIGH).
3. Arrange pineapple slices and maraschino cherries in dish.
4. Prepare cake batter following directions on package, using half of ingredient amounts; use pineapple juice and water for liquid. Fill cake dish half full with batter. (Use any remaining batter for cupcakes.) Cover with a paper towel. Cook in microwave oven 9 to 11 minutes at BAKE, or until done (see page 75); rotate dish one-quarter turn once.
5. Immediately invert cake onto serving plate.

OATMEAL CAKE WITH COCONUT-NUT TOPPING

1¼ **cups boiling water**
1 **cup quick-cooking oats**
1⅓ **cups sifted cake flour**
1 **teaspoon baking soda**
1 **teaspoon cinnamon**
½ **teaspoon salt**
½ **cup (1 stick) butter**
1 **cup packed dark brown sugar**
1 **cup granulated sugar**
2 **eggs, well beaten**
1 **teaspoon vanilla extract**
  Coconut-Nut Topping

1. Pour boiling water over oats in a bowl; allow to stand 20 minutes.
2. Line a 2-quart glass baking dish with 2 layers of paper towels cut to fit. Set aside.
3. Sift flour, baking soda, cinnamon and salt together; set aside.
4. Cream butter and sugars in a large mixer bowl on medium speed of electric mixer until light and fluffy. Add oat mixture and beat for an additional minute.
5. Add beaten eggs, vanilla extract and dry ingredients; beat 2 minutes.
6. Turn batter into the lined dish. Cook uncovered in micro-wave oven 11 to 12½ minutes at HIGH, or until done (see page 75); rotate dish one-half turn every 4 minutes.
7. Turn cake onto a heat-proof platter. Peel off paper. Spread warm topping over baked cake.
8. Brown the topping. In microwave oven with browning element, place cake on the microwave oven tray in top position under browning element and cook 5 minutes at BROWN, or until bubbly and browned. Under conventional broiler, broil until top is bubbly and browned.
9. Serve warm or cold.

12 to 15 servings

HINT: If the corners of cake are cooking too fast, cover each corner with a small piece of aluminum foil.

COCONUT-NUT TOPPING

¼ **cup (½ stick) butter**
½ **cup packed brown sugar**
¼ **cup half-and-half**
1 **cup flaked coconut**
½ **cup chopped nuts**

Melt butter in a small glass bowl in microwave oven (1 minute at HIGH). Add remaining ingredients and mix well.

EASY FUDGE FROSTING

3 **ounces (3 squares) unsweetened chocolate**
2 **tablespoons butter or margarine**
2¾ **cups sifted confectioners' sugar**
7 **tablespoons half-and-half**
  Dash salt
1 **teaspoon vanilla extract**

1. Melt chocolate and butter in a 2-quart glass bowl in microwave oven (about 1 minute at HIGH). Stir.
2. Add 1½ cups confectioners' sugar, half-and-half and salt; beat until smooth. Cook uncovered in microwave oven 1½ minutes at HIGH, or until bubbly.
3. Add vanilla extract, then remaining sugar in thirds, beating after each addition until smooth.

Enough frosting for two 8-inch round cake layers

CARAMEL FROSTING

½ cup (1 stick) butter
1 cup firmly packed brown
    sugar
¼ teaspoon salt
¼ cup milk
2½ cups sifted confectioners'
    sugar
½ teaspoon maple flavoring
1 tablespoon cream or milk
    (optional)

1. Melt butter in a 1-quart glass measuring cup in microwave oven (about 1 minute at HIGH).
2. Stir in brown sugar and salt. Cook uncovered in microwave oven 1 minute at HIGH.
3. Stir in milk gradually. Cook uncovered in microwave oven 1½ minutes at HIGH; stir every 30 seconds.
4. Blend in confectioners' sugar and maple flavoring.
5. Add cream if a thinner consistency is desired.

Enough frosting for two
8-inch round cake layers

FUDGE-FROSTED CAKE

1 package (6 ounces)
    semisweet chocolate
    pieces
2 tablespoons water
⅔ cup sweetened condensed
    milk
1 teaspoon vanilla extract
1 cup all-purpose biscuit
    mix
½ cup sugar
2 tablespoons vegetable
    shortening
1 egg
½ cup milk
1 teaspoon vanilla extract
½ cup chopped walnuts

1. Melt chocolate in a 1-quart glass measuring cup in microwave oven (2 minutes at HIGH); stir after each minute. Add water, sweetened condensed milk and 1 teaspoon vanilla extract; stir.
2. Line an 8-inch round glass cake dish with waxed paper. Pour chocolate mixture into dish. .
3. Combine biscuit mix, sugar, shortening, egg and ¼ cup milk; beat 1 minute. Add remaining milk and vanilla extract; beat 1 minute. Pour batter over chocolate mixture. Cover with waxed paper. Cook in microwave oven 6 to 8½ minutes at BAKE, or until done (see page 75); rotate dish one-quarter turn once.
4. Immediately invert cake onto serving plate, peel off paper and sprinkle with chopped nuts.
5. Serve while still warm.

BROWNIES À LA MODE

2 ounces (2 squares)
    unsweetened chocolate
⅓ cup shortening
1 cup sugar
2 eggs
¼ teaspoon vanilla extract
1 cup cake flour
¼ teaspoon baking powder
¼ teaspoon salt
1 cup chopped nuts
    Vanilla ice cream

1. Melt chocolate in a glass custard cup in microwave oven (1½ to 2 minutes at HIGH). Cool.
2. Cream shortening and sugar. Add eggs, one at a time, and beat well after each addition. Add vanilla extract and cooled chocolate; mix well.
3. Blend flour, baking powder and salt; stir into creamed mixture. Mix in nuts.
4. Turn batter into a waxed-paper-lined 8-inch round glass cake dish or 1½-quart glass baking dish. Cook uncovered in microwave oven 6 to 7 minutes at BAKE, or until done (see page 75); rotate dish one-quarter turn once.
5. Cool slightly, turn out of dish, peel off paper and cut into pieces.
6. Serve with a scoop of vanilla ice cream.

About 6 servings

Triple-Treat Walnut Bars, 82; Spicy Walnut Diamonds

SPICY WALNUT DIAMONDS

2½ cups sifted all-purpose
   flour
2 tablespoons cocoa
1½ teaspoons baking powder
1 teaspoon salt
½ teaspoon nutmeg
¼ teaspoon cloves
½ cup (1 stick) butter or
   margarine
2 cups firmly packed
   brown sugar
3 eggs
½ cup honey
1½ cups chopped walnuts
   (1 cup medium and ½
   cup fine)
½ cup confectioners' sugar
2 to 3 teaspoons milk

1. Blend flour, cocoa, baking powder, salt and spices.
2. Melt butter in a small glass bowl in microwave oven (about 30 seconds at HIGH).
3. Combine brown sugar and eggs in a large bowl; beat until well blended and light. Add honey, melted butter and flour mixture; mix until smooth.
4. Stir in the 1 cup medium chopped walnuts, and spread evenly in 2 waxed-paper-lined 2-quart glass baking dishes. Sprinkle evenly with the ½ cup finely chopped walnuts.
5. Cook uncovered, one dish at a time, in microwave oven 6 to 7 minutes at BAKE, or until done (see page 75); rotate dish one-half turn once.
6. Cool, turn out of baking dish and peel off paper.
7. Mix confectioners' sugar and enough milk to make a smooth, thin glaze. Spread over cooled layer. Cut into diamonds or bars.

About 4 dozen cookies

TRIPLE-TREAT WALNUT BARS

½ cup (1 stick) butter or margarine
1 package (3 ounces) cream cheese
½ cup packed dark brown sugar
1 cup whole wheat flour
⅓ cup toasted wheat germ
1 package (6 ounces) semisweet chocolate pieces
2 eggs
½ cup honey
⅓ cup whole wheat flour
⅓ cup instant nonfat dry milk
¼ teaspoon salt
¼ teaspoon cinnamon
¼ teaspoon mace
1½ cups chopped walnuts

1. Cream butter, cheese and brown sugar in a bowl until light. Add 1 cup whole wheat flour and wheat germ and mix until smooth. Turn into a waxed-paper-lined 2-quart glass baking dish; spread evenly.
2. Cook uncovered in microwave oven 3 minutes at HIGH; rotate dish one-half turn after each minute.
3. Sprinkle chocolate over layer in dish. Heat uncovered in microwave oven 1 minute at HIGH, or until chocolate softens, then spread it evenly over baked layer.
4. Combine eggs and honey; beat just until well blended. Add ⅓ cup whole wheat flour, dry milk, salt, spices and walnuts; mix well. Spoon over chocolate.
5. Cook uncovered in microwave oven 7 to 11 minutes at BAKE, or until done (see page 75); rotate dish one-half turn after 5 minutes.
6. Cool, turn out of dish, peel off paper and then cut into bars or diamonds.

About 3 dozen cookies

GINGER BARS

½ cup shortening
¼ cup sugar
1 egg yolk
½ cup molasses
¼ cup milk
1¾ cups cake flour
½ teaspoon baking soda
¼ teaspoon salt
¼ teaspoon nutmeg
½ teaspoon ginger
½ teaspoon cinnamon
½ cup raisins, chopped
Confectioners' Sugar Frosting

1. Cream shortening with sugar. Add egg yolk and beat well. Add molasses and milk; blend.
2. Blend flour, baking soda, salt and spices; stir into creamed mixture. Mix in raisins. Turn into a waxed-paper-lined 1½-quart glass baking dish and spread evenly. Cook uncovered in microwave oven 6 to 7 minutes at BAKE, or until done (see page 75); rotate dish one-quarter turn once.
3. Cool, turn out of dish, peel off paper and spread with Confectioners' Sugar Frosting. Cut into bars or squares.

2 to 3 dozen cookies

CONFECTIONERS' SUGAR FROSTING

1 teaspoon butter
1 tablespoon milk
½ cup confectioners' sugar
¼ teaspoon vanilla extract

Put butter and milk into a small glass mixer bowl. Heat uncovered in microwave oven only until butter melts (about 15 seconds at HIGH). Add confectioners' sugar and vanilla extract to milk; beat thoroughly. Spread thinly on cookie bars.

COCONUT NUT BARS

Base:
- ⅓ **cup shortening**
- ⅓ **cup packed brown sugar**
- ¾ **cup all-purpose flour**
- ½ **teaspoon baking soda**
- ½ **teaspoon salt**
- ¾ **cup quick-cooking oats**

Coconut Topping:
- 2 **eggs**
- 1 **cup packed brown sugar**
- 1 **tablespoon flour**
  Grated peel of 1 lemon
- 1 **tablespoon lemon juice**
- 1 **cup shredded coconut, chopped**
- ½ **cup chopped walnuts**

1. For base, cream shortening and brown sugar.
2. Blend flour, baking soda and salt; stir into creamed mixture. Add oats and mix well. Pat into a lightly greased 1½-quart glass baking dish.
3. For coconut topping, beat eggs slightly, add remaining ingredients and mix well. Pour over base. Cover with a paper towel. Cook in microwave oven 7 to 8 minutes at BAKE, or until done (see page 75); rotate dish one-quarter turn once.
4. Cool before cutting.

16 cookies

PEACH BUTTER BARS

- 1 **cup sifted all-purpose flour**
- ¼ **cup sugar**
- ½ **cup (1 stick) butter**
- ⅓ **cup sifted all-purpose flour**
- ½ **teaspoon baking powder**
- ½ **teaspoon salt**
- 2 **eggs**
- 1 **teaspoon vanilla extract**
- 1 **cup firmly packed brown sugar**
- 1 **cup dried peaches, snipped**
- ½ **cup chopped walnuts**

1. Mix 1 cup flour and the sugar in a bowl. Cut in butter with a pastry blender or two knives until the particles formed are the size of small peas. Turn into a lightly greased 8-inch square glass baking dish and press firmly into an even layer over bottom of dish.
2. Cook uncovered in microwave oven 3½ minutes at BAKE; rotate dish one-half turn after 2 minutes.
3. Meanwhile, blend remaining ⅓ cup flour, the baking powder and salt. Set aside.
4. Beat eggs with vanilla extract. Add brown sugar gradually, beating until thick. Stir in the flour mixture, peaches and nuts.
5. Remove dish from oven; turn the peach mixture onto the baked layer and spread evenly.
6. Cook uncovered in microwave oven 6 minutes at BAKE; rotate dish one-quarter turn twice. Cook 4 to 5 minutes at HIGH, or until mixture begins to pull away from sides (it will still be moist on top); rotate dish one-half turn after 2 minutes.
7. Cool completely on a rack before cutting into bars.

About 2 dozen

CHOCOLATE CHIP BARS

- ½ **cup (1 stick) butter**
- 1 **teaspoon vanilla extract**
- ⅔ **cup firmly packed dark brown sugar**
- 1 **egg**
- 1¼ **cups all-purpose flour**
- 1 **teaspoon baking powder**
- ¼ **teaspoon salt**
- 1 **package (6 ounces) semisweet chocolate pieces**

1. Cream butter with vanilla extract. Add brown sugar gradually, creaming until fluffy. Add egg and beat thoroughly.
2. Blend flour, baking powder and salt thoroughly; stir into creamed mixture. Stir in half of chocolate pieces. Turn into a greased 8-inch square glass baking dish. Sprinkle remaining chocolate pieces on top.
3. Cook uncovered in microwave oven 6 to 7 minutes at BAKE, or until edges begin to pull away from the sides of the dish; rotate dish one-quarter turn 2 or 3 times. Cool and cut into bars.

12 bars

NO-BAKE COOKIES

2 cups sugar
5 tablespoons unsweetened cocoa
½ cup milk
½ cup (1 stick) butter
½ teaspoon vanilla extract
3 cups quick-cooking oats
1½ cups shredded or flaked coconut

1. Combine sugar and cocoa in a 2-quart glass bowl. Stir in milk and add butter. Cook uncovered in microwave oven 4 minutes at HIGH, or until mixture comes to a rolling boil. Stir well. Continue cooking 1 minute at HIGH.
2. Remove mixture from oven and stir in vanilla extract. Add oats and coconut; mix thoroughly. Drop by teaspoonfuls onto waxed paper. Refrigerate to set.

3 to 4 dozen

TING-A-LINGS

1 cup salted peanuts
2 cups chow mein noodles
1 package (12 ounces) butterscotch-flavored pieces

1. Toss peanuts and noodles together in a 1-quart glass casserole.
2. Melt butterscotch pieces in a 1-quart glass measuring cup in microwave oven (3 minutes at HIGH). Stir until smooth. Add to peanut mixture; toss gently until coated.
3. Drop from teaspoon onto waxed paper. Chill to harden.

36 pieces

Chocolate-Marshmallow Ting-a-Lings: Follow recipe for Ting-a-Lings; substitute ½ **cup miniature marshmallows** for the peanuts and **semisweet chocolate pieces** for butterscotch pieces.

MARSHMALLOW-CEREAL BARS

¼ cup (½ stick) butter or margarine
1 package (10 ounces) regular marshmallows or 5 cups miniature marshmallows
1 cup (6 ounces) peanut butter pieces
5 cups ready-to-eat crisp rice cereal

1. Put butter, marshmallows and peanut butter pieces into a 2-quart glass casserole. Cook uncovered in microwave oven 1½ to 2 minutes at BAKE, or until melted and smooth; stir once.
2. Mix cereal into marshmallow mixture and press into a lightly buttered 1½-quart baking dish. Cool until set. Cut into bars.

Date-Cereal Bars: Follow recipe for Marshmallow-Cereal Bars; omit peanut butter pieces; use only 4 cups ready-to-eat crisp rice cereal and add ½ **cup granola** and ¾ **cup chopped dates**.

CHOCOLATE CRUMB CRUST

¼ cup (½ stick) butter
2 cups cream-filled chocolate sandwich-style cookie crumbs (24 cookies)

1. Melt butter in a glass bowl in microwave oven (30 seconds at HIGH).
2. Stir cookie crumbs into melted butter. Turn into a greased 10-inch glass pie plate and press onto bottom and up sides. Cook uncovered in microwave oven 2 minutes at HIGH; rotate pie plate one-half turn once. Cool.

One 10-inch crumb crust

BAKED PASTRY SHELL I

1 pie crust stick or mix (enough for a 9-inch pie shell)

1. Prepare pie crust following directions on package.
2. Roll out ⅛ inch thick and place it in a 9-inch glass pie plate; be careful not to stretch pastry.
3. Trim and flute edge. Prick bottom and sides of pie shell with a fork.
4. Cook uncovered in microwave oven 4 to 5½ minutes at BAKE, or until crust appears flaky; rotate pie plate one-quarter turn twice. Cool.
5. If browner appearance is desired, put pie plate on microwave oven tray in top position under browning element and cook 3 to 4 minutes at BROWN.

One 9-inch pastry shell

HINT: You can also use your favorite homemade pastry recipe with one addition; add **4 drops yellow food coloring** to the water before sprinkling water over flour mixture. Proceed as directed above. A brown appearance can also be obtained by brushing prepared pie shell with vanilla extract before cooking.

BAKED PASTRY SHELL II

1 frozen 9-inch deep-dish pie shell

1. Transfer frozen pie shell from aluminum pan to a 9-inch glass pie plate. Cook uncovered in microwave oven 1 minute at HIGH. Ease pastry into pie plate and prick shell thoroughly with a fork. Cook uncovered 4 minutes at HIGH; rotate pie plate one-quarter turn twice.
2. If browner appearance is desired, put pie plate on microwave oven tray in top position under browning element and cook 3 to 4 minutes at BROWN.

One 9-inch pastry shell

GRAHAM CRACKER CRUST

⅓ cup butter
¼ cup sugar
1½ cups graham cracker crumbs (about 18 graham crackers)

1. Melt butter in a 9-inch glass pie plate in microwave oven (about 45 seconds at HIGH). Mix in sugar and cracker crumbs.
2. Press evenly over bottom and sides. Cook uncovered in microwave oven 2 minutes at HIGH; rotate pie plate one-quarter turn after 1 minute.
3. Cool crust before filling.

One 9-inch crumb crust

10-Inch Graham Cracker Crust: Follow recipe for Graham Cracker Crust, increasing butter to ½ cup, sugar to ⅓ cup, and graham cracker crumbs to 1¾ cups. Cook as directed.

CHOCOLATE WAFER CRUST

⅓ cup butter
1½ cups chocolate wafer crumbs (about 40 wafers)

1. Melt butter in a 9-inch glass pie plate in microwave oven (about 45 seconds at HIGH). Mix in wafer crumbs.
2. Press evenly over bottom and sides. Cook uncovered in microwave oven 2 minutes at HIGH; rotate pie plate one-quarter turn after 1 minute.
3. Cool shell before filling.

One 9-inch crumb crust

Vanilla Wafer Crust: Substitute **vanilla wafer crumbs** for chocolate wafer crumbs.

CRUMB-TOP APPLE PIE

1 baked 9-inch pastry shell
Filling:
½ cup sugar
2 teaspoons flour
¼ teaspoon cinnamon
¼ teaspoon nutmeg
Pinch salt
6 large cooking apples
Crumb Topping:
¼ cup packed dark brown sugar
½ cup flour
1 tablespoon sugar
⅛ teaspoon cinnamon
⅛ teaspoon nutmeg
⅛ teaspoon salt
¼ cup (½ stick) butter or margarine

1. Prepare pastry shell in a glass pie plate and set aside.
2. For filling, combine sugar, flour, cinnamon, nutmeg and salt. Sprinkle 2 tablespoons of mixture over bottom of baked pastry shell. Set remaining mixture aside.
3. Wash, quarter, core, pare and thinly slice apples. Turn into pastry shell, heaping slightly at center. Sprinkle with remaining sugar mixture.
4. For crumb topping, mix brown sugar, flour, sugar, cinnamon, nutmeg and salt. Cut in butter until mixture is crumbly. Sprinkle over apples.
5. Cook uncovered in microwave oven 6 to 8 minutes at HIGH, or until apples are tender; rotate pie plate one-half turn once.
6. Remove from oven. Allow to stand 15 minutes. Serve warm.

One 9-inch pie

LUSCIOUS CHERRY PIE

1 baked 9-inch pastry shell
3½ tablespoons cornstarch
6 tablespoons sugar
2 cans (16 ounces each) red tart cherries packed in syrup, drained; reserve 1½ cups syrup
2 teaspoons lemon juice
⅛ teaspoon salt
⅛ teaspoon almond extract
Red food coloring

1. Prepare pastry shell in a glass pie plate and set aside.
2. Blend cornstarch and sugar in a 1-quart glass measuring cup. Add reserved cherry syrup gradually, stirring until smooth. Cook uncovered in microwave oven 5 to 6 minutes at HIGH, or until thickened and clear; stir frequently.
3. Stir in cherries, lemon juice, salt, almond extract and desired amount of red food coloring.
4. Turn filling into pastry shell. Cool.

One 9-inch pie

GRASSHOPPER PIE

Chocolate Crumb Crust (page 84)

30 **large or 3 cups miniature marshmallows**
½ **cup milk**
¼ **cup green crème de menthe**
2 **tablespoons white crème de cacao**
1 **cup whipping cream, whipped**
Cream-filled chocolate sandwich-style cookies, finely crushed (optional)

1. Prepare crumb crust and set aside.
2. Put marshmallows and milk into a 4-quart glass mixing bowl. Cook uncovered in microwave oven 2 minutes at HIGH, or until marshmallows bubble up and are softened.
3. Remove from oven and stir until blended. Mix in crème de menthe and crème de cacao. Chill until mixture begins to thicken (about 30 minutes); stir occasionally.
4. Fold whipped cream into thickened marshmallow mixture. Pile into cooled crumb crust. Swirl top. Decorate with crushed cookies, if desired.
5. Refrigerate until set or freeze until firm.

One 10-inch pie

PUMPKIN PIE

1 **baked 9-inch pastry shell**
1 **can (16 ounces) pumpkin**
⅔ **cup firmly packed dark brown sugar**
1 **teaspoon cinnamon**
½ **teaspoon ginger**
½ **teaspoon nutmeg**
⅛ **teaspoon cloves**
½ **teaspoon salt**
2 **eggs, slightly beaten**
1 **cup half-and-half**

1. Prepare pastry shell in a glass pie plate and set aside.
2. Combine pumpkin, brown sugar, spices and salt in a 2-quart glass bowl. Add eggs and mix well. Gradually add half-and-half, stirring until mixture is smooth.
3. Cook uncovered in microwave oven 8 to 9 minutes at HIGH, or until thickened; stir twice.
4. Pour filling into baked pastry shell. Cook uncovered in microwave oven 14 to 16 minutes at SIMMER, or until nearly set; rotate pie plate one-quarter turn 3 times.
5. Remove from oven. Allow to cool before serving.

One 9-inch pie

CHOCOLATE MALLOW PIE

1 baked 10-inch Graham
Cracker Crust (page 85)
6 (about 1 ounce each)
milk chocolate bars with
almonds, broken in
pieces
24 large marshmallows
1 cup milk
½ pint whipping cream
Whipped cream or
whipped dessert topping

1. Prepare graham cracker crust and set aside.
2. Melt the chocolate bars in a 3-quart glass casserole in microwave oven (about 2 minutes at HIGH). Add marshmallows and milk. Cook uncovered in microwave oven until marshmallows are melted (about 3 minutes at HIGH); stir occasionally. Chill until slightly thickened; stir occasionally.
3. Whip cream and fold into cooled chocolate mixture. Turn into prepared graham cracker crust and refrigerate until set.
4. Garnish with desired topping.

One 10-inch pie

LEMON MERINGUE PIE

1 baked 9-inch pastry shell
1½ cups sugar
⅓ cup cornstarch
1½ cups boiling water
3 egg yolks, slightly beaten
3 tablespoons butter
¼ cup lemon juice
1 teaspoon grated lemon
peel
Meringue

1. Prepare pastry shell in a glass pie plate and set aside.
2. Mix sugar and cornstarch thoroughly in a 1-quart glass casserole. Stir in water. Cook uncovered in microwave oven 2½ minutes at HIGH; stir. Continue cooking 1 minute at HIGH, or until thick; stir after 30 seconds.
3. Beat a small amount of the hot mixture into egg yolks, then return to mixture in casserole. Cook uncovered in microwave oven 30 seconds at HIGH.
4. Blend butter, lemon juice and lemon peel into filling. Cool slightly. Pour into baked pastry shell. Cover with Meringue and cook as directed.

One 9-inch pie

MERINGUE

3 egg whites
⅛ teaspoon salt
6 tablespoons sugar

1. Beat egg whites with salt until frothy; gradually add sugar, beating constantly until stiff peaks are formed.
2. Pile Meringue lightly over pie filling. Swirl with back of spoon; seal Meringue to edge of crust.
3. Cook and brown Meringue. In microwave oven with browning element, cook 3 minutes at HIGH; rotate pie plate one-quarter turn twice. Move the microwave oven tray to middle position, set pie under browning element and cook 3 to 3½ minutes at BROWN. In preheated conventional oven, bake at 350°F about 15 minutes.

FROZEN FRUIT PIE

Frozen fruit pie

Preheat conventional oven to 450°F. Remove frozen pie from the aluminum pie plate and place in a 7½-inch glass pie plate. Cook uncovered in microwave oven 8 to 10 minutes at HIGH; rotate pie plate halfway through cooking period. Quickly transfer pie to preheated conventional oven and bake until golden brown (about 10 minutes).

LEMON CHIFFON PIE

1 **baked 9-inch pastry shell**
1 **envelope unflavored gelatin**
⅔ **cup sugar**
¼ **teaspoon salt**
4 **egg yolks**
½ **cup lemon juice**
¼ **cup water**
2 **teaspoons grated lemon peel**
4 **egg whites**
½ **cup sugar**
  Whipped cream (optional)

1. Prepare pastry shell in a glass pie plate and set aside.
2. Mix gelatin, ⅔ cup sugar and salt in a 1-quart glass casserole.
3. Beat egg yolks, lemon juice and water together; add to gelatin mixture and stir well. Cook uncovered in microwave oven 3 minutes at BAKE, or until mixture comes to boiling; stir after 1 minute.
4. Mix lemon peel into filling. Chill until mixture is almost set; stir several times.
5. Beat egg whites until frothy. Add ½ cup sugar gradually, beating until stiff peaks form. Fold egg whites into thickened gelatin mixture. Turn filling into baked pie shell.
6. Chill pie several hours before serving. Garnish top of pie with whipped cream, if desired.

One 9-inch pie

VANILLA CREAM PIE

1 **baked 9-inch pie shell (pastry or crumb crust)**
¾ **cup sugar**
3 **tablespoons cornstarch**
¼ **teaspoon salt**
2 **cups milk**
3 **egg yolks, slightly beaten**
1 **teaspoon vanilla extract**
2 **tablespoons butter or margarine**
  Meringue (page 88)

1. Prepare pie shell in a glass pie plate and set aside.
2. Combine sugar, cornstarch and salt in a 1½-quart glass casserole. Add milk gradually, mixing well. Cook uncovered in microwave oven 7 to 8½ minutes at BAKE, or until thick; stir after each minute.
3. Beat a small amount of hot mixture into egg yolks, then return to mixture in casserole. Cook uncovered in microwave oven 2 to 3 minutes at BAKE, or until thick; stir after each minute.
4. Add vanilla extract and butter to filling and stir well. Cool filling to room temperature.
5. Pour cooled filling into the baked pie shell. Cover with Meringue and cook as directed.

One 9-inch pie

Chocolate Cream Pie: Increase sugar to 1 cup. Add **2 ounces (2 squares) unsweetened chocolate**, grated, with the milk.

Coconut Cream Pie: Mix **1 cup flaked coconut** into cream filling, and sprinkle ⅓ **cup flaked coconut** over the Meringue before cooking.

Butterscotch Pie: Substitute **dark brown sugar** for granulated sugar, and increase butter to 3 tablespoons.

Banana Cream Pie: Slice **2 medium-size ripe bananas** into the bottom of baked pie shell. Pour the pie filling over the bananas.

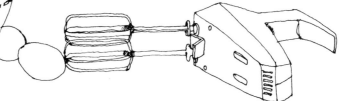

CHEESE CAKE

¼ cup (½ stick) butter
1¼ cups graham cracker crumbs (18 to 20 crackers)
½ teaspoon cinnamon
8 ounces cream cheese
¼ cup sugar
½ teaspoon vanilla extract
1 egg
1 cup dairy sour cream
2 tablespoons sugar
½ teaspoon vanilla extract

1. Melt butter in a 9-inch glass pie plate in microwave oven (about 45 seconds at HIGH). Add cracker crumbs and cinnamon to melted butter; mix well with a fork. Press crumb mixture evenly over bottom and sides of pie plate. Cook uncovered in microwave oven 2 minutes at HIGH; rotate pie plate one-quarter turn halfway through cooking period. Remove from oven and set aside.
2. Soften cream cheese in a small glass bowl in microwave oven (1 minute at HIGH).
3. Add ¼ cup sugar, ½ teaspoon vanilla extract and egg to cream cheese; mix until well blended. Pour filling into crust.
4. Cook uncovered in microwave oven 3 minutes at BAKE, or until bubbles appear on surface; rotate pie plate one-quarter turn once. Remove from oven and cool slightly.
5. Blend sour cream and remaining sugar and vanilla extract. Spoon sour cream mixture over filling. Cook uncovered in microwave oven (2½ minutes at ROAST), or until set. Cool, then chill thoroughly.

One 9-inch pie

FLAVORED GELATIN DESSERT FROM PREPARED MIX

1 cup water
1 package (3 ounces) fruit-flavored gelatin
1 cup cold water

1. Heat 1 cup water in a glass measuring cup in microwave oven to boiling (about 2 to 3 minutes at HIGH).
2. Dissolve gelatin in boiling water. Stir in cold water.
3. Pour gelatin into serving dishes and refrigerate until set.

4 servings

ORANGE-COCONUT PARFAIT

1 cup water
1 package (3 ounces) orange-flavored gelatin
1 cup cold water
1 can (11 ounces) mandarin orange sections, drained
Flaked coconut (about ½ cup)

1. Heat 1 cup water in a glass bowl in microwave oven to boiling (about 2 to 3 minutes at HIGH).
2. Dissolve gelatin in boiling water. Stir in cold water. Chill until firm.
3. Layer spoonfuls of gelatin in parfait glasses with orange sections and coconut.

4 or 5 servings

APRICOT-BANANA MOLD

1 can (17 ounces) apricot halves
1 cup water
1 package (3 ounces) lime-flavored gelatin
1 banana, peeled and sliced
Prepared whipped topping (optional)

1. Drain apricots, measuring syrup. Add water to syrup to make ¾ cup liquid.
2. Heat 1 cup water in a glass bowl in microwave oven to boiling (about 2 to 3 minutes at HIGH).
3. Dissolve gelatin in boiling water. Stir in liquid. Chill until slightly thickened.
4. Mix apricots and banana into thickened gelatin. Turn into a 4-cup mold or serving bowl. Chill until firm.
5. Unmold and, if desired, serve with prepared whipped topping.

6 to 8 servings

CHERRY-PORT DESSERT

1 cup water
1 package (3 ounces) cherry-flavored gelatin
½ cup port wine or Burgundy; or use ¾ cup ginger ale
¼ cup cold water
1 can (8¾ ounces) sliced peaches, drained
Dash cinnamon
1 cup prepared whipped topping

1. Heat 1 cup water in a 1½-quart glass bowl in microwave oven to boiling (about 2 to 3 minutes at HIGH).
2. Dissolve gelatin in boiling water. Stir in wine and cold water. Chill until slightly thickened.
3. Stir peaches into thickened gelatin. Turn into a 3-cup mold, or spoon into individual molds or dessert dishes. Chill until firm.
4. Stir cinnamon into prepared whipped topping.
5. Unmold gelatin, if molded. Garnish with spiced whipped topping and additional sliced peaches, if desired.

4 servings

JELLIED CUBES

1 cup water
1 package (3 ounces) strawberry-flavored gelatin
¾ cup cold water
Cream (optional)

1. Heat 1 cup water in a small glass bowl in microwave oven to boiling (about 2 to 3 minutes at HIGH).
2. Dissolve gelatin in boiling water. Stir in cold water. Pour into an 8- or 9-inch square pan. Chill until firm.
3. Cut gelatin into cubes, using a sharp knife which has been dipped in hot water. To remove cubes from pan, apply warm wet cloth over bottom of pan. When cubes are slightly loosened, remove with spatula. Or quickly dip pan in warm water and invert on waxed paper. Serve in sherbet glasses with cream, if desired.

4 servings

Note: For firmer cubes, decrease cold water to ½ cup, or chill overnight.

FROZEN CHOCOLATE BANANAS

6 firm ripe bananas
1 package (6 ounces) semisweet chocolate pieces

1. Peel bananas and cut crosswise into halves. Insert a wooden stick into the end of each banana piece. Place in a shallow pan; set in freezer 2 to 3 hours.
2. Melt chocolate in a small glass bowl in microwave oven (about 2 minutes at HIGH); stir occasionally. With a spatula spread chocolate over frozen bananas, using lengthwise strokes. Chocolate will become firm as it is spread.
3. Wrap in aluminum foil and store in freezer. Serve frozen.

HINT: If chocolate becomes too firm to spread, return chocolate to microwave oven and heat for a few seconds at HIGH.

Jellied Cubes; Cherry Port Dessert; Orange-Coconut Parfait, 91;
Apricot-Banana Mold, 91

BAKED APPLE

1   medium baking apple
1   tablespoon brown sugar
2   teaspoons butter
   Cinnamon

1. Wash and core apple. Pare a thin section of skin from top of apple. Place apple in a glass custard cup.
2. Fill center of apple with brown sugar and top with butter. Sprinkle with cinnamon.
3. Cook uncovered in microwave oven 2 to 2½ minutes at HIGH, or until almost tender. Let stand 5 minutes before serving.

HINT: When cooking more than one apple, follow the timing below and rearrange apples once during cooking period.

2 apples	3 to 3½ minutes at HIGH
3 apples	4 to 4½ minutes at HIGH
4 apples	5 to 5½ minutes at HIGH

BAKED GRAPEFRUIT

A very nutritious snack for after school or any time.

1   grapefruit
2   teaspoons brown sugar
1   teaspoon butter

1. Wash grapefruit and cut in half. Remove core and seeds.
2. Set grapefruit halves cut side up in a glass baking dish or on a paper towel. Sprinkle fruit with brown sugar; put butter in center. Cook uncovered in microwave oven 2 minutes at HIGH.

CHERRY-PEACH DELIGHT

½   cup water
2   tablespoons lemon juice
¼   teaspoon cinnamon
⅛   teaspoon cloves
1   can (21 ounces) cherry
   pie filling
1   can (16 ounces) peach
   halves, drained and cut in
   halves
1½   cups all-purpose biscuit
   mix
½   teaspoon cinnamon
   Milk
1   egg, beaten

1. Combine water, lemon juice, ¼ teaspoon cinnamon, cloves and cherry pie filling in a 2-quart glass baking dish. Mix in peaches. Heat uncovered in microwave oven 8 minutes at HIGH, or until boiling; stir twice.
2. Combine biscuit mix and ½ teaspoon cinnamon. Add enough milk to egg to make ½ cup. Pour liquid onto biscuit mix and cinnamon; stir with a fork until a soft dough is formed.
3. Drop dough by level measuring tablespoons evenly onto the hot mixture. Cook uncovered in microwave oven 5 minutes at BAKE; rotate dish one-half turn once.
4. Brown the topping. In microwave oven with browning element, place dish on the microwave oven tray in top position under browning element and cook 5 minutes at BROWN, or until tops of dumplings are lightly browned. Under conventional broiler, brown just until lightly browned.

6 servings

PEACH DESSERT

6 cups sweetened peeled fresh peach quarters (see Note)
⅓ cup butter or margarine
⅓ cup all-purpose flour
1 cup uncooked oats, quick or old-fashioned
½ cup firmly packed brown sugar
½ teaspoon salt
¼ teaspoon cinnamon
¼ teaspoon nutmeg

1. Put peaches into an 8-inch square glass baking dish.
2. Melt butter in a small glass bowl in microwave oven (45 to 60 seconds at HIGH).
3. Mix flour, oats, brown sugar, salt, cinnamon and nutmeg in a bowl; add melted butter and continue to mix until crumbly. Sprinkle crumb mixture over peaches.
4. Cook uncovered in microwave oven 12 to 14 minutes at BAKE; rotate dish one-quarter turn twice.

About 6 servings

Note: If desired, substitute 2 cans (16 ounces each) peach halves, drained and quartered.

PEACHES FLAMBÉE

4 medium-size ripe peaches
1 or 2 tablespoons lemon juice
⅓ cup firmly packed brown sugar
2 tablespoons butter
2 tablespoons Cointreau
¼ cup kirsch

1. Rinse peaches, peel, cut into halves and pit. Cut peaches into large pieces and put into a 1-quart glass casserole. Pour lemon juice over peaches. Cover with an all-glass lid or plastic wrap. Cook in microwave oven 2 to 3 minutes at HIGH, or until slightly cooked. Remove from oven.
2. Put brown sugar and butter into a 2-cup glass measuring cup. Cook uncovered in microwave oven 30 seconds at HIGH. Stir in Cointreau until blended. Cook uncovered 30 seconds at HIGH.
3. Stir brown sugar mixture into peaches. Cook covered in microwave oven 1 minute at ROAST.
4. Pour kirsch into a 1-cup glass measuring cup. Heat uncovered in microwave oven until warm (20 seconds at HIGH). Pour over peaches and ignite.
5. Serve plain or over vanilla ice cream.

6 servings

HINT: To remove peel from peaches, heat 1 cup water in a 2-cup glass measuring cup in microwave oven to boiling (2½ to 3 minutes at HIGH). Drop peaches in 1 or 2 at a time; let stand 45 to 60 seconds. Remove from water and peel with a knife.

FRUIT CRISP

4 cups sliced fruit, such as apples, peaches or pears
2 teaspoons cinnamon
3 tablespoons sugar
2 tablespoons lemon juice

Topping:
¾ cup corn flake crumbs
½ cup flour
½ cup packed brown sugar
¼ teaspoon baking powder
⅛ teaspoon salt
½ cup (1 stick) butter
¼ cup chopped walnuts
1 tablespoon cinnamon

1. Put fruit into an 8-inch square glass baking dish. Mix 2 teaspoons cinnamon and sugar and sprinkle over fruit. Drizzle lemon juice over top.
2. For topping, combine corn flake crumbs, flour, brown sugar, baking powder and salt. Cut in butter until mixture is crumbly. Add walnuts and toss lightly. Spoon mixture over the fruit and sprinkle with cinnamon. Cover with waxed paper.
3. Cook in microwave oven 10 minutes at BAKE; rotate dish one-quarter turn after 5 minutes. Allow to stand covered 5 minutes before serving.

6 servings

SYRUP AND CANDIES

Stage	Temperature	Test
Thread	230° to 234°F	The syrup spins a 2-inch thread when allowed to drop from fork or spoon.
Soft Ball	234° to 240°F	The syrup forms a soft ball in very cold water; it flattens when removed from water.
Firm Ball	244° to 248°F	The syrup forms a firm ball in very cold water; it does not flatten when removed from water.
Hard Ball	250° to 266°F	The syrup forms a ball which is pliable yet hard enough to hold its shape in very cold water.
Soft Crack	270° to 290°F	The syrup separates into threads which are hard but not brittle in very cold water.
Hard Crack	300° to 310°F	The syrup separates into threads which are hard and brittle in very cold water.

Note: If using a candy thermometer, do not leave thermometer in the syrup while cooking.

PENUCHE

2½ **cups packed brown sugar**
Dash salt
1 **tablespoon light corn syrup**
¾ **cup milk**
1 **tablespoon butter or margarine**
½ **cup chopped nuts**
1 **teaspoon vanilla extract**

1. Combine brown sugar, salt, corn syrup, milk and butter in a 2-quart oven-proof glass mixing bowl/pitcher. Cook uncovered in microwave oven 4 minutes at HIGH; stir until sugar is completely dissolved. Continue cooking to soft-ball stage (6 to 8 minutes at HIGH); stir occasionally.
2. Cool mixture to lukewarm, then beat. When mixture first begins to thicken, add nuts and vanilla extract; mix well. Turn into a greased 8-inch square dish. Cool and cut into squares.

About 1 pound

DIVINITY

2 **cups sugar**
½ **cup water**
½ **cup light corn syrup**
2 **egg whites**
¾ **cup chopped nuts**
¾ **cup chopped candied cherries**
1 **teaspoon vanilla extract**

1. Combine sugar, water and corn syrup in a 2-quart oven-proof glass mixing bowl/pitcher. Cook uncovered in microwave oven 6 minutes at HIGH, or until sugar is dissolved. Continue cooking to hard-ball stage (5 to 6 minutes at HIGH); stir occasionally.
2. Meanwhile, beat egg whites until stiff, not dry, peaks form.
3. Pour syrup over egg whites in a thin stream, beating constantly. Continue beating until creamy (15 to 20 minutes). Mix in nuts, cherries and vanilla extract. Turn into a buttered 11x7-inch pan. Cut into squares when firm.

About 1 pound

Note: Instead of turning candy into buttered pan, drop by teaspoonfuls onto waxed paper. Cool thoroughly.

Variation: Substitute **1 cup chopped nuts** or **2 cups flaked coconut** for the cherries.

MICROWAVE CHOCOLATE FUDGE

4 ounces (4 squares) unsweetened chocolate
2 packages (3 ounces each) cream cheese
4 cups sifted confectioners' sugar
1 tablespoon vanilla extract
¾ cup coarsely chopped nuts

1. Melt chocolate in a small glass bowl in microwave oven (2 minutes at HIGH). Set aside to cool.
2. Soften cream cheese in a 1½-quart glass bowl in microwave oven (30 to 60 seconds at SIMMER), then beat until fluffy.
3. Gradually add confectioners' sugar, beating until fluffy after each addition.
4. Blend in the cooled chocolate and vanilla extract. Stir in nuts.
5. Turn into a buttered 8-inch square pan. Chill in refrigerator until firm.

CRACKLE PEANUT BRITTLE

2 cups sugar
1 cup light corn syrup
½ cup water
2 cups salted peanuts
2 teaspoons butter or margarine
2 teaspoons baking soda
1 teaspoon vanilla extract

1. Combine sugar, corn syrup and water in a 2-quart oven-proof glass mixing bowl/pitcher. Cook uncovered in microwave oven 6 minutes at HIGH, or until sugar is dissolved.
2. Stir peanuts into syrup. Cook uncovered in microwave oven 8 minutes at HIGH; stir every 2 minutes.
3. Stir butter into mixture. Cook uncovered in microwave oven to hard-crack stage (8 to 10 minutes at HIGH); stir every 2 minutes.
4. Add baking soda and vanilla extract and mix well. Pour onto 2 lightly buttered baking sheets, spreading as thinly as possible.
5. As soon as candy is cool enough to handle, wet hands with water and stretch as thin as desired. Turn candy over and cool completely.
6. When firm and cool, break into medium-size pieces. Store in a tightly covered container.

About 2 pounds

POPCORN

We do not recommend popping corn in the microwave oven unless you use a "corn popper" designed especially for microwave oven cooking. An ordinary glass dish could become too hot and break. If a paper bag is used, the heat from the popcorn kernels can cause the bag to catch fire.

APPLESAUCE

2 pounds apples (6 to 8)
½ cup water
½ to 1 cup sugar (depending upon type of apple and sweetness desired)

1. Wash, quarter and core apples. Combine apples and water in a 2-quart glass casserole. Cover with an all-glass lid or plastic wrap. Cook in microwave oven 8 to 10 minutes at HIGH; stir once.
2. Force contents of casserole through a sieve or food mill. Add sugar and stir until sugar is dissolved.
3. Serve warm or chill before serving.

6 servings

HINTS: For 9 servings, prepare 3 pounds of apples and put into a 3-quart casserole. Cover and cook 10 to 15 minutes at HIGH; stir once. Add ¾ to 1½ cups sugar.
•Exact cooking time depends on type of apple used.

YEAR-ROUND FRUIT COMPOTE

1 cup dried apricots
1 cup golden raisins
1 package (12 ounces) pitted prunes
1 can (20 ounces) unsweetened pineapple chunks (undrained)
Lemon peel from ¼ lemon
1 cinnamon stick, broken in half

1. Put fruits, lemon peel and cinnamon sticks into a 1½-quart glass casserole. Cover with an all-glass lid or plastic wrap.
2. Cook in microwave oven 8 minutes at HIGH; rotate dish one-quarter turn once.
3. Remove lemon peel and cinnamon before serving.

8 to 10 servings

STRAWBERRY SHORTCAKE

2 cups all-purpose flour
¼ cup sugar
1 tablespoon baking powder
½ teaspoon salt
½ cup (1 stick) butter
¾ cup milk
Sweetened strawberries or other fresh fruit
Sweetened whipped cream

1. Line two 8-inch round glass cake dishes with 2 layers of paper towels cut to fit dish.
2. Combine flour, sugar, baking powder and salt in a bowl. Cut in butter until mixture resembles coarse crumbs. Add milk and mix only until the dry ingredients are moistened. Dough will be thick and lumpy.
3. Divide dough into two portions. Drop one-half of dough by teaspoonfuls into each lined cake dish. Spread evenly with moistened fingers.
4. Cook uncovered, one dish at a time, in microwave oven 2½ to 3 minutes at HIGH, or until done.
5. Remove shortcake from dishes and peel off paper.
6. Serve shortcake warm, filled and topped with fruit and whipped cream.

6 to 8 servings

PREPARED PUDDING MIX

1 package prepared pudding
2 cups milk

1. Empty contents of package into a 1-quart glass casserole or 1-quart glass measuring cup. Add enough milk to dissolve pudding, stirring constantly; stir in remaining milk. Cook uncovered in microwave oven 4 minutes at HIGH, or until pudding begins to boil; stir often. Pudding thickens as it cools.
2. Chill and serve.

4 servings

VANILLA PUDDING

⅓ cup sugar
¼ teaspoon salt
3 tablespoons cornstarch
2 cups milk
1 egg, separated
½ teaspoon vanilla extract

1. Combine sugar, salt and cornstarch in a 1-quart glass casserole. Add milk gradually and blend well. Cook uncovered in microwave oven 6 to 8 minutes at BAKE; stir often.
2. Beat egg yolk and stir a little of hot mixture into yolk. Return to casserole. Cook uncovered in microwave oven 1 to 1½ minutes at BAKE, or until mixture coats a metal spoon; do not leave spoon in mixture.
3. Beat egg white until stiff and fold into hot mixture, gently but thoroughly. Mix in vanilla extract. Pour into individual serving dishes or a large bowl to cool.

4 servings

FLUFFY TAPIOCA

1 egg, separated
⅓ cup sugar
⅛ teaspoon salt
3 tablespoons quick-cooking tapioca
2 cups milk
1 teaspoon vanilla extract

1. Mix egg yolk, 3 tablespoons of the sugar, salt, tapioca and milk in a 2-quart glass measuring cup. Cover with waxed paper. Cook in microwave oven 8 minutes at HIGH; stir occasionally.
2. Beat egg white in a bowl until frothy. Add remaining sugar and beat until soft peaks form. Add hot mixture to beaten egg white gradually, folding until blended. Mix in vanilla extract.
3. Allow to stand 20 minutes; stir. Serve warm or cool.

5 servings

BAKED CUSTARD

1⅔ cups milk
3 eggs
¼ cup sugar
¼ teaspoon salt
½ teaspoon vanilla extract
Ground nutmeg (optional)

1. Scald milk in a glass measuring cup in microwave oven (3 to 4 minutes at HIGH).
2. Meanwhile, put eggs into a 1-quart glass casserole and beat slightly. Add the sugar, salt and vanilla extract; mix well.
3. Add the scalded milk gradually to egg mixture, stirring constantly. Sprinkle with nutmeg, if desired.
4. Heat 1½ cups water in a 2-quart glass casserole in microwave oven to boiling (2 to 3 minutes at HIGH).
5. Place the casserole with custard in the hot water and cover with an all-glass lid. Cook in microwave oven 7 minutes at ROAST, or until nearly set (center of custard will become firm on cooling).
6. Remove custard from water and set on a rack to cool.

6 servings

HINT: Baked custard is easier to prepare in one dish rather than individual custard cups.

CRISPY TOPPING

1 tablespoon butter
1½ tablespoons light brown sugar
Dash salt
½ cup corn flakes, slightly crumbled
2 tablespoons chopped nuts

1. Melt butter in an 8-inch round glass cake dish in microwave oven (15 seconds at HIGH). Blend in brown sugar and salt. Cook uncovered in microwave oven 2 minutes at HIGH; stir once.
2. Stir corn flakes and nuts into butter mixture. Cool. Sprinkle on pudding.

CHOCOLATE FONDUE

12 ounces (12 squares) semisweet chocolate
1 cup whipping cream
3 tablespoons brandy or rum
Assorted dippers (marshmallows, strawberries with hulls, apple slices, banana chunks, pineapple chunks, mandarin orange segments, cherries with stems, cake cubes, melon balls)

1. Melt chocolate in a 1-quart glass measuring cup in microwave oven (3 minutes at BAKE). Stir to blend.
2. Add cream to chocolate; stir until well blended. Heat uncovered in microwave oven 1½ minutes at BAKE.
3. Add brandy to chocolate mixture and stir well.
4. Serve in fondue pot and keep warm. Accompany with desired dippers.

About 3 cups

Fish and Shellfish

It's not a fish tale! Fish and shellfish cooked in your microwave oven taste so delicious that they'll disappear as fast as the serving platter reaches your table. Quick cooking keeps these foods tender and moist, so plan to serve them often. With the many delicious fish and seafoods found in our lakes, streams and oceans, you won't want to relegate them to an occasional meal.

Whether fillets, steaks or whole, fish can be prepared with excellent results in your microwave oven. However, due to the extremely short cooking time, it is important to follow the recipes closely. Cook only for the minimum suggested time. Then check for doneness, using conventional testing methods: fish will turn opaque and flake easily with a fork. Note instructions carefully. Overcooking will result in dry, tough flesh that has lost its subtle flavor and delicate texture. Do not forget foods continue to cook even after you have removed them from the microwave oven.

When cooking fish that has been frozen, whether commercially frozen purchases or home-frozen catches from this year's vacation, be sure the fish is completely thawed before cooking. To prevent thin edges from starting to cook while the center is still frozen, thaw the fish partially, then run it under cold water to complete defrosting. Fish that has been frozen will give up extra moisture as it thaws and cooks; save this juice to flavor accompanying sauces.

Dieters will be delighted when they discover that no additional fat or oil is needed when cooking fish; it's perfect for a nutritious low-calorie meal. Sprinkle paprika or herbs on fish fillets for a pleasing appearance. What could be a tastier way to save calories?! For those who are not as calorie-conscious, fish turns into an elegant dish when smothered in a sauce or covered with melted butter and paprika.

Whole fish makes a dramatic presentation when prepared for family and friends. The stunning appearance will never betray the effortless, easy preparation. The entire fish can even be cooked right on the serving platter. A more pleasing appearance will be achieved if the delicate head and tail are shielded with aluminum foil during cooking. The eyes of the fish will turn white when cooked, so plan a creative way to cover them, such as with pimento-stuffed olive slices. For a traditional baked appearance, brush the fish with water mixed with a gravy browning sauce. You will find that a whole fish cooked in a microwave oven is more flaky and moist than when cooked conventionally. Since thinner portions tend to overcook before thick center portions are done, use the standing time to finish the center and prevent overcooking of the edges.

For both fish fillets and whole fish, proper arrangement is necessary to assure even cooking. Place thicker portions toward the outside and thinner portions toward the center of the dish. Two types of dish covers are recommended to speed cooking and prevent dehydration. Glass lids or plastic wrap will hold the steam in the cooking dish, resulting in a product similar in taste and texture to fish conventionally poached or steamed. If not using a lid, use waxed paper to prevent spatters on the oven interior. The fish will taste baked without drying the surface.

Shellfish are quick and easy to cook. They come in their own cooking container, complete with built-in cover. One great advantage of cooking shellfish in the microwave oven is the elimination of the huge quantities of boiling water that are needed for conventional cooking. Shellfish will steam in their own shells. If desired, you can use your microwave oven to open oysters. Heat just until the shells open slightly. Then continue with your favorite recipe, or serve immediately as oysters on the half shell.

When cooking shellfish, placement of the food in the cooking dish is again important. The test for doneness is similar to conventional methods: when cooked, the flesh becomes opaque in color and firm to the touch. Where applicable (shrimp, crab, lobster) the shell will also turn red. The cooking time remains the same whether cooking with the shell or without, as microwaves pass through the shell. Cleaned sea shells can also be used in place of ramekins for an elegant touch to a very special dinner.

BAKED FISH SUPREME

2 **pounds fish fillets,**
   ¾ inch thick (halibut,
   haddock or other white
   fish)
2 **grapefruit**
1 **teaspoon salt**
¼ **teaspoon pepper**
¼ **cup (½ stick) butter**
1 **can (about 10 ounces)**
   cream of asparagus,
   cream of celery or cream
   of mushroom soup
   (undiluted)
½ **cup dairy sour cream**
3 **green onions, thinly**
   sliced
1 **tablespoon chopped**
   parsley

1. Cut fish into serving-size pieces. Place in a shallow 2-quart glass baking dish.
2. Peel and section grapefruit over a bowl to retain juice. Drain sections. Pour juice over fish. Allow to marinate at room temperature 10 to 15 minutes; discard juice. Sprinkle fish with salt and pepper.
3. Melt butter in a glass measuring cup in microwave oven (about 30 seconds at HIGH); pour over the fish. Turn fish over to coat with butter. Cover dish with waxed paper and cook in microwave oven 7 to 8 minutes at HIGH.
4. Remove from oven and baste fish with pan juices.
5. Combine soup with sour cream, green onion and parsley. Spoon some over each piece of fish. Top with grapefruit sections. Cover again with waxed paper and continue cooking 6 to 7 minutes at BAKE, or until heated through.

6 to 8 servings

BUTTERED FISH FILLETS

2 **tablespoons butter**
1¼ **pounds whitefish fillets**
   Salt and pepper
   Paprika

1. Melt butter in a glass custard cup or glass measuring cup in microwave oven (about 15 seconds at HIGH).
2. Put fish into a 2-quart glass baking dish, brush with melted butter and sprinkle with salt, pepper and paprika. Cover with waxed paper. Cook in microwave oven 3 minutes at HIGH, or until fish flakes when tested with a fork.

4 or 5 servings

HINT: Other fish fillets such as halibut, haddock and flounder can be cooked using these directions.

SUNSHINE FISH FILLETS

1½ **pounds red snapper fillets**
   or other fish fillets
2 **tablespoons butter**
1½ **teaspoons grated orange**
   peel
1½ **tablespoons orange juice**
½ **teaspoon salt**
   Few grains pepper
   Freshly ground nutmeg

1. Place fish fillets in a 2-quart glass baking dish.
2. Melt butter in a small glass bowl in microwave oven (30 seconds at HIGH). Add remaining ingredients, mix well and pour over fish. Cover with waxed paper.
3. Cook in microwave oven 4 minutes at HIGH, or until fish flakes when tested with a fork.

About 6 servings

WHOLE FISH

(using Temperature Probe)

Stuffing (favorite recipe or a prepared mix), optional
1 **whole cleaned and boned fish**
Butter

1. When serving fish hot, stuff if desired.
2. Melt butter in microwave oven. Brush entire fish with melted butter. Place fish on a roast rack set in a 2-quart glass baking dish. Cover head and tail with foil.
3. Insert Temperature Probe in fish just above the gill into the meatiest area parallel to backbone (be sure it does not touch foil around head). Have the probe in the side of the fish closest to the dish. Cover tightly with plastic wrap. Cook in microwave oven set at 140°F and at HIGH.
4. Remove from oven. Allow to stand covered 5 minutes before serving. To serve fish, slide back skin and slice or serve with a spoon. If serving fish cold, accompany with Cucumber Sauce (page 105) or mayonnaise and dill or tarragon.

STUFFED FISH

1 **dressed whitefish (1 pound)**
¼ **cup (½ stick) butter**
1½ **teaspoons salt**
2 **tablespoons grated onion**
2 **cups bread cubes**
Paprika or seasoned salt

1. Wash fish and pat dry.
2. Melt butter in a glass custard cup or glass measuring cup in microwave oven (about 30 seconds at HIGH).
3. Brush inside of fish with a portion of the melted butter and sprinkle with salt.
4. Combine 2 tablespoons of the melted butter and onion in an 8-inch round glass cake dish. Cook uncovered in microwave oven 2 minutes at HIGH.
5. Add bread cubes to onion and stir. Fill cavity of fish with stuffing. Lace cavity closed using wooden picks and string.
6. Brush fish with remaining melted butter. Sprinkle with paprika.
7. Put fish on a roast rack set in a 2-quart glass baking dish. Cover with waxed paper. Cook in microwave oven 7 to 9 minutes at BAKE, or until fish flakes when tested with a fork; turn fish over and rotate dish one-half turn once during the cooking period.

About 4 servings

HINT: Any whole fish suitable for baking may be cooked following these directions. If a larger fish is cooked, add approximately 3 minutes per pound additional cooking time.

RED SNAPPER VERACRUZ STYLE

2 **tablespoons olive oil**
1 **cup chopped onion**
1 **clove garlic, minced**
1 **can (16 ounces) tomatoes, drained and coarsely chopped**
1 **teaspoon salt**
¼ **teaspoon pepper**
1½ **pounds red snapper fillets**
¼ **cup sliced pimento-stuffed olives**
Lemon wedges

1. Combine oil, onion and garlic in a 2-quart glass casserole. Cover with an all-glass lid or plastic wrap. Cook in microwave oven 2 minutes at HIGH; stir after 1 minute.
2. Add tomatoes, salt and pepper to mixture in casserole; stir. Cook covered in microwave oven 3 minutes at HIGH.
3. Arrange red snapper fillets, skin side down, in a 2-quart glass baking dish with thicker portions to the outside. Pour sauce over fish. Sprinkle with olives. Cover with plastic wrap.
4. Cook in microwave oven 8 to 9 minutes at HIGH, or until fish flakes easily with a fork; rotate dish one-half turn once.
5. Remove from oven and allow to stand 4 minutes.

About 6 servings

PLANKED HALIBUT DINNER

4 halibut steaks, fresh or
  thawed frozen
  (about 2 pounds)
¼ cup (½ stick) butter
2 tablespoons olive oil
1 tablespoon wine vinegar
2 teaspoons lemon juice
1 clove garlic, minced
¼ teaspoon dry mustard
¼ teaspoon marjoram
½ teaspoon salt
⅛ teaspoon black pepper
2 large zucchini
1 package (10 ounces)
  frozen green peas
1 can (8¼ ounces) tiny
  whole carrots
  Au Gratin Potato Puffs
  Butter
  Fresh parsley
  Lemon wedges

1. Put halibut steaks into a large glass baking dish.
2. Melt butter in a small glass dish in microwave oven (about 30 seconds at HIGH). Mix in olive oil, vinegar, lemon juice, garlic and dry seasonings. Drizzle over halibut. Cover with waxed paper. Cook in microwave oven 6½ to 8½ minutes at BAKE, or until fish flakes easily.
3. Meanwhile, halve zucchini lengthwise and scoop out center portion. Place zucchini halves back together and cook in microwave oven in a covered glass casserole 5 to 7 minutes at HIGH, or until tender.
4. Cook peas in microwave oven following directions on page 188 in Frozen Vegetable Cooking Chart; drain.
5. Turn carrots with liquid into a small glass bowl. Heat uncovered in microwave oven 2 to 3 minutes at HIGH; stir once. Drain.
6. Prepare Au Gratin Potato Puffs.
7. Arrange halibut on wooden plank and border with zucchini halves filled with peas, the carrots and potato puffs.
8. Dot peas and carrots with butter. Place under conventional broiler with top of food 4 to 6 inches from heat just until potato puffs are browned. Sprinkle carrots with chopped parsley.
9. Garnish with sprigs of parsley and lemon wedges arranged on a skewer.

4 servings

Au Gratin Potato Puffs: Pare **4 medium potatoes**; cook in microwave oven as directed on page 186 in Fresh Vegetable Cooking Chart; mash potatoes. Add **2 tablespoons butter** and ⅓ **cup milk**; whip until fluffy. Add **2 slightly beaten egg yolks**, ½ **cup shredded sharp Cheddar cheese**, **1 teaspoon salt** and **few grains pepper**; continue whipping. Using a pastry bag with a large star tip, form mounds about 2 inches in diameter on plank. Proceed as directed in recipe.

SALMON STEAKS WITH CUCUMBER SAUCE

Cucumber Sauce:
  1 cup dairy sour cream
  1 cup chopped pared
    cucumber
  1 tablespoon sugar
  2 tablespoons prepared
    horseradish
  1 tablespoon vinegar
    Salt to taste
    Dash ground red pepper

4 salmon steaks
  (about 2 pounds)

1. For sauce, combine all ingredients in a bowl; chill.
2. Arrange salmon steaks in a 1½-quart glass baking dish. Cover with waxed paper. Cook in microwave oven 4 minutes at HIGH. Turn salmon steaks over and rearrange. Continue cooking covered 3 to 4 minutes at HIGH, or until fish flakes easily when tested with a fork.
3. Remove from oven. Allow to stand covered 2 minutes. Serve with Cucumber Sauce.

4 to 6 servings

TROUT AMANDINE WITH PINEAPPLE

2 tablespoons butter
1 package (2¼ ounces)
    slivered almonds
¼ cup (½ stick) butter
1 tablespoon lemon juice
6 whole cleaned and boned
    trout (about 8 ounces
    each)
6 drained canned pineapple
    slices

1. Put 2 tablespoons butter and almonds into a glass pie plate. Cook uncovered in microwave oven 5 to 6 minutes at HIGH; stir every minute just until almonds are lightly toasted. Set aside.
2. Melt remaining butter in a 2-cup glass measuring cup in microwave oven (30 seconds at HIGH). Add lemon juice.
3. Brush whole trout inside and out with lemon-butter mixture. Arrange fish around edge of a microwave-safe serving plate in a circular pattern. Fit a small piece of foil over each head to shield. Cover with plastic wrap.
4. Cook in microwave oven 6 to 7 minutes at HIGH, or until fish flakes easily. (Be certain to check for doneness under shielded area.)
5. Remove from oven and allow to stand covered 2 minutes.
6. Meanwhile, arrange pineapple slices on toasted almonds. Cover with plastic wrap. Heat in microwave oven 2 minutes at HIGH. Garnish fish with almonds and pineapple.

6 servings

CRAB-STUFFED FILLET OF SOLE

3 tablespoons butter
3 tablespoons flour
½ teaspoon salt
1½ cups milk
⅓ cup dry white wine
1 cup shredded Swiss
    cheese
1 medium onion, peeled
    and minced
2 tablespoons butter
1 can (6½ or 7 ounces)
    crab meat, drained and
    flaked
1 can (4 ounces)
    mushrooms, drained and
    finely chopped
½ cup coarse cracker
    crumbs
    Salt and freshly ground
    white pepper
8 sole fillets
    (about 2 pounds)
    Snipped parsley

1. Melt 3 tablespoons butter in a 1-quart glass measuring cup in microwave oven (about 30 seconds at HIGH). Stir in flour and ½ teaspoon salt. Gradually add milk and wine, stirring until smooth. Cook uncovered 3 minutes at HIGH, or until thickened; stir once. Stir in cheese. Set aside.
2. Put onion and 2 tablespoons butter into a 1-quart glass casserole. Cook uncovered in microwave oven 2 minutes at HIGH, or until onion is tender; stir after 1 minute.
3. Add crab meat, mushrooms and cracker crumbs to onion; mix well. Season with salt and pepper.
4. Lay each fillet white side down and sprinkle with salt and pepper. Dividing the stuffing evenly, spread stuffing almost the full length of each fillet. Roll up and place seam side down in a 2-quart glass baking dish. Cover with waxed paper.
5. Cook in microwave oven 5 minutes at HIGH; rotate dish one-half turn after 3 minutes. With a bulb baster, draw off any juices in the baking dish and stir into the sauce. Continue cooking covered 2 to 3 minutes at HIGH.
6. Remove dish from oven. Allow to stand covered 5 minutes.
7. Meanwhile, heat sauce uncovered in microwave oven 5 minutes at HIGH, or until bubbly; stir once. Pour sauce into a sauce boat and garnish with parsley. Serve sauce with the fish.

8 servings

FILLET OF SOLE IN ALMOND SAUCE

1 package (16 ounces) frozen fillet of sole
½ cup (1 stick) butter
¼ cup toasted slivered almonds
¼ teaspoon salt
2 teaspoons lemon juice

1. Defrost fish in microwave oven following directions on page 71 in Defrosting Chart.
2. Melt ¼ cup butter in a small glass dish in microwave oven (30 seconds at HIGH).
3. Place fillets in a 2-quart glass baking dish and brush with melted butter. Cover with waxed paper. Cook in microwave oven 4 to 5 minutes at HIGH, or until fish flakes easily when tested with a fork.
4. Melt remaining ¼ cup butter in a glass measuring cup in microwave oven (30 seconds at HIGH). Add almonds, salt and lemon juice; stir.
5. To serve, pour sauce over fillets.

About 4 servings

PERCH WITH PARSLEY AND DILL

8 dressed medium-size perch
1 teaspoon salt
½ teaspoon pepper
¼ cup finely snipped parsley
2 tablespoons snipped parsley
2 tablespoons chopped fresh dill, or 1 teaspoon dill seed

1. Season fish with salt and pepper.
2. Sprinkle ¼ cup parsley over bottom of a buttered 1½-quart glass baking dish. Arrange fish in dish and top fish with remaining parsley and dill. Cover with waxed paper. Cook in microwave oven 4 to 6 minutes at HIGH, or until fish flakes easily when tested with a fork.
3. Transfer fish to serving platter and garnish with **sprigs of parsley** and **dill** and **lemon wedges**.

4 servings

MISSISSIPPI RIVER DELIGHT

4 skinned and dressed cat-fish or other fish, fresh or frozen
⅓ cup bottled French dress-ing
8 lemon slices
Paprika

1. Clean, wash and dry fish. Brush inside and out with dressing.
2. Cut 4 of the lemon slices in half and place 2 halves in each body cavity.
3. Place fish in a 2-quart glass baking dish. Pour remaining dressing over fish and sprinkle with paprika. Place lemon slice on top of each fish. Cover with waxed paper.
4. Cook in microwave oven 5 minutes at HIGH, or until fish flakes easily when tested with a fork; rotate dish one-half turn once.

4 servings

SALMON LOAF

1 can (16 ounces) salmon
⅓ cup milk
⅔ cup soft bread crumbs
2 eggs
1 teaspoon salt
½ cup chopped celery
1 tablespoon lemon juice
1 tablespoon chopped
   parsley
   Paprika for top

1. Drain fish, remove bones and skin and flake with a fork. Combine with remaining ingredients and mix well.
2. Spoon mixture into a 1-quart glass casserole. Sprinkle with paprika. Cover with an all-glass lid or plastic wrap. Cook in microwave oven <u>10 to 14 minutes at BAKE</u>, or until loaf is set around the edges; rotate casserole one-quarter turn once.
3. Let stand 5 minutes before serving and garnish with **parsley** and **lemon wedges.**

SALMON RING

½ cup chopped celery
½ cup chopped green pep-
   per
2 tablespoons minced onion
1 can (16 ounces) red
   salmon or 2 cans (6½ or
   7 ounces each) tuna
1 cup fine dry bread
   crumbs
1 tablespoon lemon juice
1 cup undiluted evaporated
   milk
1 egg, beaten

1. Combine celery, green pepper and onion in a 2-quart glass casserole. Cook uncovered in microwave oven <u>2 minutes at HIGH</u>, or until tender.
2. Add salmon, bread crumbs and lemon juice to cooked vegetables.
3. Combine milk and egg; add to salmon mixture and mix well.
4. Carefully spoon the mixture into a microwave-safe ring mold. Cover with waxed paper. Cook in microwave oven <u>8 to 9 minutes at HIGH</u>; rotate dish one-quarter turn once.

6 servings

HINT: If a microwave-safe ring mold is unavailable, form a ring mold by placing a custard cup right side up in an 8-inch round glass cake dish.

TUNA-CHIP CASSEROLE

2 cans (6½ or 7 ounces
   each) tuna, drained
1 can (about 10 ounces)
   condensed cream of
   mushroom soup
¾ cup (about 5 ounces)
   frozen green peas
⅓ cup chopped celery
1 tablespoon chopped
   onion
¼ cup milk
1 teaspoon Worcestershire
   sauce
¾ cup coarsely crushed
   potato chips

1. Combine tuna, soup, peas, celery, onion, milk and Worcestershire sauce in a 2-quart glass casserole, mixing thoroughly. Sprinkle potato chips over top of mixture.
2. Cook uncovered in microwave oven <u>10 minutes at HIGH</u>, or until thoroughly heated; rotate casserole one-quarter turn once.

About 6 servings

TUNA SUPREME

2 tablespoons oil
⅔ cup chopped onion
1 green pepper, cut in thin strips
1 can (about 10 ounces) condensed tomato soup
2 teaspoons soy sauce
2 tablespoons brown sugar
1 teaspoon grated lemon peel
3 tablespoons lemon juice
2 cans (6½ or 7 ounces each) tuna, drained
Cooked rice (page 48)

1. Heat oil in a 2-quart glass casserole in microwave oven 1 minute at HIGH. Add onion and green pepper; stir. Cook uncovered in microwave oven 2 minutes at HIGH, or until vegetables are tender; stir once.
2. Add tomato soup, soy sauce, brown sugar, lemon peel and lemon juice to mixture in casserole; mix. Cook uncovered in microwave oven 4 minutes at HIGH; stir once.
3. Mix tuna with tomato mixture. Heat uncovered in microwave oven to serving temperature (2 minutes at HIGH).
4. Serve with cooked rice.

About 6 servings

TUNA-MACARONI CASSEROLE

1 package (10 ounces) frozen chopped broccoli
2 cups (7 ounces) uncooked elbow macaroni
2 cans (6½ or 7 ounces each) tuna in vegetable oil
1 teaspoon salt
¼ cup chopped celery
1 can (about 11 ounces) condensed Cheddar cheese soup
1¼ cups milk

1. Heat frozen broccoli in microwave oven just until thawed (about 3 minutes at HIGH); drain.
2. Cook macaroni following recipe for Cooked Pasta (page 49).
3. In a 3-quart glass casserole, combine cooked macaroni, undrained tuna, salt, drained broccoli and celery.
4. Blend condensed soup and milk; add to tuna mixture and mix well. Cover with an all-glass lid or plastic wrap. Cook in microwave oven about 10 minutes at HIGH, or until thoroughly heated; stir occasionally.

About 6 servings

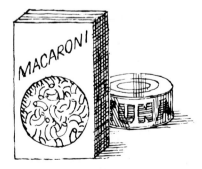

WHOLE LOBSTER

1 whole lobster
(1½ pounds)
¼ cup hot water
1 teaspoon salt
2 tablespoons butter or
margarine
Salt, pepper and paprika

1. To kill the lobster, place lobster on a cutting board with back or smooth shell up. Hold a towel firmly over head and claws. Quickly insert the point of a sharp heavy knife into center of the small cross on the back of the head; this kills the lobster by severing the spinal cord. Before removing knife, bear down heavily, cutting through entire length of body and tail. Pull halves apart; remove and discard the stomach (a small sac which lies in the head) and the spongy lungs (which lie in upper body cavity between meat and shell). Remove and discard the dark intestinal vein running through center of body. Crack claws with a nut cracker.
2. Put hot water and 1 teaspoon salt into a 2-quart glass baking dish. Put lobster into dish, shell side up. Cover with plastic wrap. Cook in microwave oven 4 minutes at HIGH.
3. Remove from oven and turn lobster over.
4. Melt butter in a small glass container in microwave oven (about 15 seconds at HIGH). Brush melted butter over lobster meat and sprinkle with salt, pepper and paprika. Continue cooking lobster covered in microwave oven 5½ to 8½ minutes at ROAST, or until flesh is white and firm and shell is red.

LOBSTER TAILS

Frozen rock lobster tails,
7 to 8 ounces each
Melted butter
Paprika (optional)

1. To thaw lobster, heat the tails in microwave oven until they feel just warm. Allow to stand about 10 minutes for heat to equalize and tails to completely defrost.
2. For "butterfly" style tails, cut hard shell down middle with sharp knife. Grasp tail in both hands and open flat. Brush flesh with melted butter and, if desired, sprinkle with paprika.
3. Place lobster tails, flesh side up, in a glass baking dish. Cook uncovered in microwave oven; rearrange tails in dish after half of cooking period is completed.

Cook as follows:

Number	Minutes
1	3 to 3½ at HIGH
2	4½ to 5 at HIGH
4	5½ to 6 at HIGH

HINT: Cooking times are approximate. Color is the best indication of proper cooking; the flesh should be opaque and the shell red.

DEVILED CRAB

3 tablespoons butter
2 tablespoons chopped onion
2 tablespoons flour
¾ cup milk
1 egg, beaten
½ teaspoon salt
Dash pepper
½ teaspoon dry mustard
½ teaspoon sage
Dash ground red pepper
1 teaspoon Worcestershire sauce
1 tablespoon lemon juice
1 tablespoon chopped parsley
1 pound crab meat (bony tissue removed)
1 tablespoon butter
¼ cup dry bread crumbs

1. Put 3 tablespoons butter and onion into a 1½-quart glass casserole. Cook uncovered in microwave oven <u>3 minutes at HIGH</u>, or until tender; stir after 1 minute.
2. Stir flour into the butter. Add milk gradually; stir constantly. Cook uncovered in microwave oven <u>2 minutes at HIGH</u>, or until thickened; stir occasionally.
3. Stir a little of the hot sauce into the egg. Add to remaining sauce, stirring constantly. Add salt, pepper, mustard, sage, red pepper, Worcestershire sauce, lemon juice, parsley and crab meat; mix well.
4. Divide mixture into 6 individual shells or glass custard cups.
5. Melt 1 tablespoon butter in a small glass dish in microwave oven (<u>30 seconds at HIGH</u>). Mix bread crumbs with melted butter and sprinkle over top of each shell. Cook uncovered in microwave oven <u>5 to 7 minutes at BAKE</u>; rearrange shells once during cooking period.

6 servings

COQUILLES ST. JACQUES

2 tablespoons butter
3 tablespoons lemon juice
1 pound fresh mushrooms, cleaned and sliced
1 cup dry white wine
¼ teaspoon thyme
1 bay leaf
½ teaspoon salt
⅛ teaspoon pepper
1 pound bay scallops
1½ tablespoons butter
1½ tablespoons flour
½ cup milk
¾ cup buttered bread crumbs

1. Put 2 tablespoons butter, lemon juice and mushrooms into a 2-quart glass baking dish. Cook uncovered in microwave oven <u>5 minutes at HIGH</u>; stir once. Drain mushrooms and set aside.
2. Combine wine, thyme, bay leaf, salt and pepper in the glass baking dish. Add scallops. Cover with plastic wrap. Cook in microwave oven <u>5 minutes at HIGH</u>, or until tender; stir once. Drain, reserving ½ cup broth. Discard bay leaf. Set scallops aside.
3. Melt remaining butter in the glass baking dish in microwave oven (<u>about 15 seconds at HIGH</u>). Add flour and blend to a smooth paste. Gradually add milk and reserved broth, stirring constantly. Cook uncovered <u>5 minutes at HIGH</u>, or until thickened; stir after 3 minutes, then at the end of each 30 seconds.
4. Add mushrooms and scallops to white sauce; mix thoroughly. Sprinkle bread crumbs over top. Cook uncovered in microwave oven <u>4 minutes at HIGH</u>; rotate dish one-half turn once.
5. Serve immediately.

6 servings

FRESH SHRIMP

Fresh shrimp can easily be cooked for use in salads, appetizers, or for serving in a sauce.

1 pound shrimp	Shrimp may be shelled before or after cooking. Arrange shrimp in a layer on bottom of a glass baking dish. Cook uncovered in micro-wave oven <u>5 to 6 minutes at HIGH</u>, or until shrimp meat turns white and opaque; stir twice.

HINT: If shrimp is frozen, follow directions on page 71 in Defrosting Chart.

SHRIMP CREOLE

1 pound fresh shrimp, cooked
2 tablespoons vegetable oil
¾ cup finely chopped onion
¾ cup finely chopped green pepper
2 tablespoons flour
1 can (16 ounces) tomatoes, sieved
1 teaspoon Worcestershire sauce
1 bay leaf
1½ teaspoons salt
¼ teaspoon pepper
½ teaspoon sugar
½ teaspoon oregano
Cooked rice (page 48)

1. Reserve 8 whole shrimp for garnish and cut remainder into pieces. Refrigerate until ready to use.
2. Heat oil in a 2-quart glass casserole in microwave oven <u>30 seconds at HIGH</u>. Mix in onion and green pepper. Cook uncovered in microwave oven <u>4 minutes at HIGH</u>, or until tender; stir after each minute.
3. Sprinkle vegetables with flour. Stir in remaining ingredients except cooked rice. Cook uncovered in microwave oven <u>6 minutes at HIGH</u>; stir once or twice.
4. Stir in shrimp pieces. Heat uncovered in microwave oven to serving temperature (<u>3 minutes at HIGH</u>).
5. Serve shrimp mixture on hot cooked rice and garnish with the whole shrimp.

About 4 servings

SHRIMP IN PATTY SHELLS

2 tablespoons butter or margarine
1 small onion, thinly sliced
1 small clove garlic, minced
1 can (about 10 ounces) condensed cream of celery soup
½ cup milk
1½ pounds cooked shrimp, peeled and deveined
½ cup cooked peas
6 to 8 refrigerated puff pastry patty shells, baked conventionally

1. Put butter, onion and garlic into a 1½-quart glass casserole. Cook uncovered in microwave oven <u>4 minutes at HIGH</u>, or until onion is tender; stir after 1 minute.
2. Add soup, milk, cooked shrimp and peas; mix. Cover with waxed paper. Cook <u>4 to 5 minutes at HIGH</u>, or until thoroughly heated; stir occasionally.
3. Serve shrimp mixture in patty shells.

6 to 8 servings

SHRIMP WITH TOMATOES AND POTATOES

1 pound cooked, shelled
shrimp (page 113)
¼ pound salt pork, diced
⅔ cup chopped onion
2 medium potatoes, pared
and diced (about 2½
cups)
1 small clove garlic, minced
1 teaspoon salt
¼ teaspoon seasoned pepper
¼ teaspoon oregano
1 bay leaf
½ cup hot water
1 can (19 or 20 ounces)
tomatoes (undrained)
4 drops Tabasco

1. Cut shrimp into pieces; set aside.
2. Put salt pork into a 2-quart glass baking dish. Cover with a paper towel. Cook in microwave oven 2 to 3 minutes at HIGH, or until fat accumulates; stir occasionally.
3. Add onion to salt pork; stir. Cook uncovered in microwave oven 2½ minutes at HIGH, or until soft.
4. Add potatoes, garlic, salt, seasoned pepper, oregano, bay leaf and hot water; mix. Cover with waxed paper. Cook in microwave oven 10 to 12 minutes at HIGH, or until potato is tender; stir occasionally.
5. Mix tomatoes, Tabasco and shrimp into potato mixture in dish. Cover with waxed paper. Heat in microwave oven to serving temperature (5 to 6 minutes at HIGH).

About 4 servings

AVOCADO VOISIN

1½ tablespoons butter
1½ tablespoons minced onion
1½ tablespoons minced celery
¾ teaspoon curry powder
¾ cup uncooked white rice
1½ cups chicken or beef
broth
Few grains each salt and
white pepper
1 small bay leaf
1½ tablespoons butter
2 tablespoons flour
Few grains each salt and
white pepper
1 cup milk
1 egg yolk
1 tablespoon butter
2 cans (about 6½ ounces
each) crab meat, drained
2 tablespoons chutney,
finely chopped
3 avocados
Lemon juice
3 tablespoons grated
Parmesan cheese
Parsley and lemon
wedges for garnish

1. Put 1½ tablespoons butter, onion and celery into a 1½-quart top-of-range glass casserole*. Cook uncovered in microwave oven about 4 minutes at HIGH, or until tender; stir after 1 minute.
2. Add curry powder to vegetables and blend thoroughly. Stir in rice, mixing to coat each grain. Add broth, few grains each salt and white pepper and bay leaf. Cover and cook, following package directions, on conventional range surface unit until rice is tender and liquid absorbed.
3. Meanwhile, melt 1½ tablespoons butter in a 1-quart glass casserole in microwave oven (about 15 seconds at HIGH). Blend in flour and remaining salt and pepper. Add milk gradually, stirring constantly. Cook uncovered 4 minutes at HIGH, or until thickened; stir after each minute.
4. Beat egg yolk slightly and stir in a small amount of hot mixture, then return to mixture in casserole and blend. Cover sauce and keep warm.
5. Melt remaining butter in a large glass pie plate in microwave oven (about 15 seconds at HIGH). Add crab meat, mix and heat uncovered in microwave oven until hot (about 2 minutes at HIGH).
6. Add chutney to crab meat and mix well. Combine rice and crab meat, tossing lightly to mix. Keep warm.
7. Halve avocados, remove seeds and peel. Cut small slice from bottoms so that avocados will be flat, arrange avocados on a glass platter and put cut-off slices in avocado cavities. Brush cut surfaces of avocado with lemon juice. Pile crab-rice mixture into avocado halves. Spoon sauce over each stuffed avocado. Cook uncovered in microwave oven 2 minutes at HIGH. Sprinkle with Parmesan cheese. Heat uncovered to serving temperature (1 to 3 minutes at BAKE).
8. Garnish with parsley and lemon wedges.

6 servings

*If you do not have top-of-range glass casserole, do steps 1 and 2 in a pan on top of a conventional range.

Avocado Voisin

SEAFOOD CASSEROLE

2 frozen rock lobster tails
1 pound scrod fillets
¼ cup white wine
2 cans (6½ ounces each)
   Alaska King crab or 2
   packages (6 ounces each)
   frozen crab, thawed
1 can (about 10 ounces)
   condensed cream of
   shrimp soup
1 can (about 10 ounces)
   condensed cream of
   mushroom soup
½ cup whipping cream
2 tablespoons sherry
   Dash pepper
2 tablespoons butter or
   margarine
¼ cup dry bread crumbs
¼ cup grated Parmesan
   cheese
   Paprika

1. Defrost lobster following directions on page 71 in Defrosting Chart. Cook following directions on page 111. Remove lobster meat and cut into small pieces. Set aside.
2. Cut scrod into serving pieces. Place in a 1½-quart glass baking dish. Add wine. Cover with plastic wrap. Cook in microwave oven 5 minutes at HIGH. Drain and break up into small pieces.
3. Combine lobster, scrod, crab, condensed soups, cream, sherry, and pepper in a 1½-quart glass casserole. Insert Temperature Probe in center of mixture, being careful that it does not rest on bottom of casserole. Cook uncovered in microwave oven set at 155°F and at HIGH.
4. Melt butter in a 2-cup glass measuring cup in microwave oven (45 seconds at HIGH). Add crumbs and Parmesan cheese. Mix well and sprinkle over seafood mixture. Sprinkle paprika over all.

6 servings

HINT: If not using Temperature Probe, cook casserole uncovered 15 minutes at HIGH; rotate dish one-half turn once.

Meat

In many homes, the meat dish stars at dinner time. Whether it is the family-favorite meat loaf, an elegant crown roast of lamb or an all-American pot roast, these delicious foods can be prepared quickly and easily in your microwave oven. Most dishes will cook in one-third to one-half the time it takes using conventional methods, retaining the natural meat juices for tender and flavorful results.

Tender cuts of meat, such as roasts, can be cooked with excellent results. A uniformly shaped roast cooks most evenly. If you notice narrow areas cooking too fast, shield them with aluminum foil tucked around the meat. Make sure the foil does not touch the sides of the microwave oven.

Defrost meat completely before cooking. Place the roast on a microwave-safe roast rack to hold the meat out of the cooking juices. During the first half of the cooking time, place the roast fat side down. Halfway through the cooking period, turn the roast so the fat side is up to prevent the surface from overcooking.

Save the tasty juices to serve as *au jus* or to make gravy. Tender cuts of meat need no additional moisture when they cook, so waxed paper is an ideal cover. It will help hold the heat around the roast and prevent the interior of your microwave oven from being spattered. Consult the charts in this chapter for time, temperature and power levels for the cut of meat you are cooking. Remember that the length of time will vary with the initial temperature, weight and shape of the meat and, of course, personal preferences for doneness. During the initial cooking, use the suggested time as a guide. When you turn the roast over, insert the Temperature Probe in the roast, making sure that the tip of the probe does not touch bone or fat. You'll find that the Temperature Probe gives you truly carefree meat cooking.

If you do not have a Temperature Probe, remove the roast from the microwave oven and use a conventional meat thermometer to test the internal temperature. If additional cooking time is needed, remove thermometer and return roast to microwave oven.

Standing time is more important with larger cuts of meat than with any other food. A standing time of twenty minutes is necessary for the temperature of the meat to equalize. During this time, the internal temperature will increase 15 to 20 degrees. For this reason, be sure you stop cooking 15 degrees below the desired serving temperature. When you remove the roast from the microwave oven, cover with aluminum foil to prevent the surface from cooling. Leave the ends open slightly to prevent the roast from getting a steamed taste.

Contrary to what friends and relatives will say, you'll find that roasts do indeed turn brown when cooked in a microwave oven. Roasts brown naturally because of their size, fat content and the length of cooking time.

The Gourmet Control feature with its range of power settings gives you the flexibility to cook less tender cuts of meat with such tasty results that your family will clamor for them to be served often. Less tender cuts of meat need to be cooked more slowly and with added moisture until they become fork tender. Some recipes call for marinating; this also adds color and flavor. These meats need to be tightly covered to hold in the steam and aid in tenderizing. Some foods, for instance stews, will cook better when the pieces are small and uniform. As with tender cuts, the meat should be completely defrosted before cooking. The food will cook more evenly if large pieces are turned and small pieces are stirred.

The versatility of ground meat makes it the basic ingredient in many favorite main dishes. These meat dishes cook quickly and easily in your microwave oven.

Utilize leftovers for an economical dish. When adapting one of your recipes you may need to cut the amount of added liquid, as it will not evaporate in a microwave oven.

Steaks, chops and hamburgers can be cooked in the microwave oven. However, these meats will cook so quickly that they won't have time to brown. You can achieve a browner appearance by using a gravy browning sauce, or by adding onion soup mix before cooking. You may also brown under the browning element, if your microwave oven has one, or in a conventional broiler for a few minutes.

Lamb Crown Roast with Apricot Stuffing, 127; Cauliflower and Peas (see Fresh and Frozen Vegetable Cooking Charts, pages 185 and 188)

MEAT COOKING

The following Chart is a guide for cooking roasts, hamburgers, steaks and chops. For best results with roasts, use your Temperature Probe for accurate cooking.

First determine the approximate cooking time by multiplying the pounds of meat by the approximate cooking minutes per pound. Divide by two to determine half the cooking time. Set time and power level for first half of the cooking time (power level is indicated on the chart) and cook without using the Temperature Probe. After the first half of the cooking time has elapsed, turn the meat over and insert Temperature Probe in the center of meat. Set Gourmet Control and Temperature Control for second half of the cooking time (see chart) and cook. When the meat interior reaches the preset temperature, the microwave oven will automatically turn off. Cover and allow the meat to stand for 15 minutes before carving. During the standing time the internal temperature will rise 15 to 20 degrees.

Meat	Power setting for first half of cooking	Power setting for second half of cooking†	Approximate cooking time	Temp. Probe setting	Internal temp. after standing time
Beef					
Rolled rib roast (3 to 5 lbs.)	High	Roast	8 to 9 min. per lb.	125°F	140°F rare
			10 to 11 min. per lb.	145°F	160°F medium
			12 to 13 min. per lb.	155°F	170°F well
Standing rib roast (4 to 6 lbs.)	High	Roast	7 to 8 min. per lb.	125°F	140°F rare
			8 to 9 min. per lb.	145°F	160°F medium
			10 to 11 min. per lb.	155°F	170°F well
Rolled rump roast, boneless (4 to 6 lbs.)	Roast	Roast	8½ to 10 min. per lb.	135°F	150°F medium-rare
			10 to 11 min. per lb.	145°F	160°F medium
			11 to 12½ min. per lb.	155°F	170°F well
Tenderloin, half (2 to 3 lbs.)	High	High	2 to 3 min. per lb.	125°F	140°F rare
Hamburgers (2)	High	High	3 min.		rare
(4)	High	High	4 min.		rare
*Steaks, T-bone, porterhouse, or sirloin (1 lb.)	*High	High	5 to 7 min.		rare to medium-rare
Lamb					
Leg (4 to 8 lbs.)	Roast	Roast	8 to 9 min. per lb.	145°F	160°F medium
			10 to 11 min. per lb.	155°-165°F	170°-180°F well

*Steaks and chops can also be done in a microwave oven Browner Grille®.
†Turn meat over for second half of cooking time.

Meat	Power setting for first half of cooking	Power setting for second half of cooking†	Approximate cooking time	Temp. Probe setting	Internal temp. after standing time
Lamb (cont.)					
Boneless leg, rolled (3 to 6 lbs.)	Roast	Roast	10 to 11 min. per lb.	145°F	160°F medium
			11 to 12½ min. per lb.	155°-165°F	170°-180°F well
Chops, loin (2)	Roast	Roast	7 to 10 min.		medium
(4)	Roast	Roast	12½ to 15 min.		medium
Pork					
Loin roast, boneless or bone in (3 to 5 lbs.)	High	Roast	10 to 12 min. per lb.	160°F	170°F well
Shoulder roast, boneless (4 lbs.)	High	Roast	10 to 11 min. per lb.	160°F	170°F well
*Chops, loin (2)	High	High	6 to 8 min.		well done
(4)	High	High	10 to 12 min.		well done
**Ham, fully cooked (2 to 5 lbs.)	Roast	Roast	9 to 11 min. per lb.	115°F	130°F
(6 to 10 lbs.)	Roast	Roast	7 to 10 min. per lb.	115°F	130°F
Veal					
Boneless shoulder roast (3 lbs.)	Roast	Roast	11 to 13 min. per lb.	155°F	170°F well

*Steaks and chops can also be done in a microwave oven Browner Grille®.
**For a cook-before-eating ham we suggest using the conventional oven.
†Turn meat over for second half of cooking time.

COOKING LESS-TENDER CUTS OF MEAT*

Meat	Power Setting	Approximate Cooking Time
Beef brisket (3-3½ lbs.; 2 cups water)	High	10 minutes
	Simmer	90 minutes or until fork tender
Beef short ribs (3 lbs.)	High	10 minutes
	Simmer	40-50 minutes or until fork tender
Corned beef (3 lbs.; 2 cups water)	High	10 minutes
	Simmer	90 minutes or until fork tender
Lamb stew (2 lbs. lamb shoulder)	High	10 minutes
	Simmer	30-40 minutes or until fork tender
Pork spareribs (2 lbs.)	Simmer	35-45 minutes or until fork tender
Pot roast (4 lbs. beef chuck pot roast)	Simmer	65-75 minutes or until fork tender
Swiss steak (2 lbs. beef round steak)	Simmer	50-60 minutes or until fork tender

*Follow favorite recipe for amount of liquid unless otherwise stated.

Beef Rolled Roast

BEEF ROLLED ROAST

3- to 5-pound beef boneless rolled rib or rump roast Salt and pepper (optional)

1. Set roast, fat side down, on a roast rack set in a 2-quart glass baking dish. Season roast, if desired, with salt and pepper. Cover roast with waxed paper. Cook in microwave oven for one-half of cooking time (see Meat Cooking Chart for time and settings).
2. After one-half of cooking time is completed, turn roast over, fat side up. Insert Temperature Probe in center of meat. Cook covered in microwave oven set at temperature for desired doneness and at ROAST.
3. Remove roast from oven. Cover meat with foil and allow to stand 20 to 30 minutes for heat to equalize; during this time internal temperature will rise.

HINTS: To add flavor and color, coat surface of roast completely with dry onion soup mix (about 1 package).
•If one side of roast appears to be cooking faster than the other side, rotate dish one-half turn.

BEEF STANDING RIB ROAST

4- to 6-pound beef standing
  rib roast
Salt and pepper
  (optional)

1. Set roast, fat side down, on a roast rack set in a 2-quart glass baking dish. Season roast, if desired, with salt and pepper. Cover any bones that extend from meat with aluminum foil. Cover roast with waxed paper. Cook in microwave oven for one-half of cooking time (see Meat Cooking Chart for time and settings).
2. After one-half of cooking time is completed, turn roast over, fat side up. Insert Temperature Probe in center of meat. Cook covered in microwave oven set at temperature for desired doneness and at ROAST.
3. Remove roast from oven. Cover meat with foil and allow to stand 20 to 30 minutes for heat to equalize; during this time internal temperature will rise.

YANKEE POT ROAST

1 beef arm chuck roast
  (4 pounds)
1 package brown gravy mix
4 small onions, cut in half
  Hot water
4 carrots, pared, halved
  and cut in thirds
4 potatoes, pared and cut
  in quarters

1. Put meat into a 4-quart glass casserole. Sprinkle gravy mix over meat. Add onion and enough hot water to cover meat. Cover casserole with an all-glass lid.
2. Cook in microwave oven 30 minutes at SIMMER.
3. Turn meat over. Add carrots and potatoes to liquid. Cook covered in microwave oven 1 hour at SIMMER, or until meat is tender.
4. Remove from oven and allow to stand covered 10 to 15 minutes.
5. If desired, thicken liquid as for Basic Gravy (page 178).

6 to 8 servings

BEEF TENDERLOIN

3-pound beef loin
  tenderloin roast
1 to 2 tablespoons butter

1. Trim any surface fat and connective tissue from exterior of roast.
2. Melt butter in a glass custard cup in microwave oven (about 30 seconds at HIGH).
3. Brush meat with melted butter and place on a roast rack set in a 2-quart glass baking dish. Cover with waxed paper. Cook in microwave oven 6 to 8 minutes at HIGH; after one-half of cooking time is completed, rotate dish one-half turn; turn roast over.
4. Remove meat from oven and allow to stand 5 minutes; meat will be rare.

HINT: If additional browning is desired, see page 117 or brown meat under microwave browning element or broiler. Be sure not to use glass baking dish under conventional broiler.

SIRLOIN STEAK WITH BLUE RIBBON SAUCE

1 beef sirloin steak
    (2 pounds), cut about ¾
    to 1 inch thick
1 cup thinly sliced onion
1 lemon, thinly sliced
¼ cup (½ stick) butter or
    margarine
2 tablespoons prepared
    mustard
1 cup chili sauce
1 tablespoon
    Worcestershire sauce
1 teaspoon chili powder
1 can (6 ounces) cocktail
    vegetable juice
Salt (optional)

1. Trim fat from steak. Cut steak into serving pieces and put into an 8-inch square glass baking dish. Arrange onion and lemon slices over meat.

2. Cream butter and mustard; blend in chili sauce, Worcestershire sauce, chili powder and vegetable juice. Pour mixture over onion and lemon. Cover with plastic wrap. Cook in microwave oven 15 minutes at HIGH, or until meat is done as desired; rearrange meat halfway through cooking period.

3. Remove from oven. Allow to stand covered 5 minutes before serving.

4. Sprinkle meat with salt, if desired.

About 6 servings

BEEF CUBED STEAKS

4 beef cubed steaks
2 tablespoons butter
Salt and pepper

1. Place steaks in a glass baking dish; steaks should not overlap.

2. Melt butter in a glass custard cup in microwave oven (about 30 seconds at HIGH).

3. Brush steaks with melted butter. Cover with waxed paper. Cook in microwave oven 3 minutes at HIGH.

4. Turn over and rearrange steaks. Cook covered in microwave oven 2 to 3 minutes at HIGH, or until done as desired.

5. Sprinkle with salt and pepper before serving.

STEAK AND VEGETABLES ON SKEWERS

2 ears corn
1 cup Burgundy
¼ cup vegetable oil
2 tablespoons onion soup
    mix
1 teaspoon salt
½ teaspoon thyme
¼ teaspoon pepper
1 clove garlic, minced
1½ pounds beef sirloin, cut
    in 1-inch pieces
2 zucchini, cut in 1-inch
    pieces
4 cherry tomatoes

1. Cook corn (see Fresh Vegetable Cooking Chart, page 185) 3 minutes at HIGH, or until just tender enough to cut through. Cut into 1-inch slices.

2. Combine Burgundy, oil, soup mix, salt, thyme, pepper and garlic. Add meat and marinate 1 hour at room temperature or 2 hours in refrigerator.

3. Remove meat and reserve marinade. Alternate meat, corn and zucchini on 4 skewers. If using metal skewers, see page 14. Arrange skewers on microwave oven cooking tray.

4. Cover with waxed paper. Cook in microwave oven 8 to 10 minutes at ROAST, or until meat is done as desired. Turn and rearrange skewers and brush with marinade twice during cooking period.

5. Place a cherry tomato at the end of each skewer for garnish. Serve on a bed of **cooked rice**.

4 servings

BEEF KABOBS

1	cup soy sauce
1/3	cup honey
1½	pounds beef sirloin, cut in 1-inch pieces
12	pineapple chunks, fresh or canned
1	green pepper, cut in squares
8	cherry tomatoes

1. Combine soy sauce and honey. Add meat and marinate 1 hour.
2. Remove meat and reserve marinade.
3. Alternate beef, pineapple and green pepper on 4 skewers. (If using metal skewers, see page 14.) Arrange kabobs in a 2-quart glass baking dish and brush with marinade.
4. Cover with waxed paper. Cook in microwave oven 6 to 7 minutes at ROAST, or until meat is done as desired; turn and rearrange skewers and brush with marinade twice during cooking period.
5. Place a cherry tomato at the end of each skewer for garnish. Serve on a bed of **cooked rice**.

4 servings

CARIBBEAN STEAK KABOBS

1¾	pounds beef sirloin, boneless, cut 1¼ inches thick
1	cup soy sauce
1/3	cup honey
2	cloves garlic, minced
¼	cup finely chopped crystallized ginger
2	firm bananas with all-yellow peel
¼	cup flaked coconut Lime juice

1. Slice meat across grain into ¼-inch strips.
2. Combine soy sauce, honey, garlic and ginger; mix well and pour over meat strips in a large shallow dish. Refrigerate about 30 minutes, turning meat once.
3. Remove meat from marinade, reserving marinade. Thread meat onto 12 (8-inch) bamboo skewers, allowing space at end of each skewer for banana pieces.
4. Peel bananas and cut into 24 pieces; dip pieces into marinade, roll in coconut and drizzle with lime juice.
5. Put banana pieces on ends of skewers; brush meat and banana pieces with marinade.
6. Arrange 6 kabobs in a large glass baking dish. Cover with waxed paper. Cook in microwave oven 2 minutes at HIGH.
7. Turn and rearrange kabobs. Cook covered in microwave oven 2 minutes at HIGH.
8. Put kabobs on heated platter and keep warm.
9. Repeat procedure for remaining 6 kabobs.

6 servings

MICROWAVE SUKIYAKI

2 **pounds beef tenderloin**
½ **cup soy sauce**
¼ **cup sherry or sake**
¼ **cup sugar**
2 **medium onions**
1 **cup drained canned sliced mushrooms**
5 **green onions, sliced**
1 **can (5 ounces) water chestnuts, drained and sliced**
1 **can (16 ounces) bean sprouts, drained and rinsed**
½ **pound spinach leaves, washed, drained and sliced**
1 **can (5 ounces) bamboo shoots, drained and sliced**
Cooked rice (page 48)

1. Cut beef into thin slices and put into 2-quart glass baking dish. Mix soy sauce, sherry and sugar; pour over meat. Set aside to marinate about 30 minutes.
2. Slice onions and put over meat. Cover with waxed paper. Cook in microwave oven 5 minutes at HIGH; stir occasionally.
3. Push meat into center of dish. Put the remaining vegetables into dish in separate piles around the edges. Spoon some of the marinade in dish over each vegetable. Cover with waxed paper. Cook in microwave oven 6 minutes at HIGH; rotate dish one-half turn once.
4. Serve with hot cooked rice.

6 to 8 servings

MICROWAVE STROGANOFF

1½ **pounds beef sirloin, boneless**
⅓ **cup flour**
¼ **teaspoon salt**
⅛ **teaspoon pepper**
⅓ **cup butter or margarine**
1 **can (about 10 ounces) condensed beef consommé or broth**
1 **can (about 10 ounces) condensed onion soup**
1 **can (3 ounces) sliced mushrooms, drained**
1 **cup dairy sour cream**
5 **drops Tabasco**
Buttered cooked noodles or rice (page 49 or 48)

1. Cut meat into 2x½x¼-inch strips. Coat with a mixture of flour, salt and pepper.
2. Melt butter in a 2-quart glass baking dish in microwave oven (about 45 seconds at HIGH). Add the meat and stir to coat with butter. Cover with waxed paper. Cook in microwave oven 5 to 6 minutes at HIGH, or until meat is no longer pink; stir occasionally.
3. Pour consommé and onion soup over meat in dish. Heat uncovered in microwave oven to boiling (8 to 10 minutes at HIGH); stir occasionally. Cook uncovered 3 minutes at HIGH; turn and rearrange strips once during cooking period.
4. Stir in mushrooms, sour cream and Tabasco. Cover with waxed paper. Heat in microwave oven to serving temperature (about 4½ minutes at ROAST); stir once.
5. Serve over buttered cooked noodles or rice.

6 to 8 servings

Pepper Steak

PEPPER STEAK

2 pounds beef flank steak
¼ cup water
¼ cup soy sauce
1 teaspoon garlic salt
½ teaspoon sugar
¼ teaspoon ginger
⅛ teaspoon pepper
2 green peppers, cut in 1-inch pieces
2 tomatoes, peeled and quartered
1 can (16 ounces) bean sprouts, drained and rinsed
1 tablespoon cornstarch
6 tablespoons cold water
Cooked rice (page 48)

1. Slice flank steak, while cold, into thin strips across the grain.
2. Mix water, soy sauce, garlic salt, sugar, ginger and pepper in a 2-quart glass baking dish. Add meat and turn once. Cover with plastic wrap. Allow to marinate in refrigerator 1 to 3 hours.
3. Add green pepper to meat. Cook covered in microwave oven 5 minutes at ROAST; stir once.
4. Add tomatoes and bean sprouts; stir. Cook covered in microwave oven 5 to 10 minutes at ROAST, or until meat is fork-tender; stir once.
5. Mix cornstarch with water and stir into meat mixture. Cook uncovered in microwave oven 2 to 3 minutes at HIGH, or until thickened.
6. Serve with rice.

6 to 8 servings

BEEF STEW

2 **pounds beef for stew**
1 **teaspoon salt**
2 **teaspoons Worcestershire sauce**
2 **cups boiling water**
2 **large potatoes, pared and cut in eighths**
2 **medium carrots, cut in thin strips**
1 **large onion, cut in eighths**

1. Put meat into a 4-quart glass casserole. Add salt, Worcestershire sauce and boiling water. Cover with an all-glass lid. Cook in microwave oven 10 minutes at HIGH.

2. Add potato, carrot and onion to liquid in casserole; stir. Cook covered in microwave oven 60 to 75 minutes at SIMMER, or until meat is tender; stir occasionally. Be sure meat and vegetables are covered with liquid during cooking; add hot water as necessary.

3. Allow to stand covered 15 to 20 minutes before serving.

About 6 servings

HINT: If desired, thicken liquid as for Basic Gravy (page 178).

EASY BEEF STEW

This is an ideal recipe for using leftover vegetable and beef.

2 **tablespoons beef drippings**
1 **medium onion, finely chopped**
1 **bay leaf**
1 **cup sliced cooked carrots**
1 **cup cooked diced potatoes**
½ **teaspoon salt**
½ **teaspoon celery seed**
2 **cups beef gravy**
2 **cups cubed cooked roast beef**
Paprika

1. Heat drippings in a 2-quart glass baking dish in microwave oven (20 to 30 seconds at HIGH).

2. Add onion to drippings. Cook uncovered in microwave oven 3 minutes at HIGH.

3. Add remaining ingredients, except paprika, to dish with onion; mix. Cover with waxed paper and cook in microwave oven 8 minutes at HIGH, or until thoroughly heated; stir occasionally.

4. Sprinkle with paprika before serving.

4 servings

EASY BEEF GOULASH

2 **tablespoons beef drippings**
2 **medium onions, peeled and sliced**
2 **medium potatoes, pared and cubed**
½ **teaspoon paprika**
2 **cups cubed cooked roast beef**
1 **tablespoon Worcestershire sauce**
¼ **cup ketchup**
½ **teaspoon dry mustard**
½ **teaspoon salt**
Dash pepper
2 **cups water**
2 **tablespoons cornstarch**

1. Heat drippings in a 2-quart glass casserole in microwave oven (20 to 30 seconds at HIGH). Add onion, potato and paprika. Cover with an all-glass lid or plastic wrap. Cook in microwave oven 3 minutes at HIGH.

2. Add meat to casserole along with Worcestershire sauce, ketchup, dry mustard, salt and pepper; mix. Cook covered in microwave oven 3 minutes at HIGH.

3. Mix about 2 tablespoons of the water with cornstarch. Stir cornstarch mixture and remaining water into casserole mixture. Cook covered in microwave oven 10 to 12 minutes at HIGH; stir occasionally.

4 servings

BEEF AND POTATO CASSEROLE

2 tablespoons beef
   drippings
2 medium onions, sliced
2 medium potatoes, pared
   and diced
½ teaspoon paprika
2 cups cubed cooked roast
   beef
1 tablespoon
   Worcestershire sauce
¼ cup ketchup
½ teaspoon dry mustard
½ teaspoon salt
   Dash pepper
2 cups water
2 tablespoons cornstarch

1. Heat drippings in a 2-quart glass casserole in microwave oven (15 to 30 seconds at HIGH).
2. Add onion, potato and paprika to drippings. Cover with an all-glass lid or waxed paper. Cook in microwave oven 3 minutes at HIGH.
3. Add meat to casserole along with Worcestershire sauce, ketchup, dry mustard, salt and pepper; mix. Cook covered in microwave oven 3 minutes at HIGH.
4. Mix about 2 tablespoons of the water with cornstarch. Stir cornstarch mixture and remaining water into casserole mixture. Cover and cook in microwave oven 10 to 12 minutes at HIGH, or until thoroughly heated; stir occasionally.

4 servings

LAMB ROAST

4- to 8-pound lamb roast
   (leg, whole or rolled)

1. Set roast, fat side down, on a roast rack set in a 2-quart glass baking dish. Cover small end of leg and any bones that extend from meat with aluminum foil. Cover with waxed paper and cook in microwave oven for one half of cooking time (see Meat Cooking Chart for time and settings).
2. After one half of cooking time is completed, remove any foil, turn roast over, fat side up. Insert Temperature Probe in center of meat. Cook covered in microwave oven set at temperature for desired doneness and at ROAST.
3. Remove roast from oven. Cover meat with foil and allow to stand 20 to 30 minutes for heat to equalize; during this time internal temperature will rise.

HINT: If one side of roast appears to be cooking faster than the other side, rotate dish one-half turn; repeat if necessary.

LAMB CROWN ROAST WITH APRICOT STUFFING

3 tablespoons butter
½ package (4 ounces)
   herb-seasoned stuffing
   mix
¼ cup water
3 tablespoons chopped
   celery
3 tablespoons chopped
   dried apricots
1 lamb rib crown roast
   (5 to 6 pounds)

1. Melt butter in a 1-quart glass casserole in microwave oven (30 to 45 seconds at HIGH). Add stuffing mix, water, celery and apricots; mix well.
2. Place lamb crown roast on a roast rack set in a 2-quart glass baking dish. Fill center cavity with stuffing. Cover with waxed paper. Cook in microwave oven 10 minutes at ROAST.
3. Rotate dish one-half turn. Insert Temperature Probe into meaty portion of roast. Shield meat and ribs as needed with foil. Cook covered in microwave oven set at 160°F and at ROAST.
4. Remove roast from oven. Cover with foil and allow to stand 10 minutes before serving.

About 8 servings

LAMB CHOPS À L'ORANGE

4 lamb loin chops
Garlic salt
3 fresh orange slices,
½ inch thick
½ cup orange marmalade

1. Sprinkle chops lightly with garlic salt.
2. Stand chops on bones, fat side up, alternately with orange slices in a glass baking dish.
3. Spoon marmalade over all. Cover with waxed paper. Cook in microwave oven <u>13 to 17 minutes at ROAST,</u> or until done as desired; rotate dish one-half turn after 8 minutes.

LAMB-PINEAPPLE KABOBS

1½ pounds boneless lamb shoulder or leg, cut in 1½-inch cubes
1 can (13½ ounces) pineapple chunks, drained (reserve ½ cup syrup)
½ cup soy sauce
¼ cup lemon juice
2 cloves garlic, minced
½ teaspoon pepper
Cooked rice (page 48)
Orange Barbecue Sauce (page 178)

1. Put lamb cubes into a large shallow dish.
2. Reserve pineapple chunks. Mix ½ cup pineapple syrup, soy sauce, lemon juice, garlic and pepper. Pour over meat. Refrigerate several hours or overnight; turn meat occasionally.
3. Remove meat from marinade; reserve marinade for brushing kabobs during cooking.
4. Alternately arrange meat pieces and the reserved pineapple chunks on 4 (8-inch) bamboo skewers; brush with marinade.
5. Arrange kabobs in a 2-quart glass baking dish. Cover with waxed paper. Cook in microwave oven <u>11 to 12 minutes at ROAST,</u> or until meat is done as desired; turn and rearrange kabobs and brush with marinade twice during cooking period.
6. Arrange kabobs on fluffy cooked rice and serve with Orange Barbecue Sauce.

4 servings

LAMB CASSEROLE

2 cups diced cooked lamb
2 cups cooked rice (page 48)
½ cup cooked peas
2 cups lamb gravy
1 tablespoon chopped pimento
½ teaspoon salt

1. Combine all ingredients in a 1½-quart glass baking dish. Cover with waxed paper.
2. Cook in microwave oven <u>10 minutes at HIGH,</u> or until thoroughly heated; stir occasionally.

4 servings

LAMB AND RICE CASSEROLE

2 cups diced cooked lamb
2 cups cooked rice (page 48)
½ cup cooked peas
2 cups lamb gravy
1 tablespoon chopped pimento
½ teaspoon salt

1. Combine all ingredients in a 1½-quart glass baking dish. Cover with plastic wrap.
2. Cook in microwave oven <u>10 minutes at HIGH,</u> or until hot; stir occasionally.

4 servings

QUICK LAMB STEW

2 tablespoons butter
2 cups cubed cooked lamb
3 tablespoons flour
1 teaspoon salt
⅛ teaspoon pepper
1¼ cups liquid
    (water or broth)
1 cup cooked diced potato
½ cup diced cooked carrots
½ cup cooked peas
1 cup chopped cooked
    onion

1. Melt butter in a 1½-quart glass casserole in microwave oven (15 seconds at HIGH).
2. Add meat to melted butter and cook uncovered in microwave oven 2 minutes at HIGH.
3. Add flour, salt and pepper; stir well. Cook uncovered in microwave oven 1 minute at HIGH.
4. Pour liquid into casserole; stir. Cook uncovered in microwave oven 2½ minutes at HIGH, or until thickened.
5. Add vegetables and stir to combine. Cover with an all-glass lid or waxed paper. Cook in microwave oven 9½ to 11 minutes at BAKE, or until thoroughly heated; stir occasionally.

4 servings

PORK ROAST

3- to 5-pound pork roast
Salt and pepper
(optional)

1. Set roast, fat side down, on a roast rack set in a 2-quart glass baking dish. Season roast, if desired, with salt and pepper. Cover any bones that extend from meat with aluminum foil. Cover with waxed paper. Cook in microwave oven for one half of cooking time (see Meat Cooking Chart for time and settings).
2. After one half of cooking time is completed, remove any foil, turn roast over, fat side up. Insert Temperature Probe in center of meat. Cook covered in microwave oven set at 160°F and at ROAST.
3. Remove roast from oven. Cover meat with foil and allow to stand 20 to 30 minutes for heat to equalize; during this time internal temperature will rise.

HINT: If one side of roast appears to be cooking faster than the other side, rotate dish one-half turn; repeat if necessary.

PORK ROAST IN ORIENTAL MARINADE

To make microwave cooking even easier, a plastic cooking bag is used for marinating as well as cooking.

1 tablespoon flour
1 pork shoulder roast,
    boneless (4 pounds)
½ teaspoon salt
1 tablespoon sugar
½ teaspoon ginger
1 clove garlic, minced
½ cup dry sherry or
    orange juice
¼ cup lemon juice
¼ cup soy sauce
2 tablespoons ketchup

1. Shake 1 tablespoon flour in a medium-size plastic cooking bag. Place bag in a glass baking dish.
2. Trim excess fat from meat and place roast in the bag.
3. Mix salt, sugar, ginger, garlic, wine, lemon juice, soy sauce and ketchup; pour over meat in the bag. Close bag securely with string *(do not use metal twist tie)*. Refrigerate several hours.
4. Make six ½-inch slits in the top of the bag. Insert Temperature Probe in center of meat. Cook in microwave oven set at 160°F and at ROAST.
5. Allow to stand 20 minutes for heat to equalize; during this time internal temperature will rise to 170°F.

ROAST PORK AND SAUERKRAUT

Leftover roast pork dressed up for a second showing.

2 tablespoons pork
   drippings
3 cups undrained
   sauerkraut
1 teaspoon caraway seed
4 servings cooked roast
   pork
¼ teaspoon salt
   Dash pepper

1. Heat drippings in a 2-quart glass casserole in microwave oven (15 to 30 seconds at HIGH).
2. Add undrained sauerkraut and caraway seed to drippings. Cover with an all-glass lid or waxed paper. Heat in microwave oven 7 minutes at HIGH; stir twice.
3. Place roast pork on top of sauerkraut. Sprinkle with salt and pepper. Heat covered in microwave oven to serving temperature (4 to 5 minutes at BAKE).

STUFFED PORK CHOPS

2 tablespoons butter or
   margarine
1 cup bread cubes
1 cup cubed pared apple
1 teaspoon salt
4 pork loin chops, 1¾
   inches thick (have chops
   cut for stuffing)

1. Melt butter in a glass custard cup in microwave oven (about 30 seconds at HIGH).
2. Combine bread, apple, melted butter and salt.
3. Stuff chops with mixture and place in a single layer in a glass baking dish. Cover with waxed paper. Cook in microwave oven 11 minutes at ROAST.
4. Turn chops over; rotate dish one-half turn. Cook covered 9 to 11 minutes at ROAST, or until well done.
5. Remove meat from oven and allow to stand 5 minutes.

HINT: If additional browning is desired, see page 117, or brown chops under microwave browning element or broiler. Be sure not to use glass baking dish under conventional broiler.

PORK CUTLETS ON PRUNES

2 packages (12 ounces
   each) pitted prunes
¾ cup water
2 pounds pork loin sirloin
   cutlets, trimmed of excess
   fat
   Salt and pepper

1. Put prunes and water into a 2-quart glass baking dish. Arrange pork cutlets over top. Cover with plastic wrap.
2. Cook in microwave oven 25 to 30 minutes at SIMMER, or until meat is fork-tender; turn cutlets over and rotate dish one-half turn halfway through cooking period.
3. Season with salt and pepper. Allow to stand covered 5 minutes.

4 to 6 servings

PORK SAUSAGE PATTIES

1 pound bulk pork sausage

Make 6 sausage patties, 3x½ inches. Put into a 2-quart glass baking dish. Cover with waxed paper. Cook in microwave oven 6 to 8 minutes at HIGH, or until well done; rearrange patties halfway through the cooking period.

6 servings

HINT: If additional browning is desired, see page 117; or brown under microwave browning element or broiler. Be sure not to use glass baking dish under a conventional broiler.

PORK CHOW MEIN

1 **pound lean pork, cut in small pieces**
2 **cups thinly sliced celery (on the diagonal)**
1 **cup chopped onion**
2 **tablespoons cornstarch**
¼ **cup water**
1 **can (19 ounces) Chinese mixed vegetables, drained and rinsed**
1 **cup beef broth**
2 **tablespoons soy sauce**
1 **tablespoon brown sauce or molasses**
¼ **teaspoon ginger**
1 **tablespoon cornstarch (optional)**

1. Put meat into a 2-quart glass casserole. Cover with an all-glass lid or plastic wrap. Cook in microwave oven 4 minutes at HIGH, or until meat begins to lose its pink color; stir once.
2. Add celery and onion to meat; mix. Cook covered in microwave oven 3 minutes at HIGH.
3. Blend 2 tablespoons cornstarch with water; stir into meat mixture. Add Chinese vegetables, broth, soy sauce, brown sauce and ginger; mix well.
4. Cook covered in microwave oven 20 to 25 minutes at SIMMER, or until meat is tender; stir twice during cooking. If sauce does not seem thick enough halfway through cooking, remove ¼ cup of cooking liquid, cool slightly and mix in remaining cornstarch. Stir into casserole mixture and continue cooking.

4 servings

SWEET-SOUR PORK

1½ **pounds pork loin, boneless, cut in thin strips**
¼ **cup firmly packed brown sugar**
¼ **cup cornstarch**
½ **teaspoon salt**
½ **cup water**
2 **tablespoons soy sauce**
1 **tablespoon red wine vinegar**
1 **can (20 ounces) unsweetened pineapple chunks (undrained)**
½ **medium green pepper, thinly sliced**
½ **medium onion, thinly sliced**
  Cooked rice (page 48)

1. Arrange pork strips in a 3-quart glass baking dish. Cover with plastic wrap. Cook in microwave oven 7 minutes at ROAST; rotate dish one-half turn once. Remove meat with a slotted spoon and set aside.
2. Combine brown sugar, cornstarch and salt. Stir in water, soy sauce and vinegar. Blend cornstarch mixture into meat juices in dish. Add pineapple with juice, reserved meat, green pepper and onion; stir.
3. Cook covered in microwave oven 15 to 18 minutes at ROAST, or until pork is tender and sauce is thickened and bubbly; stir every 3 minutes.
4. Serve over cooked rice.

About 6 servings

OLIVE PORK AND ARTICHOKES ESPAÑOL

Rice-Stuffed Artichokes
¼ cup (½ stick) butter or margarine
1 pound boneless pork, cut in ½-inch slices
⅓ cup sliced pimento-stuffed olives
1½ cups dry white wine, such as sauterne
2 cloves garlic, crushed
1½ teaspoons marjoram leaves
1 teaspoon savory leaves
¼ teaspoon pepper
2 tablespoons lemon juice
¼ cup drained canned white onions
4 whole cloves
2 teaspoons cornstarch
2 tablespoons water
2 teaspoons sugar (about)

1. Prepare Rice-Stuffed Artichokes; keep warm.
2. Melt butter in a large glass baking dish in microwave oven (30 to 45 seconds at HIGH). Arrange meat in bottom of dish. Cover with waxed paper. Cook 2 minutes at HIGH.
3. Turn meat over. Cook covered in microwave oven 2 minutes at HIGH.
4. Turn meat over. Add olives, wine, garlic, herbs, pepper, lemon juice and onions to dish. Tie cloves in a small piece of cheesecloth and add to liquid. Cook covered in microwave oven 21 minutes at ROAST, or until meat is no longer pink inside and is almost tender.
5. Place stuffed artichokes on top of pork. Using a baster or spoon, drizzle the wine mixture over the artichokes. Cook covered in microwave oven about 5 minutes at HIGH, or until meat is tender. Discard cloves.
6. Arrange artichokes, meat, sliced olives and onions on a serving platter; keep warm.
7. Blend cornstarch and water; stir into wine mixture in dish. Cook uncovered in microwave oven about 4 minutes at HIGH, or until thickened; stir frequently. Sweeten to taste with sugar.
8. Garnish platter with **olives, lemon wedges** and **watercress.** Serve sauce in a bowl to go with meat and rice and as a dipping sauce for artichoke leaves.

4 servings

RICE-STUFFED ARTICHOKES

4 artichokes
1 package (6 ounces) saffron rice mix
¼ cup toasted slivered almonds

1. Wash artichokes. Cut off stems at base and remove small bottom leaves. If desired, snip off tips of leaves with scissors and cut off about 1 inch from top. Cook artichokes following directions on page 184 in Fresh Vegetable Cooking Chart, then remove chokes.
2. Cook rice following recipe for Packaged Rice Mix (page 48). Mix in almonds. Spoon into cooked artichokes. Serve hot.

4 servings

COUNTRY-STYLE PORK RIBS WITH PLUM GLAZE

3 pounds country-style pork ribs
1 can (17 ounces) purple plums, drained (reserve ½ cup syrup)
½ cup thawed frozen orange juice concentrate
½ teaspoon Worcestershire sauce

1. Cut ribs into single-rib portions. Place on a roast rack set in a 2-quart glass baking dish with thick part of ribs to the outside. Cover with plastic wrap.
2. Cook in microwave oven 12½ minutes at ROAST. Drain off fat. Remove rack and turn ribs over in dish.
3. Purée plums with reserved syrup. Put into a 1-quart glass measuring cup. Add orange juice concentrate and Worcestershire sauce. Cook uncovered in microwave oven 3 to 5 minutes at HIGH, or until thicker; stir once.
4. Pour sauce over ribs. Cover with waxed paper. Cook in microwave oven 10 minutes at ROAST.
5. Remove from oven. Allow to stand covered 5 minutes. Serve ribs with sauce.

About 8 servings

BARBECUED RIBS

2 pounds pork spareribs
2 cups ketchup
1 tablespoon prepared horseradish
¼ cup packed light brown sugar
½ cup vinegar
½ cup water
1 tablespoon Worcestershire sauce
½ cup chopped onion
1 tablespoon celery seed
⅛ teaspoon salt
⅛ teaspoon pepper

1. Cut spareribs into individual ribs and place in bottom of a large glass baking dish.
2. Combine remaining ingredients and pour over meat. Cover with waxed paper. Cook in microwave oven 40 to 45 minutes at ROAST, or until well done. Turn ribs over after 20 minutes.

4 servings

HINT: To reduce cooking time when grilling, ribs can be partially cooked in microwave oven approximately 12 to 15 minutes at HIGH. Remove from oven, place ribs on grill and cook until well done.

BAKED HAM SLICE WITH PINEAPPLE

1 smoked ham center slice, ¾ inch thick
1 teaspoon prepared mustard
¼ cup firmly packed brown sugar
2 pineapple slices
¼ cup fine cracker crumbs

1. Put ham slice into a glass baking dish. Spread mustard over ham and sprinkle with brown sugar.
2. Cut pineapple slices in half and coat with cracker crumbs. Arrange on ham. Cover with waxed paper. Cook in microwave oven 4 minutes at HIGH.
3. Rotate dish one-half turn. Cook covered in microwave oven 6 minutes at ROAST.

About 4 servings

HAM AND YAMS

3 tablespoons butter
3 tablespoons chopped onion
2 tablespoons flour
½ cup pineapple juice
½ cup pineapple tidbits
⅓ cup packed brown sugar
2 cups chopped cooked ham
2 cups sliced (½ inch thick) cooked yams or sweet potatoes

1. Put butter and onion into a 1½-quart glass casserole. Cook uncovered in microwave oven 2 minutes at HIGH; stir after 1 minute.
2. Blend flour into onion butter and stir in pineapple juice. Cook uncovered in microwave oven 1 minute at HIGH, or until thick.
3. Stir pineapple tidbits, brown sugar and ham into sauce. Pile in center of an 8-inch round glass cake dish. Put sliced yams around outer edge. Cover with waxed paper. Heat in microwave oven to serving temperature (6 to 8 minutes at BAKE).

4 servings

Baked Ham

BAKED HAM

3- to 10-pound fully cooked smoked ham (canned or half ham)
½ cup firmly packed brown sugar
1½ teaspoons flour
½ teaspoon dry mustard
1 tablespoon cider vinegar
1 can (8 ounces) sliced pineapple, drained
4 maraschino cherries

1. Set ham, fat side down, on a roast rack set in a 2-quart glass baking dish. Cover with waxed paper. Cook in microwave oven for one half of cooking time (see Meat Cooking Chart for time and settings).

2. After one half of cooking time is completed, turn ham over, fat side up. Cook covered in microwave oven until 10 minutes before minimum recommended time is completed.

3. Mix brown sugar, flour and mustard in a small bowl. Stir in vinegar.

4. Remove ham from oven. Spread brown sugar mixture over ham. Arrange pineapple slices and cherries on ham and press firmly into glaze. Insert Temperature Probe. Cook uncovered in microwave oven set at 120°F and at ROAST.

5. Remove from oven. Cover meat with foil and allow to stand 20 minutes for heat to equalize; during this time internal temperature will rise.

HINT: If shape of ham is uneven, cover small end with aluminum foil for the first half of cooking time.

Broccoli 'n' Ham Roll-Ups

BROCCOLI 'N' HAM ROLL-UPS

1½ **pounds fresh broccoli**
3 **tablespoons butter or margarine**
3 **tablespoons flour**
1 **teaspoon prepared horseradish**
¾ **cup chicken broth**
¼ **cup Madeira**
¼ **cup half-and-half**
8 **ounces fresh mushrooms, cleaned and sliced**
24 **thin slices Swiss cheese (8 ounces)**
12 **slices (1½ pounds) cooked ham**

1. Wash and trim broccoli. Cook in microwave oven following directions on page 184 in Fresh Vegetable Cooking Chart. Drain. Allow to stand covered.
2. Melt butter in a 1-quart glass measuring cup (30 seconds at HIGH). Blend in flour. Add horseradish. Add broth and Madeira gradually, stirring until smooth. Cook uncovered in microwave oven 2½ to 3 minutes at SIMMER, or until thickened; stir twice.
3. Stir in half-and-half and mushrooms. Cook uncovered in microwave oven 1 minute at SIMMER.
4. Place 2 cheese slices and 2 broccoli spears on each ham slice. Roll up and place in a 3-quart glass baking dish. Pour sauce over all. Heat uncovered in microwave oven to serving temperature (6 to 8 minutes at DEFROST); rotate dish one-half turn once.

6 servings

HAM AND ASPARAGUS

16 asparagus spears
(about 1 pound)
2 tablespoons butter
2 tablespoons flour
1 cup milk
2 egg yolks
½ teaspoon salt
½ teaspoon dry mustard
4 slices boiled ham
¼ cup shredded Cheddar
cheese

1. Cook asparagus following directions on page 184 in Fresh Vegetable Cooking Chart.
2. Melt butter in a 1-quart glass casserole in microwave oven (15 seconds at HIGH). Stir in flour. Add milk gradually, stirring constantly. Cook uncovered in microwave oven 4 minutes at HIGH, or until thick; stir after each minute.
3. Beat egg yolks and stir into sauce; add seasoning.
4. Wrap 4 asparagus spears in each slice of ham. Lay ham rolls in a 1½-quart baking dish and pour sauce over the top. Sprinkle with cheese. Cover with waxed paper. Heat in microwave oven to serving temperature (5 to 6 minutes at BAKE).
5. Serve on toast.

4 servings

BACON

Bacon slices

1. Arrange bacon on a roast rack set in a 2-quart glass baking dish. Cover with paper towels. Cook in microwave oven at HIGH until browned.
2. Remove from oven and let stand 1 to 2 minutes for crisp bacon.

Cook as follows:

Slices	Minutes
1	2
2	2
3	3
4	4
6	5
8	7

HINT: If desired, when cooking 1 or 2 bacon slices at a time, use a paper-towel-lined paper plate.

VEAL CUTLETS IN WINE

1 pound veal cutlets
¼ cup flour
1 teaspoon salt
¼ teaspoon pepper
2 tablespoons butter
¼ cup dry Marsala
¼ cup sliced green olives

1. To increase tenderness, place meat on flat working surface and repeatedly pound with meat hammer. Turn meat and repeat process. Cut into 4 serving-size portions.
2. Mix flour, salt and pepper. Coat meat with flour mixture.
3. Melt butter in a 2-quart glass baking dish in microwave oven (15 to 30 seconds at HIGH). Arrange meat in bottom of dish. Cover with waxed paper. Cook 4 minutes at HIGH; turn meat over after 2 minutes.
4. Remove excess liquid. Cook covered in microwave oven 14 minutes at ROAST; rotate dish one-half turn after 7 minutes.
5. Turn pieces over. Add wine and olives. Cook covered in microwave oven 1 minute at HIGH.

4 servings

VEAL 'N' TOMATO

2 tablespoons butter
2 tablespoons flour
1½ cups beef broth
1 tablespoon tomato paste
1 large tomato, diced
1 onion, minced
1 cup sliced mushrooms
1 bay leaf
1½ pounds veal for stew, cut
in 1-inch pieces
1 teaspoon salt
⅛ teaspoon pepper
Cooked rice (page 48)

1. Melt butter in microwave oven in a 2-quart glass baking dish (15 seconds at HIGH). Blend in flour. Add broth gradually, stirring until smooth. Stir in tomato paste.
2. Cook uncovered in microwave oven 3 minutes at HIGH; stir once. Add tomato, onion, mushrooms and bay leaf; stir. Cook uncovered 4 minutes at HIGH; stir once.
3. Add meat, salt and pepper to sauce; stir. Cover with plastic wrap. Cook in microwave oven 25 to 30 minutes at SIMMER, or until meat is tender; stir occasionally and be sure meat is covered with sauce.
4. Remove from oven and allow to stand covered 5 to 10 minutes.
5. Serve over rice.

4 to 6 servings

KIDNEY KABOBS

8 lamb kidneys
(about 1 pound)
½ cup clear French dressing
12 medium mushrooms
8 slices bacon, cut in half
1½ tablespoons butter or
margarine
½ teaspoon salt
⅛ teaspoon pepper

1. If necessary, remove membrane from kidneys. Cut each kidney horizontally through center. Using scissors, cut away core and tubes. Rinse with cold water and drain.
2. Put kidneys into a bowl and add French dressing; stir to coat well. Cover and refrigerate at least 1 hour.
3. Clean mushrooms and reserve stems.*
4. Put bacon on a roast rack set in a 2-quart glass baking dish. Cover with a paper towel. Cook in microwave oven 4 minutes at HIGH (bacon will be partially cooked).
5. Remove kidneys from marinade and wrap each kidney with partially cooked bacon piece.
6. Alternate kidneys and mushrooms on 4 bamboo or metal skewers, beginning and ending with kidney. (If using metal skewers, see page 14.) Put into a 2-quart glass baking dish.
7. Melt butter in a glass custard cup in microwave oven (about 30 seconds at HIGH). Brush butter over mushroom caps. Cover with waxed paper. Cook in microwave oven 9 minutes at ROAST, or until kidneys are tender; turn kabobs over and rearrange after 4 minutes.
8. Season kabobs with salt and pepper. Serve with cooked rice.

4 servings

*Save mushroom stems and use in vegetable or soup recipes.

LIVER AND ONIONS

1 medium onion, thinly
sliced
½ cup beef broth
½ teaspoon Worcestershire
sauce
¼ teaspoon caraway seed
1 pound beef liver slices
(about ½ inch thick),
rinsed

1. Put onion, broth and seasonings into a 2-quart glass baking dish. Cover with waxed paper. Cook in microwave oven 7 minutes at HIGH.
2. Meanwhile, cut away tubes and outer membrane from liver, if necessary.
3. Remove the onion slices with slotted spoon. Add liver (thin ends to center of dish). Cook covered in microwave oven 2 minutes at HIGH.
4. Turn pieces over and put onion slices on top. Cook covered in microwave oven 7 minutes at ROAST, or until liver is done to taste; rotate dish one-half turn after 3½ minutes.

4 servings

HAMBURGER STROGANOFF

1 pound lean ground beef
1 large onion, chopped
1 teaspoon salt
    Dash pepper
1 can (about 10 ounces)
    condensed cream of
    chicken soup
½ pint dairy sour cream

1. Place ground beef and onion in a 2-quart glass baking dish. Cover with waxed paper. Cook in microwave oven 5 minutes at HIGH, or until meat is no longer pink; stir occasionally. Drain off excess fat.
2. Add salt, pepper and soup; mix well. Cook covered in microwave oven 6 to 8 minutes at HIGH, or until thoroughly heated; stir occasionally.
3. Stir in sour cream. Cover and allow to stand 2 minutes.

About 4 servings

WINE 'N' CHEESE BURGERS

1½ pounds ground beef
⅓ cup chopped parsley
⅓ cup chopped onion
1½ teaspoons salt
½ teaspoon pepper
1½ cups dry red wine, such
    as Burgundy
6 blue cheese cubes

1. Mix ground beef, parsley, onion, salt and pepper. Shape into 6 patties. Place patties in a 2-quart glass baking dish.
2. Make a depression in top of each patty. Pour wine over the patties; cover and refrigerate 2 hours.
3. Discard wine marinade. Cover with waxed paper. Cook in microwave oven 5 to 6 minutes at HIGH, or until done as desired; turn burgers halfway through the cooking period and rotate dish one-half turn once.
4. To serve, place a cube of blue cheese on each patty.

6 servings

MEATBALLS WITH POTATO AND MUSHROOM SAUCE

2 medium potatoes, pared
    and cut in cubes
1 pound ground beef chuck
2 tablespoons chopped
    onion
1 tablespoon chopped
    parsley
2 tablespoons dry bread
    crumbs
½ teaspoon salt
1 egg
2 tablespoons water
1 can (about 10 ounces)
    condensed cream of
    mushroom soup
¾ cup milk

1. Put potato into a 1-quart glass casserole. Cover with an all-glass lid or plastic wrap. Cook in microwave oven about 4½ minutes at HIGH, or until tender; stir once. Set aside.
2. Combine meat, onion, parsley, bread crumbs and salt. Mix egg and water. Stir into meat mixture.
3. Divide meat mixture into 12 portions. Shape each portion into a meatball, using 2 or 3 cooked potato cubes as the center. Put into a 1½-quart glass baking dish. Cover with waxed paper.
4. Cook in microwave oven 6 minutes at HIGH; rearrange after 3 minutes. Drain off fat.
5. Combine condensed mushroom soup and milk. Stir in remaining cooked potatoes. Pour over meatballs. Cover with waxed paper. Cook in microwave oven 5 minutes at BAKE; rotate dish one-quarter turn once.

4 servings

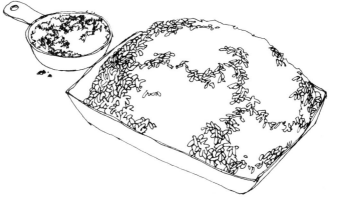

PORCUPINE MEATBALLS

1 **pound ground beef**
1 **can (about 10 ounces)**
    condensed tomato soup
¼ **cup finely chopped onion**
1 **teaspoon salt**
1 **cup packaged precooked**
    rice
1 **egg, slightly beaten**
⅔ **cup water**
1 **teaspoon prepared**
    mustard

1. Put beef into a bowl. Add ¼ cup condensed soup, onion, salt, rice and egg; mix well. Shape meat mixture firmly into 20 balls. Put meatballs into a 2-quart glass baking dish. Cover with waxed paper.
2. Cook in microwave oven 3 to 4 minutes at HIGH, or until set. Drain off fat. Turn meatballs over and rearrange them.
3. Blend remaining condensed soup, water and prepared mustard. Pour over meatballs in dish. Cover with plastic wrap.
4. Cook in microwave oven 6 to 7 minutes at ROAST, or until rice is tender; rearrange meatballs once during cooking.

4 servings

SWEDISH MEATBALLS

1 **pound ground beef round**
    steak
½ **pound ground pork**
½ **cup instant mashed**
    potatoes
½ **cup fine dry bread**
    crumbs
1 **egg, beaten**
1 **teaspoon salt**
¼ **teaspoon pepper**
½ **teaspoon brown sugar**
¼ **teaspoon allspice**
¼ **teaspoon nutmeg**
⅛ **teaspoon cloves**
⅛ **teaspoon ginger**
½ **cup fine dry bread**
    crumbs

1. Mix ground meats in a large bowl. Add potatoes, ½ cup bread crumbs, egg, and a mixture of the salt, pepper, brown sugar, allspice, nutmeg, cloves and ginger; mix lightly.
2. Shape mixture into 1-inch balls. Roll balls in remaining bread crumbs. Put meatballs into a 2-quart glass baking dish. Cover with waxed paper.
3. Cook in microwave oven 6 to 8 minutes at BAKE, or until meatballs are thoroughly cooked; rotate dish one-half turn once.

6 to 8 servings

SAUCE-CROWNED MEAT RING

¾ **cup coarse dry bread**
    crumbs
1 **cup lemon-lime**
    carbonated beverage
2 **pounds lean ground beef**
2 **eggs, slightly beaten**
1 **cup chopped onion**
2 **teaspoons salt**
1½ **teaspoons dill weed**
⅓ **cup Worcestershire sauce**
½ **cup chili sauce**

1. Soak bread crumbs in lemon-lime carbonated beverage in a bowl. Add ground beef, eggs, onion, salt, dill and Worcestershire sauce; mix lightly but thoroughly.
2. Pack meat mixture lightly into a lightly oiled deep 1½-quart ring mold. Unmold into a glass baking dish. Cover with waxed paper. Cook in microwave oven 5 minutes at HIGH.
3. Remove excess liquid from meat ring with baster; rotate dish one-half turn. Cook covered in microwave oven 3 to 4 minutes at HIGH, or until meat is no longer pink on surface.
4. Again remove excess liquid with baster and rotate dish one-half turn. Spread chili sauce over meat ring. Cook covered in microwave oven 4 minutes at HIGH.
5. Remove from oven, cover with aluminum foil and allow to stand 5 minutes for heat to equalize.

About 8 servings

Sauce-Crowned Meat Ring

MEAT LOAF

1½ **pounds ground beef**
½ **cup fine dry bread crumbs**
1 **egg, beaten**
¾ **cup milk**
¼ **cup finely chopped onion**
1½ **teaspoons salt**
¼ **teaspoon pepper**
½ **cup ketchup**

1. Mix ground beef lightly with bread crumbs, egg, milk, onion, salt and pepper in a bowl. Pack mixture lightly into a 2-quart (9x5x3 inches) glass loaf dish. Cover with waxed paper.

2. Cook in microwave oven 5 minutes at ROAST. Top with ketchup. Rotate dish one-half turn. Insert Temperature Probe at an angle near center of meat. Cook in microwave oven set at 170°F and at ROAST.

3. Remove from oven, cover with aluminum foil and allow to stand 5 minutes.

6 servings

CHILI CON CARNE

1 **pound ground beef**
¼ **cup chopped onion**
1½ **tablespoons flour**
½ **teaspoon chili powder (or more to taste)**
1½ **teaspoons salt**
⅛ **teaspoon black pepper**
⅛ **teaspoon garlic salt**
1 **can (about 16 ounces) kidney beans, drained**
1½ **cups tomato purée**
1 **cup water**

1. Combine beef and onion in a 2-quart glass baking dish. Cover with waxed paper. Cook in microwave oven 5 minutes at HIGH, or until meat is no longer pink; stir several times.

2. Remove excess fat from dish. Stir flour and seasonings into meat mixture, then remaining ingredients. Cook uncovered in microwave oven 16 to 18 minutes at ROAST; stir occasionally.

About 6 servings

STUFFED CABBAGE ROLLS

8 **cabbage leaves**
1 **pound ground beef**
½ **cup cooked rice (page 48)**
1 **teaspoon instant minced onion**
1 **egg**
½ **teaspoon poultry seasoning**
1 **can (8 ounces) tomato sauce**
1½ **teaspoons light brown sugar**
2 **tablespoons lemon juice or vinegar**
2 **tablespoons water**

1. In a large saucepan on a conventional range surface unit, bring **6 cups water** and **1 teaspoon salt** to boiling. Add cabbage leaves and simmer about 2 or 3 minutes, or just long enough to make leaves pliable. Drain leaves on paper towels.

2. Put beef into a 1½-quart glass baking dish. Cover with waxed paper. Cook in microwave oven 4 minutes at HIGH, or until meat is no longer pink; stir occasionally.

3. Add rice, onion, egg and poultry seasoning to beef; mix. Divide meat mixture into 8 even portions.

4. Cut the core out of the cabbage leaf. Place one portion of meat in center of each cabbage leaf. Fold 2 sides of leaf over meat and roll up leaves from the end. Arrange cabbage rolls, seam side down, in a 2-quart glass baking dish.

5. Combine tomato sauce, brown sugar, lemon juice and water in a 2-cup glass measuring cup or small bowl. Pour over cabbage rolls. Cover with waxed paper. Cook in microwave oven 10 minutes at HIGH, or until heated; rearrange once during the cooking period.

6. Remove from oven, cover with plastic wrap and allow to stand 10 minutes before serving.

8 servings

STUFFED PEPPERS

3 medium green peppers,
cut in half
¼ cup chopped onion
¾ pound ground beef
1 can (8 ounces) tomato
sauce
¼ cup water
1 cup cooked rice (page 48)
1 egg
1 teaspoon salt
⅛ teaspoon pepper

1. Remove seed section from cut green peppers. Put pepper halves, skin side up, on paper towels and cook uncovered in microwave oven 6 minutes at HIGH. Set aside.
2. Combine onion and beef in an 8-inch round glass cake dish. Cover with waxed paper. Cook in microwave oven 4 minutes at HIGH, or until meat is no longer pink; stir several times.
3. Mix tomato sauce with water.
4. Combine onion-beef mixture with cooked rice, half of tomato mixture, egg, salt and pepper. Stuff pepper halves and place in a 2-quart glass baking dish. Pour remaining sauce over top. Cover with waxed paper. Cook in microwave oven 12 to 14 minutes at BAKE, or until thoroughly heated; rotate dish one-half turn after 5 minutes.

6 servings

ITALIAN TOMATO MEAT SAUCE

1 cup chopped onion
1 clove garlic, minced
1½ tablespoons olive oil
1 pound ground beef
1 can (28 ounces)
Italian-style tomatoes,
drained and cut in pieces
2 cans (6 ounces each)
tomato paste
1 cup water
1½ teaspoons salt
½ teaspoon pepper
1 teaspoon oregano

1. Combine onion, garlic and oil in a 2-quart oven-proof glass mixing bowl/pitcher. Cook uncovered in microwave oven 3 to 5 minutes at HIGH, or until onion is soft; stir once.
2. Add meat and mix well. Cover with waxed paper. Cook in microwave oven 4 to 5 minutes at HIGH, or until meat is no longer pink; stir once. Remove excess fat.
3. Stir remaining ingredients into meat mixture. Cook covered in microwave oven 5 to 8 minutes at HIGH, or until bubbly; stir once.

1½ quarts

LASAGNA

6 ounces uncooked lasagna
noodles
1½ tablespoons olive oil
½ pound ground beef
4 cups spaghetti sauce
6 ounces mozzarella, sliced
2 hard-cooked eggs*,
chopped
¼ cup grated Parmesan
cheese
1 cup ricotta

1. Cook noodles following recipe for Cooked Pasta (page 49).
2. Put olive oil and beef into a 9-inch glass pie plate. Cover with waxed paper. Cook in microwave oven 2½ minutes at HIGH, or until meat is no longer pink; stir occasionally.
3. Pour 1½ cups spaghetti sauce over bottom of a 2-quart glass baking dish. Put one-third of cooked noodles in a layer over sauce, then one-half of mozzarella slices. Add half each of cooked beef and chopped hard-cooked egg. Sprinkle with half of Parmesan cheese. Top with half of ricotta.
4. Repeat the layers. Put remaining noodles and then sauce on top. Cover with waxed paper. Cook in microwave oven 14 to 20 minutes at BAKE, or until heated; rotate dish one-half turn after 7 minutes.
5. Remove from oven, cover dish with aluminum foil and allow to stand 10 minutes.

8 servings

*Do *not* hard-cook the eggs in the microwave oven; cook them conventionally on top of the range.

MEAT-STUFFED MANICOTTI

8 manicotti shells
(two-thirds of 5½-ounce
package)
2 tablespoons olive oil
½ pound fresh spinach,
washed, dried and finely
chopped
2 tablespoons chopped
onion
½ teaspoon salt
½ teaspoon oregano
½ pound ground beef
2 tablespoons fine dry
bread crumbs
1 egg, slightly beaten
2 tablespoons tomato paste
1½ tablespoons butter or
margarine, softened
Grated Parmesan or
Romano cheese (about 2
tablespoons)

1. Cook manicotti following recipe for Cooked Pasta (page 49).
2. Combine olive oil, spinach, onion, salt, oregano and meat in a 2-quart glass casserole. Cover with waxed paper. Cook in microwave oven 6 to 7 minutes at HIGH, or until meat is no longer pink; stir occasionally.
3. Remove from oven; set aside to cool slightly. Add bread crumbs, egg and tomato paste; mix well. Stuff manicotti with mixture. Put side by side in a greased 2-quart glass baking dish.
4. Spread butter over stuffed manicotti and sprinkle with cheese. Cover with waxed paper. Cook in microwave oven until thoroughly heated (about 4 minutes at HIGH); rearrange manicotti after 2 minutes.
5. If desired, serve topped with tomato sauce and additional cheese.

4 servings

MARZETTI

2 tablespoons butter or
margarine
½ cup chopped onion
½ cup chopped green
pepper
1 can (3 ounces) chopped
mushrooms, drained
1 pound ground beef
1 teaspoon salt
⅛ teaspoon pepper
½ teaspoon garlic salt
(optional)
3 cups cooked noodles
(page 49)
2 cans (8 ounces each)
tomato sauce
1 cup shredded Cheddar
cheese
1 cup soft bread crumbs

1. Put butter, onion, green pepper and mushrooms into a 2-quart glass baking dish. Cook uncovered in microwave oven 6 minutes at HIGH, or until onion is soft; stir after 1 minute.
2. Add meat, salt, pepper and garlic salt; mix well. Cover with waxed paper. Cook in microwave oven 5 minutes at HIGH; stir occasionally.
3. Alternate layers of noodles and meat mixture in a 2-quart glass casserole. Top with tomato sauce, cheese and bread crumbs. Cover with an all-glass lid or plastic wrap. Cook in microwave oven 7 minutes at HIGH, or until hot throughout and cheese is melted; rotate casserole one-half turn once.

6 servings

TACO CASSEROLE

1 **pound ground beef**
1 **package (1.25 ounces) taco seasoning mix**
¾ **cup water**
1 **can (15 ounces) refried beans**
2 **cups shredded lettuce (dried if necessary)**
¼ **cup chopped onion**
1 **tablespoon chopped green chilies**
1 **cup shredded Cheddar cheese**
 Nacho-flavored tortilla chips
 Chopped tomato
 Sliced ripe olives
 Dairy sour cream
 Taco sauce

1. Put meat into a 2-quart glass casserole. Cover with waxed paper. Cook in microwave oven 3½ minutes at HIGH, or until meat is no longer pink; stir once. Drain fat from meat.
2. Mix taco seasoning mix and water and add to ground beef; stir. Cover with an all-glass lid or plastic wrap. Cook in microwave oven 5 minutes at SIMMER; stir once.
3. Lightly grease bottom of a 2-quart glass baking dish. Spread refried beans evenly over the bottom. Sprinkle with shredded lettuce, onion and chilies; top with ground beef mixture. Cover with waxed paper.
4. Cook in microwave oven 5 minutes at BAKE, or until dish feels warm on bottom; rotate dish one-half turn once during cooking. Sprinkle cheese on top. Cook uncovered 1 minute at BAKE, or until cheese is melted.
5. Garnish with tortilla chips. Serve with chopped tomato, sliced olives, sour cream and taco sauce in separate serving dishes.

4 to 6 servings

CHEESE-TORTILLA CASSEROLE

1 **pound ground lean pork**
½ **pound smoked ham, ground**
1 **green pepper, finely chopped**
1 **small onion, finely chopped**
3 **cloves garlic, minced**
2 **tablespoons snipped parsley**
½ **cup dark seedless raisins**
¼ **cup chopped pimento-stuffed olives**
1 **tablespoon capers**
1 **can (16 ounces) tomatoes, well drained**
2 **tablespoons tomato juice**
2 **teaspoons sugar**
½ **teaspoon salt**
¼ **teaspoon pepper**
2 **cups shredded tortillas**
1 **egg, beaten**
 Tortillas, cut in quarters
¼ **pound sharp Cheddar cheese, thinly sliced**

1. Put pork and ham into a 1½-quart glass casserole. Cover with waxed paper. Cook in microwave oven 5 minutes at HIGH; stir once.
2. Add remaining ingredients except tortilla quarters and cheese; mix well. Cook uncovered in microwave oven 5 to 8 minutes at ROAST, or until thoroughly cooked.
3. Arrange tortilla quarters around edge of casserole and top with cheese. Heat uncovered in microwave oven 1½ minutes at ROAST, or until cheese melts and mixture bubbles.
4. Serve with warm tortillas (heat in microwave oven 15 to 30 seconds at HIGH).

8 servings

MOCK DRUMSTICKS

2 pounds ground pork
2 eggs, beaten
½ cup finely chopped onion
2 teaspoons prepared
 mustard
1 teaspoon Worcestershire
 sauce
1½ teaspoons salt
 Few grains pepper
1 cup fine dry bread
 crumbs

1. Put meat into a large bowl and add remaining ingredients except bread crumbs; mix lightly until well blended. Divide into 8 portions. Shape each portion evenly and firmly around a flat or round wooden stick. Roll meat in crumbs until well coated.
2. Arrange "drumsticks" on a roast rack set in a 2-quart glass baking dish, alternating meat ends and stick ends. Cover with a paper towel.
3. Cook in microwave oven about 15 minutes at ROAST, or until meat is done; turn drumsticks over and rotate dish one-half turn after 10 minutes.

8 servings

HOT DOGS AND BEANS

1 package (16 ounces)
 frankfurters
2 cans (about 16 ounces
 each) pork and beans in
 tomato sauce
1 envelope (about 1½
 ounces) dry onion soup
 mix
¼ cup packed dark brown
 sugar
¼ to ½ cup chili sauce
 Parsley sprigs

1. Diagonally cut half of the frankfurters into bite-size pieces; set aside 5 of the pieces and remaining whole franks for top of casserole.
2. Mix frankfurter pieces, pork and beans, soup mix, brown sugar and chili sauce in a 2-quart glass casserole. Cover with all-glass lid or plastic wrap. Cook in microwave oven 8 to 10 minutes at HIGH; stir once.
3. Arrange reserved franks on top of beans and cover. Continue cooking 5 minutes at HIGH, or until thoroughly heated; rotate the dish one-half turn at least once. Garnish with parsley.

About 6 servings

Poultry

There is a wealth of flavorful dishes for those who enjoy poultry. Whether you favor chicken, turkey, duck, Cornish hens or pheasant, you'll find a recipe for your taste in this chapter. If your family favorite is' not here, find a recipe with similar ingredients and serving sizes to use for a time guide. You'll want to serve poultry often after you sample the moist and tender results achieved in a microwave oven.

Whole poultry can be cooked with excellent results, but be sure it is completely thawed or it will cook unevenly. Then continue to prepare as you would when cooking with conventional heat. Fill the cavity with your favorite stuffing (don't worry, the stuffing won't add any extra cooking time) or season as you like. Then secure the opening with wooden picks or metal poultry pins. The large mass of food permits the use of poultry pins; just be careful not to let them touch the microwave oven walls. Next, cover the wing and leg tips with small pieces of aluminum foil to shield the thinner areas and prevent overcooking. Place the poultry on a roast rack set in a baking dish to catch the drippings. (Save the drippings for gravy.) Place the poultry breast-side-down for the first half of the cooking period. Cover with waxed paper to prevent spatters.

Follow the recipe instructions for cooking time and power level. After the first half of the cooking period, turn the poultry over and remove the foil. If you notice an area that is starting to overcook, cover that area with a small piece of foil. For the most accurate results, insert the Temperature Probe in the thickest part of poultry to indicate the exact degree of doneness. If you do not have a Temperature Probe or a thermometer designed for microwave cooking, remove poultry from microwave oven and check internal temperature with a conventional meat thermometer. If the temperature is below 165°F, remove the thermometer and return poultry to microwave oven for additional cooking. When correct temperature has been reached, remove from microwave oven, cover with aluminum foil and let stand to allow internal temperature to equalize. While the poultry is standing, use the microwave oven to finish cooking the rest of your meal.

If you would like a more traditional golden color for your chicken or turkey, brush poultry with a mixture of equal parts of butter and gravy browning sauce before cooking. Turkeys frequently feature pop-out "cooking gauges." They may be left in the turkey, but do not use them to indicate when the correct temperature is reached. Duck and goose contain more fat than chicken or turkey, so be sure to drain the excess fat as it accumulates.

Chicken pieces, like whole poultry, need to be completely defrosted before cooking. Cook the chicken pieces in a glass dish; you may even want to cook directly in your serving dish. Arrange the pieces in one layer so that the thicker portions are to the outside of the dish while the thin areas are toward the center. Halfway through the cooking, rearrange the pieces, keeping thicker portions to the outside. A waxed paper cover will keep spatters controlled. At the end of the cooking time, test for doneness by either piercing the meat deeply with a fork (juices should run clear) or cutting near the bone (no pinkness should be observed). When finished cooking, cover and let stand.

Use your microwave oven for combination cooking, too. If you like crispy fried chicken, brown your chicken pieces on top of the stove and finish cooking in the microwave oven. Shorten barbecue time by partially cooking the food in your microwave oven and then moving the pieces to the grill. Do not deep-fat-fry in your microwave oven since the temperature of the fat cannot be controlled.

Food	Approximate Cooking Time per Pound
Chicken	9½ min.
Turkey - 10 lb.	9½ min.
Turkey - 16 lb.	8½ min.
Pheasant	11 min.

Roast Turkey, 161; Cranberry Sauce, 177

ROAST CHICKEN

5-pound roasting chicken

1. Remove giblets from chicken and wash chicken. (It is recommended that giblets be cooked conventionally.)
2. Secure openings of chicken with wooden picks or poultry pins. If poultry pins are used, do not allow them to touch one another or side of oven. Cover ends of wings and legs of chicken with aluminum foil.
3. Place chicken, breast side down, on roast rack set in a 2-quart glass baking dish. Cover chicken with waxed paper. Cook in microwave oven 28 minutes at ROAST.
4. Remove foil and turn chicken over. Insert Temperature Probe in thickest part of breast.
5. Cook covered in microwave oven set at 170°F and at ROAST, or cook for an additional 28 minutes at ROAST (total cooking time is approximately 11 minutes per pound).
6. Cover chicken with foil and allow to stand at room temperature 15 to 20 minutes for heat to equalize; during this time internal temperature will rise.

HINT: If desired, stuff bird with your favorite stuffing; secure the openings. Center of stuffing must be at least 160°F when chicken is removed from oven.

HERBED DRUMSTICKS

½ **cup (1 stick) butter or margarine**
2 **teaspoons finely chopped parsley**
2 **teaspoons finely chopped chives**
½ **teaspoon tarragon**
½ **teaspoon thyme**
½ **teaspoon salt**
¼ **teaspoon pepper**
8 **chicken drumsticks**

1. Melt butter in a shallow glass baking dish in microwave oven (about 45 seconds at HIGH). Add herbs, salt and pepper; stir.
2. Add drumsticks and turn to coat with butter mixture.
3. Arrange each drumstick with thin portion toward the center. Cover with waxed paper. Cook in microwave oven 16 to 18 minutes at ROAST, or until tender; rotate the dish one-half turn twice and turn chicken pieces over once.

MICROWAVE OVEN-FRIED CHICKEN

1 **broiler-fryer chicken (about 2½ pounds), cut in serving pieces**
Milk
1 **package seasoned coating mix for chicken**
Paprika

1. Rinse chicken pieces and pat dry.
2. Dip chicken pieces in milk and then shake in a bag with coating mix. Place breaded pieces, skin side up, in a 2-quart glass baking dish with thin end toward center and thicker end toward outside. Sprinkle with paprika. Cover with waxed paper. Cook in microwave oven 12 minutes at HIGH.
3. Rearrange chicken pieces and cook covered in microwave oven about 8 to 10 minutes at HIGH, or until done.
4. Remove from oven, cover with aluminum foil and allow chicken to stand 5 minutes before serving.

About 4 servings

DO NOT DEEP-FAT FRY IN THE MICROWAVE OVEN.

Baked Chicken Pieces

BAKED CHICKEN PIECES

2 tablespoons butter
2 pounds chicken pieces
   Paprika

1. Melt butter in a custard cup or glass measuring cup in micro-wave oven (about 15 seconds at HIGH).
2. Place chicken pieces, skin side up, in a 2-quart glass baking dish with thin end toward center and thicker end toward outside. Brush pieces with melted butter and sprinkle with paprika. Cover with waxed paper and cook in microwave oven 12 minutes at HIGH.
3. Turn chicken pieces over and rearrange. Cook covered in micro-wave oven 8 to 10 minutes at HIGH, or until done.
4. Remove from oven, cover with aluminum foil and allow chicken to stand 5 minutes before serving.

About 4 servings

FIESTA CHICKEN KIEV

4 whole chicken breasts, halved, boned and skinned
3 tablespoons butter
3 tablespoons pasteurized process sharp Cheddar cheese spread
2 teaspoons instant minced onion
1 teaspoon salt
2 tablespoons chopped green chilies
3 tablespoons butter
1 cup Cheddar cheese cracker crumbs
1 package (1.25 ounces) taco seasoning mix
Shredded lettuce
1 tomato, diced
Chopped ripe olives

1. Pound each raw chicken piece with a meat hammer to flatten.
2. Mix 3 tablespoons butter and cheese spread until well blended. Mix in onion, salt and chilies.
3. Divide mixture equally onto the 8 flattened chicken pieces, placing a portion at one end of each piece. Roll up, tucking in ends to completely enclose filling. Fasten rolls with wooden picks.
4. Melt remaining butter in a 2-quart glass baking dish in microwave oven (30 seconds at HIGH). Coat each roll with melted butter, then roll in a mixture of cheese cracker crumbs and taco seasoning mix.
5. Arrange rolls in the baking dish. Cover with waxed paper. Cook in microwave oven 10 to 12 minutes at HIGH; rotate dish one-half turn twice.
6. Serve chicken on a bed of shredded lettuce and diced tomato. Top with chopped olives. If desired, serve with additional whole olives, tomato wedges and taco sauce.

8 servings

GREEK-STYLE CHICKEN

1 broiler-fryer chicken (2 to 3 pounds), cut in serving pieces
1½ tablespoons olive oil
3 tablespoons fresh lemon juice
1½ teaspoons oregano
Salt and pepper to taste
Paprika
Cooked rice or noodles (page 48 or 49)

1. Rinse chicken pieces and pat dry.
2. Combine olive oil, lemon juice and oregano in a 2-quart glass baking dish. Add chicken pieces and turn to coat. Arrange chicken pieces, skin side up, in a single layer with thin end toward center and thicker end toward outside. Sprinkle with salt and pepper. Cover with plastic wrap. Allow to marinate in refrigerator 1 hour; turn pieces over once.
3. Cook covered in microwave oven 6 minutes at HIGH.
4. Turn pieces over and rearrange them. Sprinkle with paprika. Cook covered in microwave oven 3 to 4 minutes at HIGH, or until thoroughly cooked. Allow to stand 5 minutes before serving.
5. Serve with rice.

4 servings

ORANGE-BURGUNDY CHICKEN

1 broiler-fryer chicken (about 2½ pounds), cut in pieces
½ cup orange marmalade
½ cup orange juice
⅓ cup Burgundy
2 tablespoons cornstarch
2 tablespoons brown sugar
2 tablespoons lemon juice
1 teaspoon salt

1. Arrange chicken pieces, skin side down, in a 2-quart glass baking dish with thin part toward the center and thicker part toward the outside.
2. Mix marmalade, orange juice, Burgundy, cornstarch, brown sugar, lemon juice and salt in a bowl. Pour sauce over chicken. Cover with waxed paper.
3. Cook in microwave oven 10 minutes at HIGH. Turn chicken over. Cook covered 15 minutes at ROAST, or until tender.

4 to 6 servings

CHICKEN HAWAIIAN

¼ cup (½ stick) butter
1 can (20 ounces) unsweetened pineapple chunks
1 tablespoon cider vinegar
1 tablespoon brown sugar
2 teaspoons salt
⅛ teaspoon white pepper
1 broiler-fryer chicken (about 3 pounds), cut in serving pieces
3 tablespoons cornstarch
¼ cup cold water

1. Melt butter in a 2-quart glass baking dish in microwave oven (30 to 45 seconds at HIGH).
2. Drain pineapple, reserving juice. Set pineapple chunks aside. Add juice, vinegar, brown sugar, salt and pepper to melted butter; stir. Place chicken pieces, skin side down, in mixture with thin part toward inside and thicker part toward outside. Cover with plastic wrap.
3. Cook in microwave oven 6 minutes at HIGH. Turn over and re-arrange chicken pieces. Cook uncovered 3 to 4 minutes at HIGH, or until chicken is thoroughly cooked. Keep chicken warm.
4. Pour cooking liquid into a 1-quart glass measuring cup. Add water to make 2 cups. Dissolve cornstarch in remaining water and stir into cooking liquid. Cook uncovered in microwave oven 2 minutes at HIGH, or until thickened; stir after 1 minute. Add pineapple chunks to sauce and heat uncovered 30 seconds at HIGH; stir. Pour over chicken.

4 to 6 servings

CHICKEN AND DUMPLINGS

2 tablespoons butter or margarine
¼ cup chopped onion
2 tablespoons chopped celery
1 tablespoon chopped celery leaves
1 small clove garlic, minced
2 tablespoons flour
2 cups chicken broth
½ teaspoon sugar
1 teaspoon salt
⅛ teaspoon pepper
½ teaspoon basil leaves
1 bay leaf
2 tablespoons chopped parsley
1 broiler-fryer chicken, cut in serving pieces
Basil Dumplings
1 package (10 ounces) frozen green peas

1. Put butter, onion, celery, celery leaves and garlic into a 3-quart glass baking dish. Cook uncovered until crisp-tender (2½ to 3½ minutes at HIGH); stir after 1 minute.
2. Sprinkle flour over vegetables and mix well. Add chicken broth, sugar, salt, pepper, basil, bay leaf and parsley; stir. Cook uncovered in microwave oven 8 to 10 minutes at HIGH, or until thickened; stir occasionally.
3. Arrange chicken pieces in dish with thin part toward inside and thicker part toward outside. Spoon sauce over chicken. Cover with plastic wrap. Cook in microwave oven 10 minutes at HIGH. Turn pieces over in dish. Cook covered in microwave oven 8 to 10 minutes at ROAST.
4. Prepare Basil Dumplings.
5. Remove chicken and keep warm. Add peas and break apart with a fork. Cook uncovered in microwave oven 13 to 15 minutes at HIGH, or until boiling.
6. Return chicken to dish. Drop dumpling dough next to chicken. Cover with plastic wrap. Cook in microwave oven 5 minutes at HIGH. Remove from oven and allow to stand covered 5 minutes before serving. (Dumplings when done should lose their moist look and spring back when touched.)

About 6 servings

Basil Dumplings: Combine **1 cup all-purpose biscuit mix** and ½ **teaspoon basil leaves** in a bowl. Add ⅓ **cup milk** and stir with a fork until a dough is formed. Proceed as directed in recipe.

CHICKEN CACCIATORE

1 broiler-fryer chicken
(2½ to 3 pounds), cut up
1 can (15 ounces) tomato
sauce
1 can (6 ounces) tomato
paste
½ cup finely chopped onion
½ teaspoon garlic powder
1 teaspoon salt
¼ teaspoon pepper
¼ teaspoon powdered
thyme
1½ cups water
½ cup red wine
1 can (4 ounces) sliced
mushrooms, drained

1. Cut large pieces of chicken in half for uniform size. Set aside.
2. Combine remaining ingredients, except mushrooms, in a 3-quart glass casserole.
3. Add chicken pieces and coat with sauce; arrange pieces with thin end toward center and thicker end toward outside. Cover with waxed paper. Cook in microwave oven 10 minutes at HIGH.
4. Turn and rearrange chicken pieces. Cook chicken covered in microwave oven 10 minutes at HIGH.
5. Add mushrooms to sauce; stir. Cook uncovered in microwave oven 5 to 10 minutes at HIGH, or until chicken is tender.

4 servings

BARBECUED CHICKEN

1 broiler-fryer chicken
(2½ to 3 pounds), cut in
serving pieces
¾ cup bottled barbecue
sauce (or use a favorite
recipe)
Parsley

1. Rinse chicken pieces and pat dry.
2. Arrange chicken pieces in a single layer in a 2-quart glass baking dish with thin end toward center and thicker end toward outside. Spread one third of the sauce on the chicken. Cover with waxed paper. Cook in microwave oven 8 minutes at HIGH.
3. Turn chicken pieces over and rearrange them, then spread with one third of the sauce. Cook covered in microwave oven 8 minutes at HIGH.
4. Again turn chicken over, rearrange pieces and spread with remaining sauce. Cook covered in microwave oven 8 minutes at HIGH, or until tender.
5. Remove from oven, cover with aluminum foil and allow chicken to stand 5 minutes before serving.
6. Arrange chicken on a platter and garnish with parsley.

4 servings

CHICKEN TERIYAKI

1 broiler-fryer chicken
(2½ pounds), cut in
pieces
¼ cup soy sauce
¼ cup sake or cooking
sherry
1 tablespoon vegetable oil
¾ teaspoon ground ginger
¼ cup sugar
¼ teaspoon salt

1. Cut large pieces of chicken in half for uniform size. Combine remaining ingredients and marinate chicken for several hours in refrigerator.
2. Place chicken pieces in a 2-quart glass baking dish with thin end toward center and thicker end toward outside. Reserve marinade. Cover with waxed paper and cook in microwave oven 10 minutes at HIGH.
3. Turn and rearrange chicken pieces. Cook covered in microwave oven 8 to 10 minutes at HIGH, or until chicken is tender; rotate dish one-half turn once. Brush the chicken occasionally with the reserved marinade.

4 servings

CHICKEN BREASTS IN MUSHROOM CREAM

2 **whole chicken breasts,
split lengthwise**
1 **pound fresh mushrooms**
3 **tablespoons butter**
1 **tablespoon flour**
1 **teaspoon salt**
1 **cup half-and-half or
cream**
1 **tablespoon sherry**

1. Rinse chicken breasts and pat dry.
2. Place chicken, skin side down, in a 2-quart glass baking dish. Cover with waxed paper. Cook in microwave oven 8 minutes at HIGH.
3. Turn chicken over; cook covered in microwave oven 4 minutes at HIGH, or until tender.
4. Clean and slice mushrooms. Put mushrooms and butter into a 1-quart glass casserole. Cook uncovered in microwave oven 4 minutes at HIGH; stir after 1 minute.
5. Add flour and salt to mushrooms; mix well. Add half-and-half and sherry; stir. Cook uncovered in microwave oven 4 to 6 minutes at HIGH, or until thickened. Stir after 2 minutes, then stir at the end of each 30 seconds.
6. Pour sauce over chicken. Cover baking dish with plastic wrap. Cook in microwave oven 2 minutes at HIGH.

4 servings

CHICKEN DIVAN

1½ **pounds broccoli, trimmed**
4 **chicken breasts
(about 2 pounds)**
¼ **cup (½ stick) butter or
margarine**
¼ **cup flour**
¼ **teaspoon salt**
1 **cup milk**
1 **cup chicken broth**
2 **tablespoons lemon juice**
1 **teaspoon Worcestershire
sauce**
½ **cup grated Parmesan
cheese**
½ **cup crushed cereal flakes**

1. Cook broccoli following directions on page 184 in Fresh Vegetable Cooking Chart. Drain if necessary. Cover and keep warm.
2. Arrange chicken in a 2-quart glass baking dish with thin part toward inside and thicker part toward outside. Cover with plastic wrap. Cook in microwave oven 7 minutes at HIGH, or until tender; rearrange pieces once.
3. Remove chicken from oven and uncover. Allow to stand until cool enough to handle. Skin, bone and thickly slice chicken. Arrange slices in a 2-quart glass baking dish. Cover and keep warm.
4. Melt butter in a 1-quart glass measuring cup in microwave oven (45 seconds at HIGH). Add flour and salt; blend. Add milk and broth gradually, stirring constantly.
5. Cook uncovered in microwave oven 4 to 6 minutes at HIGH, or until thickened; stir after 2 minutes, then at the end of each 30 seconds.
6. Remove from oven. Stir lemon juice and Worcestershire sauce into sauce.
7. Arrange broccoli over chicken. Sprinkle half of cheese over broccoli. Pour sauce over all. Mix remaining cheese and crushed cereal; sprinkle over sauce. Cover with waxed paper.
8. Heat in microwave oven to serving temperature (3 to 5 minutes at HIGH).

6 servings

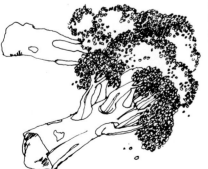

STEWED CHICKEN

1 stewing chicken (4 to 5 pounds), cut in pieces
3 small onions, sliced
3 stalks celery with leaves, sliced diagonally
2 medium carrots, pared and thinly sliced
1 tablespoon dried parsley
1 tablespoon salt
¼ teaspoon pepper
6 cups boiling water, or enough to cover chicken

1. Combine all ingredients in a 4-quart glass casserole. Cover with an all-glass lid. Cook in microwave oven 1½ hours at SIMMER, or until thickest pieces are tender; stir every 20 minutes. Add 1 cup boiling water, if needed, to keep chicken covered with broth.

2. If not serving immediately, allow chicken to cool in broth. When cool, remove skin and bones from chicken. Keep chicken in as large pieces as possible. Skim fat from broth. Refrigerate broth and chicken pieces separately in covered containers; use within several days. For longer storage, package chicken and broth together and freeze.

About 5 cups cubed chicken
and 5 to 6 cups broth

SCALLOPED CHICKEN

2 tablespoons butter
½ cup finely chopped celery
1 tablespoon chopped onion
2 cups cooked chicken cubes
1 cup soft bread crumbs
1 tablespoon flour
½ teaspoon salt
1 teaspoon instant chicken bouillon
1 teaspoon poultry seasoning
1½ cups milk
2 tablespoons butter
½ cup bread crumbs

1. Put 2 tablespoons butter, celery and onion into a small glass bowl. Cook uncovered in microwave oven 3 minutes at HIGH, or until vegetables are soft; stir after 1 minute.

2. Put chicken and bread crumbs into a 1½-quart glass baking dish; add cooked celery and onion and mix lightly. Set aside.

3. Combine flour, salt, chicken bouillon and poultry seasoning in a 1-quart glass measuring cup; stir in milk. Cook uncovered in microwave oven 4 to 5 minutes at HIGH, or until mixture comes to a boil; stir every minute.

4. Pour sauce over chicken.

5. Melt 2 tablespoons butter in a small glass dish in microwave oven (15 seconds at HIGH). Mix in bread crumbs and sprinkle on top of chicken. Cover with waxed paper.

6. Heat in microwave oven to serving temperature (6 to 7 minutes at HIGH); rotate dish one-quarter turn twice.

7. Allow to stand covered 2 minutes before serving.

About 6 servings

CHICKEN À LA KING

¼ cup (½ stick) butter or margarine
3 tablespoons flour
1 cup chicken broth
1 cup milk
½ teaspoon celery seed
½ teaspoon salt
¼ teaspoon pepper
2 cups diced cooked chicken
1 cup cooked peas
¼ cup chopped pimento
1 tablespoon grated Cheddar cheese
Toast, biscuits or patty shells

1. Melt butter in a 1½-quart glass casserole in microwave oven (30 to 45 seconds at HIGH).

2. Blend flour into melted butter. Add chicken broth and milk gradually, stirring until smooth. Cook uncovered in microwave oven 6 to 7 minutes at HIGH, or until thickened; stir after each minute.

3. Add seasonings, chicken, peas and pimento to sauce. Cook uncovered in microwave oven 5 minutes at HIGH, or until thoroughly heated.

4. Stir cheese into chicken mixture. Serve over toast or biscuits or in patty shells.

About 6 servings

CHICKEN 'N' MUSHROOM SAUCE

1 **can (about 10 ounces) condensed cream of mushroom soup**
1 **cup shredded Cheddar cheese**
3 **slices toast, cut in 1-inch pieces**
2 **cups cooked chicken pieces**

1. Combine mushroom soup and cheese in a 1-quart glass casserole. Cook uncovered in microwave oven 2 minutes at HIGH, or until cheese is melted.
2. Put pieces of toast (reserve 6 pieces for top) in bottom of an 8-inch round glass cake dish.
3. Put chicken on toast and pour sauce over all. Garnish with remaining toast pieces. Heat uncovered in microwave oven 8½ to 9½ minutes at ROAST, or until chicken is hot.

About 6 servings

CHICKEN CURRY AND PINEAPPLE

¼ **cup (½ stick) butter or margarine**
½ **cup slivered almonds**
2 **cans (13¼ ounces each) pineapple chunks, drained**
2 **to 3 tablespoons chutney**
3 **tablespoons butter or margarine**
1 **cup diced onion**
⅔ **cup diagonally sliced celery**
1 **to 2 tablespoons curry powder**
1 **can (about 10 ounces) condensed cream of chicken soup**
1 **can (about 10 ounces) condensed cream of mushroom soup**
2½ **cups diced cooked chicken**
½ **cup dairy sour cream**
  Cooked rice (page 48)

1. Put ¼ cup butter and almonds into a 1-quart glass casserole. Cook uncovered in microwave oven 2 minutes at HIGH; stir after 1 minute. Remove almonds with a slotted spoon and place on absorbent paper.
2. Add pineapple and chutney to butter in the casserole; mix well. Heat uncovered in microwave oven 2 minutes at HIGH, or until pineapple is glazed. Remove from oven and keep warm.
3. Put 3 tablespoons butter, the onion, celery and curry powder into a 2½-quart glass casserole. Cook uncovered in microwave oven 4 to 6 minutes at HIGH, or until onion is tender; stir after 1 minute.
4. Put condensed soups and cooked chicken into casserole; mix well. Cover with an all-glass lid or plastic wrap. Heat in microwave oven to serving temperature (6 to 8 minutes at HIGH); stir occasionally.
5. Remove casserole from oven, stir in sour cream and allow to stand 1 minute.
6. Serve curry over rice and top with the pineapple and almonds.

6 to 8 servings

TOMATO SHELLS STUFFED WITH CURRIED CHICKEN

4 **medium-size firm ripe tomatoes**
2 **tablespoons butter or margarine**
3 **tablespoons flour**
1 **teaspoon minced onion**
¼ **to ½ teaspoon curry powder**
1 **cup milk**
1½ **teaspoons salt**
⅛ **teaspoon pepper**
⅛ **teaspoon garlic powder**
1 **cup diced cooked chicken**

1. Cut a slice from stem end of each tomato; scoop out pulp and invert tomatoes to drain.
2. Melt butter in a 1½-quart glass casserole in microwave oven (30 seconds at HIGH). Blend in flour, onion and curry powder. Stir in milk. Cook uncovered 2½ to 3½ minutes at HIGH, or until thickened and smooth; stir occasionally.
3. Stir in mixture of salt, pepper and garlic powder and then chicken.
4. Fill tomato shells with chicken mixture and place in a 1½-quart glass baking dish. Heat uncovered in microwave oven 4 to 6 minutes at HIGH, or until thoroughly heated; rotate dish one-quarter turn once.

4 servings

PHEASANT MARSALA

2 ready-to-cook pheasants
(1½ to 2 pounds each)
2 cups dry Marsala
½ cup chopped onion
1 teaspoon salt
¼ teaspoon pepper
¼ teaspoon fennel seed
3 small carrots, pared and
cut in 1½-inch chunks
3 small potatoes, pared and
quartered
2 medium zucchini,
quartered lengthwise and
cut in 1½-inch chunks
½ pound mushrooms,
cleaned (cut large ones in
half lengthwise)
Butter or margarine
Flour

1. Remove giblets and neck from pheasants (it's recommended that giblets be cooked conventionally). Rinse birds with water and pat dry. Remove all visible fat and discard. Secure neck openings with wooden picks.
2. Put each pheasant into a cooking bag and set in a glass baking dish. Pour half of a mixture of Marsala, onion, salt, pepper and fennel into each bag. Close openings of bags with cotton thread. Cut 6 slits in top of each bag. Cook in microwave oven 42 minutes at ROAST; rotate dish one-half turn once.
3. Insert a meat thermometer through bag into meaty portion of each pheasant; internal temperature should be 170°F. If additional cooking is needed, *remove thermometer* and return pheasants to oven and continue cooking several minutes. Check temperature again. Repeat if necessary.
4. Remove pheasants from bags to baking dish (reserve cooking liquid in a measuring cup), cover pheasants with aluminum foil and allow to stand 15 to 20 minutes for heat to equalize; during this time internal temperature will rise.
5. Put carrots, potatoes and zucchini into a 2-quart glass baking dish. Pour ¼ cup reserved cooking liquid over vegetables. Cover with plastic wrap. Cook in microwave oven 10 minutes at HIGH, or until vegetables are almost tender; stir once. Add mushrooms and continue cooking covered 10 minutes at HIGH, or until all vegetables are crisp-tender; stir once or twice. Allow to stand covered 5 minutes.
6. For each cup of remaining cooking liquid, melt 2 tablespoons of butter in a glass bowl in microwave oven (30 to 45 seconds at HIGH). Stir in the same amount of flour as butter and cook uncovered in microwave oven 1 minute at HIGH, or until bubbly; stir once.
7. Add remaining cooking liquid gradually to butter-flour mixture, stirring until smooth. Cook uncovered in microwave oven (4 minutes at HIGH), or until thickened; stir frequently.
8. Spoon some of the gravy over pheasants on a platter and pour the remainder into a gravy boat. Surround pheasants with some of the vegetables. Serve remaining vegetables in a bowl.

4 to 6 servings

HINT: If pheasants are frozen, unwrap them and put them into a glass baking dish. Cover leg tips and wing tips with small pieces of aluminum foil. Heat at DEFROST just enough to remove giblets from cavities; follow directions for chicken on page 71 of Defrosting Chart.

Chicken Marsala: Follow recipe for Pheasant Marsala, substituting 2 broiler-fryer chickens (about 2 pounds each) for pheasants and omitting fennel seed.

Rock Cornish Hens Marsala: Follow recipe for Pheasant Marsala, substituting 4 frozen Rock Cornish hens (about 1 pound each), defrosted following directions on page 71 in Defrosting Chart and omitting fennel seed.

ROAST DUCKLING

**5-pound duckling
4 medium oranges,
   quartered**

1. Remove giblets from duckling and wash duckling. (It's recommended that giblets be cooked conventionally.)
2. Stuff duckling with orange quarters. Secure openings with heavy round wooden picks or metal poultry pins. If using poultry pins, do not allow them to touch one another or the sides of oven. Cover ends of wings, legs and tail of duckling with aluminum foil.
3. Place duckling, breast side up, on a roast rack set in a 2-quart glass baking dish. Cook uncovered in microwave oven 10 minutes at HIGH.
4. Brush bird with drippings. Remove foil and turn bird, breast side down. Cook uncovered in microwave oven 14 minutes at ROAST.
5. Brush bird with drippings. Cook uncovered in microwave oven 14 minutes at ROAST.
6. Turn duck, breast side up; brush with drippings. Cook uncovered in microwave oven 14 minutes at ROAST, or until drumstick feels very soft when pressed between protected fingers.
7. Remove from oven. Cover duckling with foil and allow to stand 15 to 20 minutes for heat to equalize.

About 4 servings

HINT: Use paper towels for turning and testing duckling.

LIME-GLAZED ROCK CORNISH HENS

**2 frozen Rock Cornish
  hens (about 1 pound
  each)
1 teaspoon salt
¼ cup (½ stick) butter
1 tablespoon brown sugar
1½ tablespoons lime juice
1 teaspoon soy sauce**

1. Defrost Rock Cornish hens following directions on page 71 in Defrosting Chart.
2. Remove giblets from hens; rinse hens and pat dry. Rub cavities with salt.
3. Melt butter in a glass bowl in microwave oven (30 seconds at HIGH). Mix in brown sugar, lime juice and soy sauce. Brush cavities with some of the butter mixture.
4. Tie legs and tail together with cotton thread. Cover ends of wings and legs with aluminum foil.
5. Place hens, breast side down, on a roast rack set in a 2-quart glass baking dish. Cover with waxed paper. Cook in microwave oven 8 minutes at HIGH.
6. Remove foil, turn hens over, brush with butter mixture and cover again with waxed paper. Cook in microwave oven 11 minutes at HIGH, or until tender.
7. Remove from oven. Cover hens with foil and allow to stand 15 to 20 minutes for heat to equalize.

ROAST TURKEY

10-pound turkey
Favorite stuffing
(optional)

1. Remove giblets from turkey and wash turkey. (It's recommended that giblets be cooked conventionally.)
2. Fill cavities of turkey with stuffing, if desired. Secure openings with heavy round wooden picks or metal poultry pins. If using poultry pins, do not allow them to touch one another or the sides of oven. Cover ends of wings and legs of turkey with aluminum foil.
3. Place turkey, breast side down, on a roast rack set in a 2-quart glass baking dish. Cover with waxed paper. Cook in microwave oven 40 minutes at HIGH; rotate dish one-half turn halfway through cooking period.
4. Remove foil, turn turkey over and cover again with waxed paper. Cook in microwave oven 28 minutes at ROAST.
5. Rotate dish one-half turn. Insert Temperature Probe in inside thigh muscle. Cook covered in microwave oven set at 165°F and at ROAST.
6. Remove turkey from oven. Cover turkey with foil and allow to stand 20 to 30 minutes for heat to equalize; during this time internal temperature will rise.

HINTS: Stuffing temperature must be at least 160°F when turkey is removed from oven.
•Use several layers of paper towels for turning turkey.
•Slightly reduce minutes per pound for larger turkeys.

COOKED TURKEY BREAST

1 turkey breast
(about 5 pounds)

1. Rinse turkey breast and pat dry.
2. Put turkey, skin side down, on a roast rack set in a 2-quart glass baking dish. Cover with waxed paper. Cook in microwave oven 15 minutes at HIGH.
3. Turn turkey breast over and cover exposed bone with aluminum foil. Cook covered in microwave oven 15 minutes at ROAST.
4. Rotate dish one-half turn. Insert Temperature Probe, if using, in thickest part of breast. Cook covered in microwave oven set at 165°F and at ROAST, or cook for an additional 10 minutes at ROAST.
5. Remove turkey from oven. Cover turkey with foil and allow to stand 15 minutes for heat to equalize; during this time internal temperature will rise.

TURKEY TETRAZZINI

1 package (7 or 8 ounces) thin spaghetti
2 tablespoons butter or margarine
1 tablespoon finely chopped onion
½ pound fresh mushrooms, sliced
¼ cup each chopped green pepper and red pepper (see Note)
¼ cup (½ stick) butter or margarine
¼ cup flour
½ teaspoon salt
¼ teaspoon white pepper
1 cup chicken broth
1 cup milk
3 tablespoons sherry
¼ cup snipped parsley
3 cups cooked turkey pieces
Grated Parmesan cheese

1. Cook spaghetti following recipe for Cooked Pasta (page 49). Keep warm until ready to use.
2. Put 2 tablespoons butter, onion, mushrooms and green and red pepper into a 2-quart glass casserole. Cook uncovered in microwave oven 3 minutes at HIGH, or until mushrooms are tender; stir after 1 minute.
3. Set mushroom mixture aside. Melt ¼ cup butter in the casserole in microwave oven (1 minute at HIGH). Add flour, salt and pepper and blend well. Add broth and milk gradually, stirring constantly. Cook uncovered in microwave oven 4 to 6 minutes at HIGH, or until thickened; stir after 2 minutes, then after each 30 seconds.
4. Add mushroom mixture, sherry, parsley and turkey pieces to sauce; mix well. Mix in cooked spaghetti. Heat uncovered in microwave oven 3 minutes at HIGH.
5. Stir mixture well and sprinkle with Parmesan cheese. Heat uncovered in microwave oven to serving temperature (3 to 5 minutes at HIGH).

6 to 8 servings

Note: If desired, substitute drained chopped pimento for red pepper.

ROAST TURKEY LEGS

1 tablespoon gravy
browning sauce
1 tablespoon oil
2 turkey legs (about 10
ounces each)

1. Mix browning sauce and oil for brushing sauce.
2. Put turkey legs on a roast rack set in a 2-quart glass baking dish. Brush with sauce. Cover leg bones with foil. Cover with waxed paper.
3. Cook in microwave oven 10 minutes at ROAST, or until tender; turn twice and brush with sauce.

HINT: If turkey legs are frozen, defrost following directions on page 71 in Defrosting Chart.

TURKEY-POTATO CASSEROLE

3 tablespoons butter or
margarine
¾ cup sliced mushrooms
½ cup finely chopped onion
2 cups diced cooked turkey
2 cups diced cooked
potatoes
1 tablespoon snipped
parsley
1½ teaspoons seasoned salt
⅛ teaspoon pepper
⅔ cup (1 small can)
undiluted evaporated
milk

1. Put butter, mushrooms and onion into a 2-quart glass casserole. Cook uncovered in microwave oven about 4 minutes at HIGH, or until mushrooms are tender; stir after 1 minute.
2. Put turkey, potatoes, parsley, seasoned salt and pepper into casserole. Add evaporated milk gradually, stirring gently. Heat mixture uncovered in microwave oven to serving temperature (about 5 minutes at HIGH); stir once during heating.

4 to 6 servings

CHICKEN LIVERS AND MUSHROOMS

1 pound chicken livers
¼ cup flour
½ teaspoon salt
⅛ teaspoon white pepper
2½ tablespoons butter or
margarine
½ cup orange sections, cut
in halves
1 can (3 ounces) sliced
mushrooms, drained
Snipped parsley

1. Rinse chicken livers and drain on absorbent paper.
2. Mix flour, salt and pepper; coat chicken livers evenly.
3. Melt butter in a 2-quart glass baking dish in microwave oven (30 seconds at HIGH).
4. Add livers and coat with butter. Cover with waxed paper. Cook in microwave oven 6 to 7 minutes at BAKE; stir once.
5. Spoon orange pieces and mushrooms on top of livers. Heat uncovered in microwave oven to serving temperature (3½ to 4½ minutes at BAKE); stir once.
6. Sprinkle with parsley. Serve immediately.

About 4 servings

Preserving

Jars of homemade jams and jellies with their sparkling jewellike colors tempt you to taste their flavorful delights. Just imagine spreading some on freshly baked bread! Or, think of munching a crisp homemade pickle! All of these creations are perfect for gift giving; watch your friends' faces light up.

Fruit jams and jellies are quick and easy to make in your microwave oven. You'll be delighted that you won't have to stand over a steaming pot stirring constantly; an occasional stir will do. And you won't have to worry about the sugar mixture scorching, either.

The recipes in this chapter use a variety of fruits: fresh, frozen and dried and also fruit juices. Be sure to use fresh fruits at the height of their season for the best color and flavor. The recipes that utilize convenience foods let you make homemade jellies all year long.

The short cooking time doesn't allow fruit juice to evaporate, so we recommend using commerical fruit pectin to thicken your preserves. As in conventional range-top jelly making, be sure you use a large enough container. Sugar solutions could boil over if the container is too small. Pour the cooked fruit mixture into hot, sterilized jars or glasses, seal and store. Sterilize jars conventionally by immersing in boiling water on your range top. Keep the jars in hot water until just before they are ready to be filled. Do not sterilize jars in the microwave oven. If desired, seal the jars with paraffin. Melt paraffin in the top of a double boiler; do not melt paraffin in the microwave oven. The jars may then be stored at room temperature. Or you can simply cover the jars with lids and store in the refrigerator. You may use either method of storage with all the fruit preserves in this book except the Apricot-Apple Butter, which requires refrigeration because it does not have enough sugar to prevent the food from spoiling at room temperature.

Homemade pickles are a delightful addition to an otherwise plain lunch. The smaller-than-conventional batches let you keep homemade pickles at their freshest and cook up another batch quickly, whenever you want more. The pickles and brines cook rapidly in your microwave oven. When the pickles are finished cooking, ladle them into hot, sterilized jars. Cover and store these pickles in your refrigerator. However, the Freezer Dill Pickles should be stored in the freezer and defrosted just before using.

Preserve your garden produce for use all year long and make your own convenience foods by freezing your fresh vegetables. Before freezing it is necessary to blanch most vegetables. Blanching will prevent flavor and quality changes. After blanching, plunge the vegetables into cold water to stop the cooking. When cool, package for freezing. Remember, if you use boilable freezer pouches, be sure to puncture the bag when you are cooking your own frozen vegetables.

Drying herbs fresh from your garden will save summer's freshness all winter long. Drying herbs requires no special equipment. Be sure the leaves are washed and excess moisture is dried off before starting. Dry your favorite herbs for seasoning in your favorite soups, main dishes and other foods. Give your friends bouquets of herbs you've dried. Follow the directions in the Drying Herbs Chart for drying other herbs; the technique is the same, but timings may vary.

Note: Home canning is not recommended for the microwave oven. Special range-top utensils bring the water and jars to a boil and maintain heat and pressure necessary for safe canning. A hot water bath is necessary to process home canned foods.

GRAPE JELLY

1 package (1¾ ounces) powdered fruit pectin
2 cups grape juice
1 cup water
3½ cups sugar

1. Stir powdered pectin into grape juice and water in a 2-quart oven-proof glass mixing bowl/pitcher. Cover with plastic wrap. Cook in microwave oven 8 to 10 minutes at HIGH, or until bubbles appear at edges of bowl; stir well after 3 minutes.
2. Add sugar gradually, mixing well. Cook covered in microwave oven 6 to 7 minutes at HIGH, or until mixture has boiled at least 1 minute. Stir well.
3. Skim off foam with metal spoon. Pour jelly into hot sterilized glasses or jars; cover. Cool. Store in refrigerator.
4. If desired, seal jelly with paraffin. Melt paraffin over hot water in a double boiler set over low heat. *Never* melt paraffin over direct heat or in microwave oven. Pour enough melted paraffin on top of jelly to make a layer about ⅛ inch thick. Tilt to seal to edge of glass. Cool, then cover. Store at room temperature if desired.

About 4 half-pints

STRAWBERRY JAM

4 packages (10 ounces each) frozen sliced strawberries
5 cups sugar
1 tablespoon lemon juice
1 package (3 ounces) liquid fruit pectin

1. Put frozen berries into a 3-quart glass casserole. Cook uncovered in microwave oven 6 minutes at HIGH; stir after 3 minutes to separate berries.
2. Add sugar and stir well. Cook uncovered in microwave oven 19 to 20 minutes at HIGH; or until mixture has boiled at least 1 minute; stir every 5 minutes.
3. Add lemon juice and liquid pectin. Stir well. Allow to stand uncovered 5 minutes. Skim off foam with metal spoon and stir well.
4. Pour jam into hot sterilized jars; cover. Cool. Store in refrigerator.

About 7 half-pints

CITRUS MARMALADE

1 large grapefruit
1 medium orange
1 medium lemon
1 medium lime
1½ cups water
⅛ teaspoon baking soda
5 cups sugar
1 package (3 ounces) liquid fruit pectin

1. Wash fruit. Peel each one, trim off white membrane and cut rind into slivers. Section fruit; discard seeds and dice fruit. Set aside. Combine rinds, water and baking soda in a 2-quart oven-proof glass mixing bowl/pitcher. Cover with plastic wrap. Cook in microwave oven 10 minutes at HIGH, or until rind is tender.
2. Add sugar and reserved fruit. Cook uncovered in microwave oven 18 minutes at HIGH, or until sugar is dissolved and fruit is soft; stir 3 times. (Syrup should boil at least 1 minute.)
3. Add liquid pectin and stir well. Allow to stand uncovered 5 minutes; stir occasionally. Skim off foam with metal spoon.
4. Pour marmalade into hot sterilized glasses or jars; cover. Cool. Store in refrigerator.
5. If desired, seal marmalade with paraffin. Melt paraffin over hot water in a double boiler set over low heat. *Never* melt paraffin over direct heat or in microwave oven. Pour enough melted paraffin on top of marmalade to make a layer about ⅛ inch thick. Tilt to seal to edge of glass. Cool, then cover. Store at room temperature if desired.

4 half-pints

PEACH PRESERVES

4 medium peaches, peeled and cut in pieces (about 4 cups) **6 cups sugar** **¼ cup lemon juice** **1 package (3 ounces) liquid fruit pectin**	1. Mix peaches, sugar and lemon juice in a 3-quart glass casserole. Cover with an all-glass lid or plastic wrap. Cook in microwave oven 14 minutes at HIGH, or until peaches are soft and sugar is dissolved; stir every 3 minutes. (Mixture should boil at least 1 minute.) 2. Stir in liquid pectin. Allow to stand uncovered 10 minutes. Stir to distribute fruit. 3. Pour preserves into hot sterilized jars; cover. Cool. Store in refrigerator. *6 half-pints*

APRICOT-APPLE BUTTER

1 package (11 ounces) dried apricots **2 cups apple juice** **10 cooking apples, pared, cored and cut in eighths** **4 teaspoons lemon juice** **½ teaspoon cinnamon** **Dash ground cloves**	1. Combine ingredients in a 4-quart glass casserole. Cook uncovered in microwave oven 15 to 18 minutes at HIGH, or until apples are soft; stir several times. 2. Purée in blender or food processor. Pour back into the glass casserole. Cook uncovered in microwave oven 15 minutes at HIGH, or until thick; stir several times. 3. Pack butter into hot sterilized jars; cover. Cool. Store in refrigerator. *4 half-pints*

CRANAPPLE RELISH

2 cups fresh cranberries **1 cup chopped pared apples** **1 cup sugar** **2 teaspoons grated lemon peel** **4 teaspoons lemon juice** **½ teaspoon butter or margarine**	1. Wash cranberries. Combine all ingredients in a 3-quart glass casserole. Cook uncovered in microwave oven 8 to 10 minutes at HIGH, or until mixture reaches desired thickness; stir every 2 minutes. 2. Spoon relish immediately into hot sterlized jars; cover. Cool. Store in refrigerator. 3. Serve relish warm or cool. *2 half-pints*

CHILI SAUCE

2½ pounds ripe tomatoes, peeled (about 7 medium) **2 medium green peppers, membrane and seeds removed** **2 medium onions, peeled** **1 stalk celery** **⅔ cup cider vinegar** **⅔ cup sugar** **2 teaspoons salt** **¼ teaspoon pepper** **¼ teaspoon cloves** **⅛ teaspoon cinnamon**	1. Finely chop vegetables. Combine in a 4-quart glass casserole with vinegar and a mixture of the remaining ingredients. 2. Cook uncovered in microwave oven 40 minutes at HIGH, or until thick; stir several times. 3. Pour sauce into hot sterilized jars; cover. Cool. Store in refrigerator. *About 4 pints*

WATERMELON RIND PICKLES

10 to 12 cups pared
   watermelon rind cubes
   (1 inch)*
½ cup pickling salt
2 quarts water
2 cups vinegar
6 cups sugar
1 tablespoon whole cloves
2 or 3 sticks cinnamon

1. Soak watermelon rind in a mixture of salt and water in a covered 3-quart glass casserole 2 hours. Drain; rinse with cold water. Return rind to casserole.
2. Cover rind with fresh water. Cook uncovered in microwave oven 20 to 22 minutes at HIGH, or until tender; stir once. Drain; return rind to casserole and set aside.
3. Combine vinegar and sugar in a 2-quart oven-proof glass mixing bowl/pitcher. Tie spices in cheesecloth bag. Add to vinegar and sugar. Cook uncovered in microwave oven 15 minutes at HIGH, or until sugar is dissolved and mixture is boiling; stir 3 times. Remove spice bag.
4. Pour syrup over rind. Cook uncovered in microwave oven 3 minutes at HIGH.
5. Pack pickles into hot sterilized jars; cover. Cool. Store in refrigerator.

4 pints

*Leave a thin line of pink with the watermelon rind.

BREAD AND BUTTER PICKLES

2 quarts ¼-inch cucumber
   slices (about 16
   cucumbers, 4 to 5 inches
   each)
½ cup pickling salt
1 quart boiling water
2 cups chopped onion
2 cups chopped green
   pepper
¾ cup chopped red pepper
2 cups cider vinegar
2 cups sugar
1 teaspoon celery seed
1 teaspoon mustard seed
½ teaspoon turmeric

1. Combine cucumber slices, salt and boiling water in a 4-quart glass casserole. Cover and allow to stand overnight.
2. The next day, drain the cucumbers and return to the glass casserole; add chopped vegetables. Set aside.
3. Combine remaining ingredients in a 1-quart glass measuring cup. Cook uncovered in microwave oven 8 to 9 minutes at HIGH, or until sugar is dissolved; stir twice.
4. Pour syrup over cucumber mixture; stir. Cook uncovered in microwave oven 6 minutes at HIGH; stir once.
5. Pack pickles into hot sterilized jars; cover. Cool. Store in refrigerator.

About 3 quarts

FREEZER DILL PICKLES

1 quart ¼-inch cucumber
   slices
2 cups sliced onions
4 teaspoons pickling salt
2 tablespoons water
¾ cup sugar
½ cup cider vinegar
1 teaspoon dill weed

1. Mix cucumber, onion, salt and water in a 2-quart glass casserole. Allow to stand 2 hours.
2. Combine sugar, vinegar and dill weed in a 2-cup glass measuring cup. Cook uncovered in microwave oven 3 minutes at HIGH, or until sugar dissolves completely. Allow to cool.
3. Drain cucumber-onion mixture; do not rinse. Return to casserole. Add cooled liquid; mix.
4. Pack mixture into freezer containers; cover. Freeze.

2 pints

BLANCHING VEGETABLES

Wash and cut vegetables as indicated. Put into a 1½- or 2-quart glass casserole. Add water; do not add salt. Cover with an all-glass lid or plastic wrap. Cook in microwave oven at <u>HIGH</u>; stir halfway through blanching time and at end of blanching. Plunge into cold water to stop cooking. Allow to cool, then package for freezing.

Vegetable	Amount	Amount of Water	Blanching Time
Asparagus spears	1 pound	¼ cup	3 minutes
Beans, green (whole or cut)	1 pound	½ cup	3½ minutes
Broccoli (cut in spears)	1 bunch (about 1¼ pounds)	½ cup	3 minutes
Carrots (pared and sliced)	1 pound	¼ cup	3½ minutes
Cauliflower (cut in flowerets)	1 pound	½ cup	3 minutes
Corn (cut from cobs)	cut from 4 ears	¼ cup	4 minutes
Spinach (leaves with stems removed)	1 pound	none	2 minutes
Squash, yellow summer (sliced)	1 pound	¼ cup	3 minutes

DRYING HERBS

Wash herb leaves and pat dry. Spread leaves evenly on paper-towel-lined microwave oven tray. Cover with paper towels. Cook at <u>HIGH</u> as directed below until almost dry and easy to crumble; rearrange as necessary for even cooking. Allow to stand uncovered to complete drying. Store in covered container away from light.

Herb	Amount	Time for Drying
Basil	1 cup leaves	2 to 2½ minutes
Mint	1 cup leaves	1½ to 2 minutes
Parsley (stems removed)	1 cup	2 to 2½ minutes

Soups and Sauces

What more elegant way to impress your guests than by serving a hot soup as the first course, or a savory sauce to accompany the main dish? Soups and sauces made in the microwave oven let you cook with an ease that you never dreamed possible. Many can be cooked and served right in the same dish. With microwave cooking, you needn't worry about your soups or sauces scorching. They need less attention than when cooked conventionally and, best of all, need less stirring. Soups and sauces with a milk base and sauces with a high sugar content boil over quickly, so use a container that is twice the ingredient volume.

A steaming cup of soup makes a tasty and nutritious between-meal snack. It can also dress up an ordinary lunch or stand on its own as a hearty meal. Soup can be made in the microwave oven right in the serving dish; individual servings can be made in bowls or mugs so there is an absolute minimum of cleanup.

Instant soups can be added to individual cups of boiling water (heated of course in your microwave oven). Canned soups can be prepared as easily; merely add water or milk and heat. For added convenience, use the Temperature Probe for truly carefree heating. To reheat individual servings of soup, set the temperature at 160°F and at HIGH. Many tempting soups can be made from fresh ingredients. The quick cooking helps keep colors bright and flavors fresh. Some slow-cooking soups that Grandma simmered on the back of the stove all day may take almost as long in the microwave oven, but the kitchen will stay cool. Stir soups occasionally as they cook to distribute the heat throughout.

Sauces added to meat or vegetables turn ordinary food into tasty delights. Or you can create a scrumptious dessert sauce as the crowning glory for the end of a meal. Sauces can be measured, mixed and cooked all in a glass measuring cup. Even pouring the cooked sauce will be convenient. And you save on cleanup time by cooking and serving in the same dish. Be sure the measuring cup is large enough to hold the sauce as it bubbles and cooks. Remember sugar- and milk-base sauces need large containers.

Microwave cooking heats the sauces from all sides, rather than just the bottom. It eliminates scorching and requires less attention; however, sauces do need to be stirred often to prevent lumps from forming. For easy handling, wooden and plastic spoons may be left in the sauce as it cooks. A wire whisk is invaluable when used to stir sauces and make them smooth. However, it cannot be left in the microwave oven as the sauce cooks.

Gravies are easy to make without the worry of scorching or the bother of constant stirring. If you are adapting a favorite gravy recipe for use in the microwave oven, remember that because it cooks so quickly, the liquid doesn't evaporate. Therefore, reduce the amount of liquid you are using.

You can have a hot fudge sundae any time you want. Sauces can be reheated quickly and easily in your microwave oven. They can even be heated in the storage container, providing it is microwave-safe. Stir the sauce before serving to equally distribute the heat.

FRESH VEGETABLE-BEEF SOUP

Beef Broth:
- 1½ **pounds beef shank cross cuts**
- 1½ **tablespoons butter or margarine**
- 1 **onion, peeled and cut in quarters**
- 1 **small clove garlic, peeled**
- 1 **small bay leaf**
- ¾ **teaspoon thyme leaves**
- 1 **parsley sprig**
- 2 **beef bouillon cubes**
- 3 **peppercorns**
- 1½ **teaspoons salt**
- 2 **quarts water**

Vegetables for soup:
- ¾ **cup sliced celery**
- ¾ **cup sliced pared carrot**
- 1½ **cups chopped cabbage**
- 1 **cup fresh green beans, cut in 1-inch pieces**
- 2 **large potatoes, pared and cut in 1-inch cubes**
- ¾ **cup fresh or frozen whole kernel corn**
- 1½ **teaspoons salt**
- 2 **tomatoes, peeled and chopped**

1. For broth, put meat and butter into a 4-quart glass casserole. Cover with an all-glass lid. Cook in microwave oven 6 minutes at HIGH, or until meat starts to brown; stir once. Add remaining ingredients for broth. Cook covered 8 to 10 minutes at HIGH, or until mixture boils.

2. Stir broth. Cook covered in microwave oven 60 minutes at SIMMER, or until meat is fork-tender; stir occasionally. Remove from oven.

3. Put celery, carrot, cabbage, green beans, potato and corn into a 2-quart glass casserole. Add 1 cup broth. Cover with an all-glass lid or plastic wrap. Cook in microwave oven 8 to 10 minutes at HIGH, or until tender; stir twice.

4. Remove meat from broth and cut meat into pieces. Add to broth along with cooked vegetables, salt and tomatoes; stir. Cook covered in microwave oven 10 minutes at SIMMER; stir once.

2 to 2½ quarts

NEW ORLEANS GUMBO

- ½ **cup (1 stick) butter or margarine**
- 2 **onions, peeled and chopped**
- ¼ **cup flour**
- 2 **quarts chicken broth**
- 1 **can (28 ounces) tomatoes (undrained)**
- ½ **pound okra, sliced**
- 1 **stalk celery, thinly sliced**
- ½ **teaspoon thyme**
- 1 **bay leaf**
- ½ **teaspoon salt**
  Pinch pepper
  Pinch ground red pepper
- 24 **large peeled and deveined shrimp**
- 24 **oysters**
- 2 **cups cooked rice (page 48)**

1. Put butter and onion into a 4-quart glass bowl. Cook uncovered in microwave oven 3 to 4 minutes at HIGH, or until tender; stir after 1 minute.

2. Mix flour into onion mixture. Cook uncovered in microwave oven about 30 seconds at HIGH, or until bubbly.

3. Add chicken broth gradually, stirring constantly. Add tomatoes, okra, celery, seasonings, shrimp and oysters; stir. Cook uncovered in microwave oven 30 minutes at SIMMER.

4. Put ¼ cup cooked rice into each soup bowl; ladle in hot gumbo.

8 servings

CLAM CHOWDER

2 tablespoons butter
½ cup diced celery
¼ cup minced onion
¼ cup minced green pepper
1¾ cups milk
1 cup cream or
   half-and-half
3 tablespoons flour
½ cup diced potato
2 cans (7½ ounces each)
   minced clams, drained;
   reserve liquid
½ teaspoon salt
⅛ teaspoon thyme
3 drops Tabasco
½ teaspoon Worcestershire
   sauce

1. Put butter, celery, onion and green pepper into a 3-quart glass casserole. Cook uncovered in microwave oven <u>3 minutes at HIGH</u>, or until vegetables are tender; stir after 1 minute. Remove from oven.
2. Combine milk and cream in a glass bowl. Scald uncovered in microwave oven (<u>2½ minutes at HIGH</u>).
3. Blend flour into the vegetable-butter mixture. Add the scalded milk and cream gradually, stirring constantly. Cook uncovered in microwave oven <u>2½ minutes at HIGH</u>, or until boiling.
4. Stir potato, reserved clam liquid, salt, thyme and Tabasco into sauce. Cook uncovered in microwave oven <u>3 minutes at HIGH</u>, or until boiling. Stir. Cook uncovered <u>15 minutes at SIMMER</u>; stir 3 times.
5. Add clams and Worcestershire sauce to mixture in casserole; stir. Cook uncovered in microwave oven to serving temperature (<u>1½ minutes at HIGH</u>).

4 to 6 servings

VEGETABLE OYSTER SOUP

4 cups chopped head let-
   tuce
2 cups chopped spinach
1 cup chopped carrots
½ cup chopped onion
1½ cups chicken broth or 1
   can (about 10 ounces)
   chicken broth
1 can (10 ounces) frozen
   oysters, thawed
2 tablespoons butter
2 tablespoons flour
1¼ teaspoons salt
2 cups milk
1 teaspoon grated lemon
   peel
1 tablespoon lemon juice
Freshly ground pepper
Lemon slices

1. Put lettuce, spinach, carrots, onion, ½ cup chicken broth and oysters into a 4-quart glass bowl. Cover with waxed paper. Cook in microwave oven <u>12 to 14 minutes at HIGH</u>, or until carrots are crisp-tender; stir occasionally.
2. Turn half of mixture into an electric blender container and blend a few seconds; repeat for second half of mixture. Set blended mixture aside.
3. Melt butter in a 1½-quart glass bowl in microwave oven (<u>30 seconds at HIGH</u>).
4. Stir flour and salt into melted butter. Gradually stir in milk and remaining 1 cup chicken broth. Cook uncovered in microwave oven <u>about 10 minutes at HIGH</u>, or until thickened; stir occasionally.
5. Add vegetable mixture, lemon peel and juice and pepper. Heat uncovered in microwave oven to serving temperature (<u>3 to 4 minutes at HIGH</u>).
6. Serve garnished with lemon slices.

About 7 cups

CREAMY CHEDDAR CHEESE SOUP

2 tablespoons butter
2 tablespoons chopped onion
⅓ cup flour
1¼ teaspoons dry mustard
¼ teaspoon garlic powder
¼ teaspoon paprika
6 cups milk
3 tablespoons chicken seasoned stock base
2 teaspoons Worcestershire sauce
1½ cups thinly sliced celery
10 ounces Cheddar cheese, shredded (2½ cups) Chopped green pepper, pimento strips, toasted slivered almonds or cooked crumbled bacon for garnish

1. Put butter and onion into a 4-quart glass bowl. Cook uncovered in microwave oven 4 minutes at HIGH, or until tender; stir after 1 minute.
2. Stir flour, mustard, garlic powder and paprika into onion butter. Add 3 cups milk gradually, stirring constantly. Mix in chicken stock base, Worcestershire sauce and celery. Cook uncovered in microwave oven 10 minutes at HIGH, or until slightly thickened; stir occasionally.
3. Stir remaining milk and cheese into sauce. Heat uncovered in microwave oven to serving temperature (about 8 minutes at HIGH), or if using Temperature Probe, set at 160°F and at HIGH; stir occasionally.
4. Serve soup topped with desired garnish.

About 2 quarts

CREAM OF POTATO-ONION SOUP

4 medium baking potatoes, pared and cut in pieces
2 medium onions, peeled and cut in pieces
¾ teaspoon salt
¼ cup water
3 tablespoons butter
2 tablespoons flour
3 cups milk
2 tablespoons snipped parsley
½ teaspoon celery salt
Few grains white pepper

1. Put potato and onion pieces, salt and water into a 3-quart glass casserole. Cover with an all-glass lid or plastic wrap. Cook in microwave oven 10 to 12 minutes at HIGH, or until tender; stir once.
2. Purée potato mixture in a food mill, electric blender or food processor. Set aside.
3. Melt butter in the glass casserole in microwave oven (about 30 seconds at HIGH). Blend in flour. Add milk gradually, stirring constantly. Add reserved purée, parsley, celery salt and pepper; mix well. Cook uncovered in microwave oven 5 minutes at HIGH, or until thoroughly heated; stir occasionally.

About 1½ quarts

FRENCH ONION SOUP

2 tablespoons butter
3 medium onions, sliced
⅓ cup sliced celery
4 cups beef broth
Salt to taste
4 to 6 French bread slices, toasted
Grated Parmesan cheese

1. Put butter, onion and celery into a 3-quart glass casserole. Cover with all-glass lid or plastic wrap. Cook in microwave oven 6 to 7 minutes at HIGH, or until vegetables are tender; stir occasionally.
2. Add broth and salt to onion mixture. Cook covered in microwave oven 6 to 8 minutes at HIGH, or until piping hot.
3. Ladle soup into bowls and add toasted bread slices. Sprinkle with cheese.

4 to 6 servings

EASY VEGETABLE SOUP

1 package (10 ounces)
  frozen chopped broccoli
1 can (15½ ounces) green
  beans (undrained)
4 cups shredded cabbage
2 cups chopped celery
4½ cups beef broth
  (homemade, canned or
  from bouillon cubes)
2 tablespoons instant
  minced onion
2 cups tomato juice

1. Heat frozen broccoli in a 4-quart glass casserole in microwave oven just until thawed (3 to 4 minutes at HIGH); stir often to separate.
2. Add green beans with liquid, cabbage, celery, beef broth and onion. Cover with all-glass lid or plastic wrap. Cook in microwave oven 16 to 18 minutes at HIGH, or until vegetables are tender.
3. Stir in tomato juice. Heat uncovered in microwave oven to serving temperature, using Temperature Probe set at 160°F and at HIGH.
4. Ladle hot soup into bowls. *2½ quarts*

CANNED SOUP

1 can (about 10 ounces)
  condensed soup
1 soup can water

Combine soup and water in a 1-quart glass casserole or 1-quart measuring cup. Cover with plastic wrap. Heat in microwave oven until piping hot (3 to 4 minutes at HIGH, or if using Temperature Probe, set at 160°F and at HIGH); stir occasionally.

HINTS: Check label of can; if liquid is not called for, thoroughly heat soup as is, stirring occasionally.
•Soak dehydrated soups in liquid 30 minutes before heating.

THIN WHITE SAUCE

1 tablespoon butter
1 tablespoon flour
½ teaspoon salt
1 cup milk

1. Melt butter in a 1-quart glass casserole in microwave oven (about 15 seconds at HIGH). Add flour and salt and blend to a smooth paste. Add milk gradually, stirring constantly.
2. Cook uncovered in microwave oven 4 minutes at HIGH, or until thickened; stir after 2 minutes, then at the end of each 30 seconds.
About 1 cup

Medium White Sauce: Use 2 tablespoons butter and 2 tablespoons flour with salt and 1 cup milk.

Thick White Sauce: Use 3 tablespoons butter and 3 tablespoons flour with salt and 1 cup milk.

Sour Cream Sauce: Substitute **1 cup dairy sour cream** for the milk. When sauce is thickened, add **2 teaspoons lemon juice** and mix well.

Cheese Sauce: To 1 cup hot Medium White Sauce, add ¼ **teaspoon dry mustard** and ½ **cup shredded sharp Cheddar cheese**; mix. Cook uncovered in microwave oven 1 minute at HIGH, then stir.

Olive Sauce: To 1 cup Medium White Sauce, add ¼ **cup sliced pimento-stuffed olives.**

BÉCHAMEL SAUCE

2 tablespoons butter
1 teaspoon grated onion
1 tablespoon flour
½ cup chicken broth
½ cup half-and-half
¼ teaspoon salt
⅛ teaspoon white pepper
Dash thyme

1. Melt butter in a 1-quart glass measuring cup in microwave oven (30 seconds at HIGH). Add onion and flour; mix well. Add broth and half-and-half gradually, stirring constantly.
2. Cook uncovered in microwave oven 4 to 5 minutes at HIGH, or until thickened; stir after 2 minutes, then at the end of each 30 seconds.
3. Remove from oven. Add seasonings and mix well.

About 1 cup

MOCK HOLLANDAISE SAUCE

1 cup Medium White Sauce (page 176)
2 egg yolks, beaten
2 tablespoons butter
1 tablespoon lemon juice

1. Prepare white sauce.
2. Stir ¼ cup of the white sauce into egg yolks, then blend into remaining sauce in casserole. Add butter and lemon juice; mix well. Cook uncovered in microwave oven 1 minute at HIGH, or until hot.

About 1¼ cups

HOLLANDAISE SAUCE

¼ cup (½ stick) butter
¼ cup cream or half-and-half
2 egg yolks, beaten
1 tablespoon lemon juice or vinegar
¼ teaspoon salt
Dash ground red pepper

1. Melt butter in a 1-quart glass measuring cup in microwave oven (about 30 seconds at HIGH). Add cream, egg yolks, lemon juice, salt and red pepper; mix thoroughly. Cook uncovered in microwave oven 1½ minutes at SIMMER; stir once.
2. Remove from oven and beat until light.

⅔ cup

HINT: If sauce separates, beat in cream until the consistency is smooth.

CRANBERRY SAUCE

1½ cups raw cranberries
¼ cup water
½ cup sugar

1. Put cranberries, water and sugar into a 1-quart glass measuring cup. Cover cup loosely with plastic wrap. Cook in microwave oven 3 to 5 minutes at HIGH, or until cranberries have popped; stir once.
2. Allow to stand several minutes after cooking; stir well and pour into sauce dish.

BARBECUE SAUCE

1 cup ketchup
¼ cup packed brown sugar
¼ cup vinegar
1½ teaspoons celery seed
Dash garlic powder
¼ teaspoon salt
Dash pepper
1½ teaspoons Worcestershire
sauce
1½ teaspoons horseradish
1 medium onion, chopped
¼ cup water

1. Combine all ingredients in a 2-quart glass casserole. Cover with waxed paper.
2. Cook in microwave oven 3 minutes at HIGH, or until hot; stir occasionally.

About 1½ cups

ORANGE BARBECUE SAUCE

¼ cup packed brown sugar
½ teaspoon dry mustard
⅛ teaspoon cloves
½ teaspoon Worcestershire
sauce
⅓ cup chopped onion
1½ teaspoons grated orange
peel
⅓ cup orange juice
¾ cup ketchup
1½ cups water

1. Mix all ingredients in a 1-quart glass measuring cup. Cover with waxed paper.
2. Cook in microwave oven 4 minutes at HIGH; stir occasionally.

About 2¼ cups

BASIC GRAVY

2 tablespoons flour
¼ teaspoon salt
¼ cup water
¾ cup liquid*

1. Combine flour, salt and water in a 2-cup glass measuring cup to make a smooth mixture. Add liquid gradually, stirring until smooth.
2. Cook uncovered in microwave oven 2½ minutes at HIGH, or until thickened; stir after 1 minute, then at the end of each 30 seconds.

About 1 cup

*For liquid, use pan drippings plus water, 1 bouillon cube dissolved in ¾ cup water, or reserved vegetable cooking liquid and gravy browning sauce.

MUSHROOM SAUCE

8 **ounces fresh mushrooms, cleaned and sliced**
2 **tablespoons butter or margarine**
¼ **cup flour**
¼ **teaspoon salt**
1 **cup chicken or beef broth**
1 **cup half-and-half**
1 **tablespoon snipped parsley**

1. Put mushrooms, butter, flour and salt into a 1½-quart glass casserole. Cover with an all-glass lid or plastic wrap. Cook in microwave oven 2 to 3 minutes at HIGH, or until tender; stir well after each minute.
2. Add broth gradually to mushroom mixture, stirring constantly. Cook uncovered in microwave oven 8 minutes at HIGH; stir every 2 minutes.
3. Add half-and-half gradually to mushroom mixture, stirring constantly. Cook uncovered in microwave oven to serving temperature (2 to 3 minutes at HIGH).
4. Remove sauce from oven and stir in parsley.

About 2½ cups

LEMON SAUCE

1 **tablespoon cornstarch**
¾ **cup sugar**
¾ **cup hot water**
2 **egg yolks**
1 **tablespoon butter**
3 **tablespoons lemon juice**
⅛ **teaspoon salt**

1. Combine cornstarch and sugar in a 1-quart glass casserole; add water and mix well. Cook uncovered in microwave oven 2 minutes at HIGH; stir frequently.
2. Beat egg yolks and add a small amount of hot mixture to egg yolks, then blend into mixture in casserole. Cook uncovered in microwave oven 1 minute at HIGH, or until thickened.
3. Add butter, lemon juice and salt and beat until blended.

1½ cups

APRICOT FRUIT SALAD DRESSING

2 **eggs, beaten**
1 **cup apricot nectar**
1½ **tablespoons lemon juice**
⅓ **cup sugar**
1 **teaspoon flour**
⅛ **teaspoon salt**
1 **tablespoon butter**
⅓ **cup chilled whipping cream**

1. Mix eggs, apricot nectar and lemon juice in a 1½-quart glass casserole.
2. Combine sugar, flour and salt and gradually add to liquid, stirring constantly. Cook uncovered in microwave oven 7 minutes at HIGH, or until thickened; stir occasionally.
3. Stir butter into dressing. Cool; chill.
4. Just before serving, whip cream and fold into chilled apricot mixture. Serve on fruit salad.

About 2 cups

PEANUT BUTTER SUNDAE SAUCE

1¼ **cups firmly packed light brown sugar**
⅔ **cup light corn syrup**
¼ **cup (½ stick) butter**
⅔ **cup (1 small can) undiluted evaporated milk**
¼ **cup peanut butter**

1. Put brown sugar, corn syrup and butter into a 2-quart ovenproof glass mixing bowl/pitcher. Cook uncovered in microwave oven 9 minutes at HIGH; stir once.
2. Remove from oven and blend in evaporated milk and peanut butter.

About 2 cups

BUTTERSCOTCH DESSERT SAUCE

1 **cup firmly packed light brown sugar**
⅓ **cup butter**
⅓ **cup cream or half-and-half**
Few grains salt

1. Mix brown sugar, butter, cream and salt in a 1½-quart glass casserole. Cook uncovered in microwave oven 2 minutes at HIGH, or until sugar is dissolved and butter is melted; stir after each minute. Cook about 1 minute at HIGH, or until sauce comes to boiling.
2. Serve warm over cake or ice cream.

About 1¼ cups

MELBA SAUCE

¼ **cup sugar**
2 **teaspoons cornstarch**
1 **package (10 ounces) frozen red raspberries**
½ **cup currant jelly**

1. Mix sugar and cornstarch. Set aside.
2. Put frozen raspberries into a 1-quart glass casserole. Heat uncovered in microwave oven 1 minute at HIGH. Stir to break berries apart. Cook uncovered 30 seconds at HIGH, or until thawed.
3. Mix the sugar-cornstarch mixture into raspberries, then currant jelly. Cook uncovered in microwave oven 6 minutes at HIGH, or until sauce is thickened and clear; stir every minute.
4. Sieve mixture to remove seeds. Cool sauce before serving.

About 1½ cups

CHOCOLATE FUDGE SAUCE

3 **ounces (3 squares) unsweetened chocolate**
¼ **cup (½ stick) butter**
⅔ **cup sugar**
⅛ **teaspoon salt**
⅔ **cup (1 small can) undiluted evaporated milk**
1 **teaspoon vanilla extract**
Few drops almond extract

1. Melt chocolate and butter in a 2-quart oven-proof glass mixing bowl/pitcher in microwave oven (about 2 minutes at HIGH); stir twice.
2. Add sugar, salt and evaporated milk to melted mixture; stir. Cook uncovered in microwave oven 3 minutes at HIGH, or until mixture comes to boiling; stir every minute.
3. Stir extracts into sauce. Serve warm.

About 1½ cups

CHOCOLATE PEPPERMINT SAUCE

3 **ounces (3 squares) unsweetened chocolate**
¼ **cup water**
1 **cup sugar**
½ **cup corn syrup**
⅛ **teaspoon salt**
⅔ **cup cream or half-and-half**
⅛ **teaspoon peppermint extract**

1. Combine chocolate and water in a 1½-quart glass casserole. Cook uncovered in microwave oven 2½ minutes at HIGH, or until chocolate melts; blend well.
2. Add sugar, corn syrup and salt to chocolate mixture; mix well. Cook uncovered in microwave oven 4 minutes at HIGH; stir occasionally.
3. Remove from oven and gradually add cream and peppermint extract, stirring until blended.

About 2 cups

Butterscotch Dessert Sauce; Melba Sauce; Chocolate Fudge Sauce

Vegetables

Vegetables have never tasted so fresh or looked so vibrant as they do when cooked in the microwave oven. They retain their attractive color, fresh taste and natural texture. Because vegetables cook so quickly in very little liquid, there is high vitamin retention.

If you follow the charts and recipes in this chapter, the vegetables will be cooked to the crisp-tender stage: tender to bite but without loss of texture. If you prefer your vegetables crisper, reduce the cooking time. If you like a softer texture, add cooking time. When cooking fresh vegetables, add just enough water to produce steam. There is no reason to add excess water and drain away your valuable nutrients. Most frozen vegetables do not need additional water. The ice crystals around the vegetables will supply sufficient moisture. Put salt and water in the bottom of the dish before adding vegetables. It is not advisable to put salt on top of the vegetables because salt tends to dehydrate the vegetables, making them tough. Other seasonings can be sprinkled on top of the vegetables as they cook with no adverse effects. Cover the dish with a glass lid or plastic wrap to hold in the steam and speed the cooking. Use caution when removing the cover from the dish to avoid a steam burn. Be sure to open it away from you.

When indicated, stir the vegetables halfway through the cooking time and again just before serving to assure even cooking and to equalize the temperature throughout.

Vegetables are removed from the microwave oven when they are still slightly crisp. Five minutes of standing time will let them finish cooking completely. Leave the vegetables covered to hold heat.

Fresh vegetables taste so delicious you'll be tempted to serve them with every meal. The cooking times indicated in the chart are only a guide. You may find that the time will vary with the age of the vegetable, freshness, size, shape and also the starting temperature. Remember to consider your personal taste regarding crispness or softness.

Vegetables will cook more quickly and evenly if they are cut into small, uniform-size pieces. When cooking large, uneven pieces, such as broccoli or asparagus, you should arrange the pieces with the thinner, tender areas toward the center and the stalks toward the outside. Rotate the dish, instead of stirring the vegetables halfway through the cooking period. Fresh whole vegetables can be cooked right in their skins with their own natural moisture. When cooking vegetables that have a tight skin, like potatoes and squash, you must prick the skin to release the steam. You will probably notice your microwave oven steaming up as the vegetables cook; in that case, place a paper towel on the oven tray to absorb the extra moisture. If cooking more than one potato, arrange in a circle with a one-inch space between potatoes. Halfway through the cooking time, turn the potatoes and rearrange. Potatoes hold heat for a long time, so you may want to cook them first and let them stand covered while you finish cooking the rest of your meal.

Frozen vegetables will taste garden fresh when cooked in the microwave oven. For absolutely minimum cleanup, cook the frozen vegetables right in the box; merely puncture the carton so the steam can escape. Or empty the box into a glass dish, preferably your serving dish, and cover. Cook for a few minutes and then stir to separate the frozen vegetables. Continue cooking covered. Don't overcook; remember vegetables continue to cook after they have been removed from the microwave oven, even in the short time it takes to serve them.

Many frozen vegetables are packed in plastic pouches. To cook these in the microwave oven, cut an "X" in the pouch and place the pouch "X" side down in the glass serving dish; or pierce the plastic to let the steam escape. Flex the pouch halfway through the cooking time. When cooked, merely pour the contents into a serving dish.

You can freeze surplus vegetables from your garden and keep that fresh taste the year round. The vegetables need to be blanched before freezing; see Preserving chapter for guidelines.

Canned vegetables heat very quickly; see how to do it in the Convenience Foods Chart.

Sweet-Sour Red Cabbage; 191; Glazed Carrots and Pineapple, 193; Baked Stuffed Potatoes, 196

FRESH VEGETABLE COOKING CHART

When a cover is called for, cover with an all-glass lid or plastic wrap. Stir halfway through cooking time. Slightly undercook vegetables; allow to stand covered 5 minutes before serving.

Vegetable	Quantity	Cooking Time at HIGH	Cooking Instructions
Artichokes (3 inches in diameter)	1	5-6 minutes	2 teaspoons lemon juice and 2 tablespoons water in deep 1½-qt. covered glass casserole. Cook artichoke upside down.
	2	7-8 minutes	Same as above.
	4	12-14 minutes	2 teaspoons lemon juice plus 1 cup boiling water in 3-qt. covered glass casserole. Cook artichokes upside down.
Asparagus pieces	16 (4-inch pieces)	5-7 minutes	¼ cup water, ¼ teaspoon salt in 1½-qt. covered glass casserole.
spears	1 lb.	8-10 minutes	¼ cup water, ¼ teaspoon salt in 1-qt. covered glass casserole.
Beans Green or Wax	1 lb.	10-12 minutes	¼ cup water, ¼ teaspoon salt in 1½-qt. covered glass casserole.
	2 lbs.	16-18 minutes	Same as above except use 2-qt. covered glass casserole.
Lima or Butter (shelled)	1 lb.	6-8 minutes	½ cup water, ½ teaspoon salt in 1-qt. covered glass casserole.
	2 lbs.	9-11 minutes	Same as above except use 1½-qt. covered glass casserole.
Beets	4 medium size (whole)	15-17 minutes	Cover with water, add ¼ teaspoon salt, and cook in 2-qt. covered glass casserole.
	4 (sliced)	11-13 minutes	½ cup water, ¼ teaspoon salt in 1-qt. covered glass casserole.
Broccoli	1 small bunch (1½ lbs.)	8-10 minutes	Trim tough part off stalk; split broccoli, ½ cup water, ½ teaspoon salt in 2-qt. covered glass casserole.
Brussels Sprouts	½ lb.	4-6 minutes	2 tablespoons water in 1-qt. covered glass casserole.
	1 lb.	5-7 minutes	3 tablespoons water in 1½-qt. covered glass casserole.
Cabbage	Small head, chopped or shredded	7-9 minutes	Place ½ teaspoon salt and 2 tablespoons water in bottom of 1½-qt. covered glass casserole and add cabbage.
	Medium head, whole	12-14 minutes	Same as above except use 2-qt. covered glass casserole.

Vegetable	Quantity	Cooking Time at HIGH	Cooking Instructions
Carrots	4 (cut in thin strips or diced)	7-9 minutes	¼ cup water, ¼ teaspoon salt in 1-qt. covered glass casserole.
	6 whole	10-14 minutes	Same as above except use a 1½-qt. covered glass casserole.
Cauliflower	1 medium head, cut in flowerets	7-9 minutes	¼ cup water, ¼ teaspoon salt in 2-qt. covered glass casserole.
	1 medium head, whole	9-11 minutes	Same as above.
Celery	4 cups (cut in 1-inch pieces)	8-10 minutes	¼ cup water, ½ teaspoon salt in 1½-qt. covered glass casserole.
	6 cups (cut in 1-inch pieces)	12-14 minutes	Same as above except use 2-qt. covered glass casserole.
Corn on the cob	2 ears	4½-6½ minutes	Place corn in the husk on microwave oven cooking tray or place husked corn in glass baking dish, cover dish with waxed paper. Turn after ½ the cooking period.
	4 ears	8-10 minutes	Same as above.
cut from the cob	1½ cups	4-6 minutes	¼ cup water, ½ teaspoon salt in 1-qt. covered glass casserole.
Eggplant	1 small or 3 cups, peeled and diced	5-7 minutes	Add ¼ cup water, ½ teaspoon salt in 1½-qt. covered glass casserole.
Okra whole	½ lb.	4-5 minutes	¼ cup water, ¼ teaspoon salt in 1-qt. covered glass casserole.
sliced	½ lb.	3-4 minutes	Same as above.
Onions	2 large, cut in eighths	6-8 minutes	½ cup water, ½ teaspoon salt in 1-qt. covered glass casserole.
	4 large, cut in eighths	8-10 minutes	Same as above except use a 2-qt. covered glass casserole.
Parsnips	4 split, core removed, if desired	7-9 minutes	¼ cup water, ½ teaspoon salt cooked in 1½-qt. covered glass casserole.
	8 split, core removed, if desired	10-13 minutes	Same as above except use 2-qt. covered glass casserole.
Peas shelled	2 cups	4-6 minutes	2 tablespoons water in 1-qt. covered glass casserole.
	3 cups	6-8 minutes	Same as above except use 1½-qt. covered glass casserole.

Fresh Vegetable Cooking Chart (cont.)

Vegetable	Quantity	Cooking Time at HIGH	Cooking Instructions
Potatoes baked	1 medium	4-6 minutes	Scrub and pierce potatoes. Place in a circle on paper towel on oven cooking tray, leaving 1-inch space between each potato. Turn potatoes over and rearrange after ½ of the cooking time has elapsed.
	2 medium	7-8 minutes	
	3 medium	9-10 minutes	
	4 medium	11-13 minutes	
	5 medium	14-15 minutes	
	6 medium	16-18 minutes	
boiled	4 medium, whole	10-12 minutes	¼ cup water, ½ teaspoon salt in 1½-qt. covered glass casserole.
	4 medium, pared and cut in half	8-10 minutes	Same as above.
	6 medium, pared and cut in half	12-14 minutes	Same as above except use a 2-qt. covered glass casserole.
buttered	4 medium, sliced thin	10-12 minutes	2 tablespoons butter in 1½-qt. glass baking dish. Add potatoes, ½ teaspoon salt, and dot with butter. Cover with plastic wrap.
	6 medium, sliced thin	15-17 minutes	Same as above.
Pumpkin	1 (2 lbs.), whole	6-8 minutes per lb.	Pierce skin of pumpkin. Place on paper towel. Cook 7 min.; turn over once. Cut in half; discard peel and seedy center. Cook pumpkin in 1-qt. covered glass casserole 6 more min. until tender.
Rutabaga	1 lb.	5-7 minutes	Pierce skin through waxy coating. Place on paper towel. Cook. Allow to stand 5 minutes. Cut in quarters, peel and dice.
Spinach	1 lb.	6-7 minutes	Wash, cook in water that clings to the leaves, in 2-qt. covered glass casserole.
Squash Acorn or Butternut	1, whole	6-8 minutes	Wash and pierce skin in several places. Place on paper towel on oven cooking tray.
	2, whole	12-14 minutes	Same as above.
Hubbard	2 lbs., peeled and cut in 1-inch cubes	6-8 minutes	¼ cup water, 1 teaspoon salt, cook in 1½-qt. covered glass casserole.
Zucchini	2 medium, sliced	5-6 minutes	¼ cup water, ½ teaspoon salt in 1½-qt. covered glass casserole.
	4 medium, whole	7-9 minutes	Wash and pierce zucchini. Place on paper-towel-covered roast rack. Turn and rearrange twice during cooking period.
	6 medium, whole	10-12 minutes	Same as above.

Vegetable	Quantity	Cooking Time at HIGH	Cooking Instructions
Sweet Potatoes baked	1 medium, whole	3-5 minutes	Scrub and pierce potatoes. Place in a circle on paper towel on oven cooking tray, leaving 1-inch space between each potato. Turn potatoes over and rearrange after ½ of the cooking time has elapsed.
	2 medium, whole	5-7 minutes	
	4 medium, whole	9-11 minutes	
	6 medium, whole	13-15 minutes	
boiled	4 medium, peeled, cut in half	7-9 minutes	¼ cup water, ½ teaspoon salt in 1½-qt. covered glass casserole.
	6 medium, peeled, cut in half	10-12 minutes	Same as above except use a 2-qt. covered glass casserole.
Swiss Chard	1 lb.	6-7 minutes	Wash, cook in water that clings to the leaves in 3-qt. covered glass casserole.
Tomatoes	2, cut in half	2½-4 minutes	Place in 1-qt. covered glass casserole.
	4, cut in half	4-6 minutes	Same as above except use 1½-qt. covered glass casserole.
Turnip Greens	1 lb.	12-14 minutes	½ cup water in 3-qt. covered glass casserole.
Turnips	4 medium, cut in eighths	10-12 minutes	¼ cup water, ½ teaspoon salt in 1½-qt. covered glass casserole.

FROZEN VEGETABLE COOKING CHART

Slightly undercook vegetables; allow to stand covered 5 minutes before serving.

Vegetable	Quantity	Cooking Time at HIGH	Cooking Instructions
Asparagus	10-oz. pkg.	5-7 minutes	Place in 1-qt. covered glass casserole. Stir after 3 minutes to separate.
Beans Green or Wax	9-oz. pkg.	6-7 minutes	Place in 1-qt. covered glass casserole. Add 2 teaspoons water and stir after 3½ minutes to separate.
Broccoli	10-oz. pkg.	7-8 minutes	Place in 1-qt. covered glass casserole. Stir after 4 minutes to separate.
Brussels Sprouts	10-oz. pkg.	4-6 minutes	Place in 1-qt. covered glass casserole. Add 2 tablespoons water and stir after 2 minutes to separate.
Carrots	10-oz. pkg.	5-7 minutes	Place in 1-qt. covered glass casserole. Add 2 tablespoons water and stir after 3 minutes to separate.

Frozen Vegetable Cooking Chart (cont.)

Vegetable	Quantity	Cooking Time at HIGH	Cooking Instructions
Cauliflower	10-oz. pkg.	4-6 minutes	Place in 1-qt. covered glass casserole. Stir after 2 minutes to separate.
Corn cut off the cob	10-oz. pkg.	4-6 minutes	Place in 1-qt. covered glass casserole. Add 2 tablespoons water and stir after 2 minutes to separate.
Corn on the cob	2 ears	4-6 minutes	Place ears of corn in 1-qt. covered glass casserole. Add ¼ cup hot water. Turn ears after 2 minutes.
Onions in cream sauce	10-oz. pkg.	5-6 minutes	Place in 1-qt. covered glass casserole. Stir after 3 minutes to separate.
Peas	10-oz. pkg.	4-6 minutes	Place in 1-qt. covered glass casserole. Stir after 2 minutes to separate.
Peas and Carrots	10-oz. pkg.	5-7 minutes	Place in 1-qt. covered glass casserole. Stir after 3 minutes to separate.
Peas, Black-eye	10-oz. pkg.	8-10 minutes	Place in 1-qt. covered glass casserole. Add ¼ cup water. Stir after 4 minutes to separate.
Spinach	10-oz. pkg.	4-6 minutes	Place in 1-qt. covered glass casserole. Stir after 2 minutes to separate.
Vegetables, Mixed	10-oz. pkg.	4-6 minutes	Place in 1-qt. covered glass casserole. Add 2 tablespoons water. Stir after 2 minutes to separate.

HINT: If any of the above vegetables are in a pouch, cut a large "X" in the pouch with a knife to let steam escape and place the pouch, "X" side down, in a glass casserole; add *no* water. Reduce cooking time slightly from time shown in the chart for vegetables in a package.

DRIED BEAN COOKING CHART

Rinse beans and put into indicated amount of water in a 4-quart glass casserole. Cover with an all-glass lid or plastic wrap and soak overnight. The next day, cook covered following indicated cooking times; stir at the end of each cooking time.

Type of Beans	Weight of Beans	Amount of Water	Cooking Time at HIGH	Cooking Time at ROAST	Cooking Time at SIMMER
Pinto	1 pound	1½ quarts	15 minutes	15 minutes	30 minutes
Navy	1 pound	1½ quarts	15 minutes	15 minutes	15 minutes
Black-eye pea	1 pound	3 quarts	15 minutes	15 minutes	none

VEGETABLE-CHEESE CASSEROLE

2 cans (15 ounces each) green asparagus spears
1 can (about 11 ounces) condensed Cheddar cheese soup
2 cans (16 ounces each) petite peas
2 tablespoons butter
1 cup soft bread crumbs Paprika

1. Drain asparagus spears and arrange half the spears in a buttered 2-quart glass baking dish.
2. Turn soup into a bowl. Drain peas and mix with soup. Spoon half the mixture into baking dish. Add remaining asparagus spears and spoon remaining soup mixture over all.
3. Melt butter in a small glass bowl in microwave oven (about 15 seconds at HIGH). Add bread crumbs and toss until well mixed. Sprinkle crumbs over top of casserole mixture. Sprinkle with paprika. Cover with waxed paper. Cook in microwave oven 12 to 14 minutes at BAKE, or until thoroughly heated; rotate dish one-half turn once.

6 servings

ASPARAGUS AND CHEESE

1 package (10 ounces) frozen asparagus spears or 1½ pounds fresh asparagus
2 tablespoons butter
4 mushroom caps
¼ cup flour
1 teaspoon salt
1 cup milk
⅛ teaspoon dry mustard
2 tablespoons sherry
½ cup toasted slivered almonds
¼ cup shredded sharp Cheddar cheese

1. Cook asparagus following directions in Frozen or Fresh Vegetable Cooking Chart. Drain and keep warm.
2. Put butter and mushroom caps into a 1-quart glass casserole. Cook uncovered in microwave oven 3 minutes at HIGH; stir after 1 minute.
3. Remove mushrooms and set aside. Stir flour and salt into butter in casserole. Cook uncovered in microwave oven 1½ minutes at HIGH.
4. Add milk gradually, stirring until smooth. Cook uncovered in microwave oven 2 minutes at HIGH, or until thickened; stir frequently.
5. Add mustard and sherry to sauce; mix well.
6. Place cooked asparagus in a 9-inch glass pie plate. Cover with almonds and top with mushroom caps. Pour sauce over all and sprinkle with cheese. Heat uncovered in microwave oven 1 minute at HIGH.

4 servings

GREEN BEAN AND CHEESE CASSEROLE

2 packages (9 ounces each) frozen cut green beans
1 can (about 10 ounces) condensed cream of mushroom soup
1 can (5 ounces) water chestnuts, drained and sliced
½ cup shredded Cheddar cheese
1 can (3½ ounces) french fried onion rings

1. Put beans into a 2-quart glass casserole. Cover with an all-glass lid or plastic wrap. Cook in microwave oven 9 minutes at HIGH, or until beans are tender; stir once. Drain.
2. Add mushroom soup, water chestnuts and cheese to beans; mix. Cover with an all-glass lid or plastic wrap. Cook in microwave oven 5½ to 6½ minutes at ROAST. Stir. Top with onion rings. Heat uncovered 1½ minutes at ROAST, or until bean mixture is hot.

About 6 servings

GREEN BEAN AND BACON CASSEROLE

1 package (9 ounces) frozen cut green beans
4 slices bacon, cut into small pieces
2 slices bread, cut in ½-inch cubes
⅓ cup condensed cream of mushroom soup

1. Cook green beans following directions in Frozen Vegetable Cooking Chart. Drain.
2. Put bacon into a shallow glass baking dish. Cover with a paper towel. Cook in microwave oven <u>about 2½ minutes at HIGH</u>, or until browned.
3. Remove bacon from dish. Add bread cubes to bacon fat in dish; mix well. Cook uncovered in microwave oven <u>2 minutes at HIGH</u>; stir occasionally.
4. Mix bacon with the beans in casserole, spoon undiluted soup over beans and top with the bread cubes. Cover with waxed paper. Heat thoroughly in microwave oven (<u>3 to 4 minutes at HIGH</u>).

4 servings

OLD-FASHIONED BAKED BEANS

1 pound dried navy beans
1½ quarts water
½ pound salt pork, rinsed
½ cup chopped celery
½ cup chopped onion
1 cup ketchup
½ cup molasses
3 tablespoons brown sugar
1 teaspoon dry mustard
½ teaspoon pepper
¼ teaspoon ginger

1. Put dried beans and water into a 3-quart glass casserole. Cover and soak overnight.
2. Cut salt pork into ¼-inch slices, then cut into pieces. Spread on a roast rack set in a 2-quart glass baking dish. Cover with a paper towel. Cook in microwave oven <u>5 minutes at HIGH</u>. Reserve 1 teaspoon drippings and the salt pork.
3. Combine reserved drippings, celery and onion in a 2-cup glass measuring cup. Cook uncovered in microwave oven <u>2 minutes at HIGH</u>.
4. Add the vegetables to beans; stir. Cover with an all-glass lid or plastic wrap. Cook in microwave oven <u>15 minutes at HIGH</u>. Stir. Cook covered <u>30 minutes at SIMMER</u>; stir after 15 minutes.
5. Drain beans, reserving 1 cup liquid. Combine remaining ingredients, reserved salt pork and reserved bean liquid. Add to beans; mix well. Cook covered in microwave oven <u>45 minutes at SIMMER</u>, or until beans are tender and sauce has thickened; stir every 15 minutes.

8 to 10 servings

BAKED BEANS

4 slices bacon, chopped
1 can (14 to 17 ounces) pork and beans with tomato sauce
½ teaspoon dry mustard
1 small onion, finely chopped
¼ cup ketchup
2 tablespoons brown sugar

1. Put bacon into a glass baking dish. Cover with a paper towel. Cook in microwave oven <u>3 minutes at HIGH</u>.
2. Combine beans, mustard, onion, ketchup and brown sugar in a 1-quart glass casserole. Cover with an all-glass lid or plastic wrap. Cook in microwave oven <u>8 minutes at HIGH</u>; stir occasionally.
3. Top with cooked bacon. Cook covered in microwave oven <u>2 minutes at HIGH</u>.

4 servings

HARVARD BEETS

⅓ cup sugar
1 tablespoon cornstarch
¼ teaspoon salt
¼ cup cider vinegar
1 can or jar (16 ounces) diced or crinkle-cut style beets, drained; reserve ¼ cup liquid
1 tablespoon butter

1. Combine sugar, cornstarch and salt in a 1-quart glass casserole. Stir in vinegar and reserved liquid, then beets. Cover with an all-glass lid or waxed paper. Cook in microwave oven 6 to 7 minutes at HIGH, or until mixture boils and thickens slightly; stir occasionally.
2. Add butter to beets and stir until melted.

6 servings

BROCCOLI CASSEROLE

1 small bunch broccoli, trimmed and coarsely chopped
¼ cup (½ stick) butter or margarine
1 medium onion, chopped
2 tablespoons flour
½ cup milk
1 jar (8 ounces) pasteurized process cheese spread
3 eggs, slightly beaten
¼ teaspoon salt
¼ teaspoon nutmeg
⅛ teaspoon pepper
¾ cup finely crushed herbed croutons

1. Cook broccoli following directions in Fresh Vegetable Cooking Chart. Drain thoroughly.
2. Put butter and onion into a 2-quart glass casserole. Cook uncovered in microwave oven 2 to 3 minutes at HIGH, or until onion is tender; stir after 1 minute.
3. Stir flour into butter mixture. Cook uncovered in microwave oven 2 minutes at BAKE.
4. Add milk gradually to flour mixture, stirring constantly. Cook uncovered in microwave oven 1 minute at HIGH, or until thickened.
5. Add cheese to sauce and stir until well blended. Mix in the drained cooked broccoli, eggs, salt, nutmeg and pepper. Cook uncovered in microwave oven 6 minutes at HIGH; stir after 3 minutes.
6. Stir mixture. Sprinkle crushed croutons over top. Cook uncovered in microwave oven 3 to 4 minutes at HIGH, or until casserole mixture is set in center.

6 servings

SWEET-SOUR RED CABBAGE

1 head red cabbage, coarsely shredded
½ teaspoon salt
3 tablespoons water
6 tablespoons white vinegar
3 tablespoons sugar

1. Combine cabbage, salt and water in a 3-quart glass casserole. Cover with an all-glass lid or plastic wrap. Cook in microwave oven 10 to 12 minutes at HIGH, or until crisp-tender; stir once.
2. Add a mixture of vinegar and sugar to crisp-tender cabbage; mix well. Cook covered in microwave oven 1 to 2 minutes at HIGH, or until tender.

About 8 servings

GLAZED CARROTS AND PINEAPPLE

1 **pound carrots, pared and cut in julienne strips**
1 **can (20 ounces) unsweetened pineapple chunks, drained; reserve ¼ cup juice**
¼ **cup firmly packed dark brown sugar**
¼ **teaspoon salt**
2 **tablespoons cold water**
1½ **teaspoons cornstarch**

1. Put carrot strips into a 2-quart glass baking dish. Mix reserved pineapple juice, brown sugar and salt. Pour over carrots. Cover with plastic wrap. Cook in microwave oven 5 minutes at HIGH.
2. Add pineapple to carrots; mix well. Cook covered in microwave oven 10 to 15 minutes at HIGH, or until carrots are tender; stir several times.
3. Mix cold water and cornstarch until smooth. Stir into carrot mixture. Cook uncovered in microwave oven 3 minutes at HIGH, or until thickened; stir once.

6 servings

BUTTERED SLICED CAULIFLOWER

1 **small head (about 1 pound) cauliflower**
2 **tablespoons sesame seed**
2 **tablespoons butter or margarine**
⅓ **cup sliced green onion**
½ **cup water**
¼ **cup snipped parsley**
½ **teaspoon salt**
⅛ **teaspoon pepper**
Lemon juice (optional)

1. Trim cauliflower and break into flowerets. Cut flowerets lengthwise into ¼-inch slices. Set aside.
2. Spread sesame seed in a 1½-quart glass baking dish. Heat uncovered in microwave oven 3 to 4 minutes at HIGH; stir once. Set sesame seed aside.
3. Put butter, sliced cauliflower, green onion and water into the glass baking dish. Cover with plastic wrap. Cook in microwave oven 4 to 5 minutes at HIGH, or until cauliflower is crisp-tender; stir after 1 minute.
4. Add parsley, salt, pepper and sesame seed to cauliflower; mix well. Heat uncovered in microwave oven 1 minute at HIGH.
5. If desired, drizzle lemon juice over top before serving.

About 6 servings

CREAMED CAULIFLOWER

1½ **pounds fresh cauliflower**
½ **cup (1 stick) butter**
½ **cup all-purpose flour**
1 **teaspoon salt**
1¾ **cups milk**
Paprika

1. Clean cauliflower and cut into flowerets. Cook following directions in Fresh Vegetable Cooking Chart; omit salt. Allow to stand covered while preparing sauce.
2. Melt butter in a 1-quart glass casserole in microwave oven (1 minute at HIGH). Add flour and salt and blend well. Gradually add milk, stirring constantly. Cook uncovered 4 minutes at HIGH, or until sauce bubbles and thickens; stir after the first 2 minutes, then at end of each 30 seconds.
3. Add sauce to cauliflower. Sprinkle lightly with paprika.

About 6 servings

Corn, Sweet Potatoes and Asparagus (see Fresh Vegetable Cooking Chart, 184)

CELERY AND ALMONDS AU GRATIN

4 cups 1-inch celery pieces
2 tablespoons chicken broth
½ cup coarsely chopped blanched almonds
3 tablespoons butter
3 tablespoons flour
¼ teaspoon salt
Few grains pepper
1¼ cups chicken broth
½ cup cream or half-and-half
1½ cups shredded sharp Cheddar cheese
2 tablespoons butter
½ cup dry bread crumbs

1. Put celery and 2 tablespoons chicken broth into a 2-quart glass casserole. Cover with an all-glass lid or plastic wrap. Cook in microwave oven 7 to 8 minutes at HIGH; stir twice. Drain celery. Stir in almonds, leave uncovered and set aside.
2. Melt 3 tablespoons butter in a 1-quart glass measuring cup in microwave oven (45 seconds at HIGH). Add flour, salt and pepper; mix well. Gradually add broth and cream, stirring constantly. Cook uncovered 4 minutes at HIGH, or until thickened; stir after 2 minutes, then at end of each 30 seconds.
3. Add ½ cup cheese to sauce and stir until melted. Pour over celery and almonds in casserole. Sprinkle with remaining cheese.
4. Melt remaining butter in a small glass dish in microwave oven (15 seconds at HIGH). Combine melted butter and bread crumbs; sprinkle over cheese. Cover with waxed paper. Cook 1 to 2 minutes at HIGH, or until cheese is melted.

About 6 servings

CORN ON THE COB

For real freshlike flavor, cook corn on the cob in the husk.

4 ears corn (in husks)
Butter
Salt

1. Leave husks on the corn. Remove silk either before or after cooking.
2. Place corn in a circle on the microwave oven cooking tray. Cook in microwave oven 8 to 10 minutes at HIGH; rearrange and turn ears over once.
3. Butter and salt before serving.

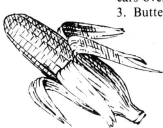

SCALLOPED CORN

1 can (16 ounces) whole kernel corn, drained
½ cup chopped onion
1½ tablespoons chopped green pepper
½ cup soda cracker crumbs
1 teaspoon salt
Dash pepper
½ cup milk
1 egg

1. Combine all ingredients thoroughly and turn into a greased 1½-quart glass casserole. Cover with an all-glass lid or plastic wrap.
2. Cook in microwave oven 6 to 8 minutes at HIGH; stir occasionally.

4 to 6 servings

CORN RELISH

1 **can (17 ounces) whole
kernel corn, drained;
reserve ¼ cup liquid**
¼ **cup vinegar**
1 **cup sweet pickle relish**
¼ **cup minced onion**
2 **canned pimentos, diced**
¼ **cup sugar**
2 **teaspoons celery seed**
½ **teaspoon salt**

1. Combine all ingredients in a 2-quart glass casserole. Cover with waxed paper. Cook in microwave oven 10 minutes at HIGH; stir after 5 minutes.
2. Allow to stand covered 5 minutes before serving.

About 6 servings

BRAISED CUCUMBER STICKS

2 **medium cucumbers**
2 **tablespoons butter**
1 **teaspoon instant chicken
bouillon**
2 **tablespoons boiling water
Salt and pepper to taste**

1. Wash cucumbers, score peel with a fork and cut off ends. Cut cucumbers in half crosswise, then cut into narrow sticks.
2. Melt butter in a 1½-quart glass baking dish in microwave oven (about 15 seconds at HIGH).
3. Dissolve instant bouillon in water. Add to melted butter and mix well. Add cucumber sticks and turn to coat with butter mixture. Cover with plastic wrap.
4. Cook in microwave oven 6 to 7 minutes at HIGH, or until cucumber is crisp-tender. Season with salt and pepper to taste. Garnish with **snipped parsley**.

6 servings

EGGPLANT PARMESAN

1 **eggplant (1 pound)**
2 **eggs, beaten**
¼ **cup undiluted evaporated
milk**
⅔ **cup fine dry bread
crumbs**

Tomato Sauce:
2 **tablespoons finely
chopped onion**
1 **small clove garlic, minced**
1 **tablespoon olive oil**
3 **cups chopped fresh
tomatoes**
½ **teaspoon salt**
⅛ **teaspoon pepper**

1 **cup grated Parmesan
cheese**
6 **slices Mozzarella cheese**

1. Remove peel from eggplant; cut into ½-inch slices. Coat with a mixture of egg and evaporated milk, then coat with crumbs.
2. For sauce, mix onion, garlic and olive oil in a 1-quart glass measuring cup. Cook uncovered in microwave oven 3 minutes at HIGH; stir once. Add tomatoes, salt and pepper; stir. Cook uncovered in microwave oven 15 minutes at HIGH; stir once.
3. Layer eggplant slices, Parmesan cheese and one half of sauce in a 2-quart glass casserole. Cover with remaining sauce. Cover with waxed paper.
4. Cook in microwave oven 8 to 12 minutes at HIGH, or until eggplant is fork-tender; rotate dish one-half turn once.
5. Top eggplant mixture with cheese slices. Heat uncovered in microwave oven 45 seconds at HIGH, or until cheese melts.

6 servings

HOMINY AND TOMATOES

1 cup shredded sharp
  Cheddar cheese
1 can (15 ounces) whole
  hominy, drained
1 can (16 ounces) tomatoes,
  drained and cut in pieces
¼ cup chopped onion
1 teaspoon chili powder
½ teaspoon salt

1. Reserve ½ cup shredded cheese for topping. Combine remaining ingredients in a 1-quart glass casserole. Cook uncovered in microwave oven 6 minutes at HIGH; stir twice.
2. Sprinkle remaining cheese on top. Cover with plastic wrap. Cook in microwave oven 1 to 1½ minutes at ROAST, or until cheese is melted.

About 6 servings

WILTED LETTUCE

1 large head leaf lettuce
6 slices bacon
½ cup cider vinegar
¼ cup water
3 tablespoons sugar
½ teaspoon salt

1. Wash lettuce, drain and pat dry. Tear lettuce into large pieces; put into a bowl and set aside.
2. Arrange bacon on a roast rack set in a 2-quart glass baking dish. Cover with a paper towel. Cook in microwave oven 6 to 7 minutes at HIGH, or until crisp. Reserve ¼ cup bacon drippings. Crumble bacon and add to lettuce.
3. Combine bacon drippings and remaining ingredients in a 1-quart glass measuring cup. Cook uncovered in microwave oven 3 to 5 minutes at HIGH, or until mixture boils. Pour over lettuce and bacon; toss lightly. Serve immediately.

About 6 servings

BAKED STUFFED POTATOES

4 medium potatoes,
  scrubbed
1 tablespoon butter
¼ cup chopped onion
½ to ¾ cup milk
2 tablespoons butter
  Salt and pepper to taste
½ cup shredded pasteurized
  process Cheddar cheese

1. Bake potatoes following directions in Fresh Vegetable Cooking Chart. Remove potatoes from oven and allow to stand 5 minutes.
2. Meanwhile, put 1 tablespoon butter and onion into a glass dish. Cook uncovered in microwave oven 4 to 5 minutes at HIGH, or until tender; stir occasionally.
3. Cut a thin slice from top of each potato. Scoop potato from shells, being careful to keep shells intact. Mash or rice potato thoroughly.
4. Heat milk in glass measuring cup in microwave oven about 30 seconds at HIGH.
5. Add milk, 2 tablespoons butter, salt, pepper and onion to potato. Whip until fluffy. Spoon into potato shells. Top with cheese. Arrange on a microwave-safe serving plate. Heat uncovered in microwave oven 2 to 3 minutes at HIGH, or until cheese is melted.

4 servings

HINT: Potatoes may be prepared in advance and reheated just before serving. Heat uncovered in microwave oven 3 to 4 minutes at HIGH, or until hot.

SAUTÉED MUSHROOMS

8 ounces mushrooms,
cleaned and sliced
1 tablespoon butter

1. Put mushrooms and butter into a 1-quart glass casserole. Cover with an all-glass lid or plastic wrap.
2. Cook in microwave oven 3 to 4 minutes at HIGH, or until tender; stir after 1 minute.

SAUTÉED ONIONS

1 medium onion, sliced
1 tablespoon butter

1. Put onion slices and butter into a 1-quart glass casserole. Cover with an all-glass lid or plastic wrap.
2. Cook in microwave oven 4 to 6 minutes at HIGH, or until tender; stir after 1 minute.

TIFFANY CHIPS

2 medium Idaho potatoes
Corn flake or wheat flake
crumbs (about 1 cup)
3 tablespoons grated
Parmesan cheese
1 tablespoon sesame seed
½ cup (1 stick) butter

1. Scrub but do not pare potatoes. Cut in half lengthwise, then cut each half lengthwise into 4 or 5 wedges.
2. Combine half of crumbs with cheese and half with sesame seed.
3. Melt butter in a shallow glass dish in microwave oven (45 seconds at HIGH).
4. Dip potato wedges in melted butter and generously coat half with each crumb mixture. Arrange in a shallow glass baking dish. Cover with waxed paper. Cook in microwave oven 6 to 7 minutes at HIGH, or until potato is tender.

About 4 servings

SCALLOPED POTATOES

3 tablespoons butter or
margarine
3 tablespoons flour
1 teaspoon salt
¼ teaspoon pepper
2½ cups milk
6 medium potatoes
(about 2 pounds)
2 tablespoons chopped
onion (optional)
Paprika

1. Melt butter in a 1-quart glass casserole in microwave oven (about 30 seconds at HIGH). Add flour, salt and pepper; mix well. Add milk gradually, stirring constantly. Cook uncovered in microwave oven 3 to 4 minutes at HIGH, or until thickened; stir after the first 2 minutes, then after each 30 seconds.
2. Pare potatoes and thinly slice them. Put half the potatoes into a greased 2-quart glass casserole. Cover with half the onion (if used) and half the sauce. Repeat layers. Cover with an all-glass lid or plastic wrap. Cook in microwave oven 15 to 17 minutes at HIGH, or until potatoes are tender; stir every 5 minutes.
3. Remove from oven and sprinkle with paprika.

About 8 servings

Au Gratin Potatoes: Follow recipe for Scalloped Potatoes and add **1 cup shredded Cheddar cheese** (¾ cup for layering and ¼ cup for top).

MASHED POTATOES

6 **medium potatoes**
 (about 2 pounds), pared
 Milk (⅓ to ½ cup)
3 **to 4 tablespoons butter**
 Salt and pepper to taste

1. Cook potatoes following directions in Fresh Vegetable Cooking Chart. Drain.
2. Heat milk in a 1-cup glass measuring cup in microwave oven (15 to 30 seconds at HIGH).
3. Mash or rice potatoes thoroughly. Whip in hot milk, butter, salt and pepper until fluffy.

About 8 servings

HINT: Mashed potatoes may be prepared in advance and reheated in microwave oven. Heat 3 minutes at HIGH; stir once.

GERMAN POTATO SALAD

4 **medium potatoes**
6 **slices bacon**
½ **cup finely diced celery**
½ **cup finely diced onion**
½ **teaspoon salt**
¼ **teaspoon hickory salt**
½ **cup white vinegar**
2½ **tablespoons sugar**

1. Cook potatoes following directions in Fresh Vegetable Cooking Chart. Cool slightly, peel and thinly slice. Set aside.
2. Arrange bacon on a roast rack set in a 2-quart glass baking dish. Cover with a paper towel. Cook in microwave oven 4 to 6 minutes at HIGH, or until crisp. Reserve 2 tablespoons drippings. Crumble bacon and set aside.
3. Alternate layers of potatoes, celery and onion in a 2-quart glass casserole, sprinkling each layer with salt or hickory salt.
4. Mix vinegar and sugar. Pour over potatoes; mix carefully. Sprinkle crumbled bacon over top and drizzle with reserved bacon drippings; mix carefully.
5. Heat uncovered in microwave oven to serving temperature (5 minutes at HIGH); mix carefully once.

4 to 6 servings

SPICED SPINACH

1 **pound fresh spinach**
¼ **cup (½ stick) butter**
½ **to 1 teaspoon ground**
 coriander
½ **teaspoon salt**
⅛ **teaspoon seasoned pepper**
1 **clove garlic, minced**
1 **teaspoon lemon juice**
1 **hard-cooked egg, peeled**
 and chopped

1. Wash and drain spinach. Cook following directions in Fresh Vegetable Cooking Chart. Drain.
2. Melt butter in a small glass bowl in microwave oven (30 seconds at HIGH).
3. Mix remaining ingredients, except egg, into melted butter.
4. Pour butter mixture over drained spinach and toss lightly. Sprinkle with chopped egg. (Cook egg on top of conventional range.)

4 servings

Stuffed Tomatoes, 202; Spiced Spinach

BAKED ACORN SQUASH

   1 acorn squash
1½ tablespoons butter
1½ teaspoons brown sugar
 ¼ teaspoon salt
 ⅛ teaspoon ginger

1. Cook squash following directions in Fresh Vegetable Cooking Chart.
2. Cut squash in half. Scoop out seedy center. Divide butter, brown sugar, salt and ginger in squash cavities. Cover with plastic wrap.
3. Cook in microwave oven 2 minutes at HIGH. Allow to stand 5 minutes before serving.

2 servings

SWEET-SOUR SPINACH

   1 pound fresh spinach, washed and chopped
   2 slices bacon, cut into small pieces
   1 teaspoon flour
   1 teaspoon sugar
 ¼ cup cream or half-and-half
   1 tablespoon vinegar

1. Cook spinach following directions in Fresh Vegetable Cooking Chart. Drain.
2. Put bacon into a 1½-quart glass casserole. Cover with a paper towel. Cook in microwave oven about 1½ minutes at HIGH, or until bacon is crisp.
3. Pour off all but 1 tablespoon fat. Add flour to fat and blend. Stir in sugar and cream. Cook uncovered in microwave oven 1½ minutes at HIGH, or until thickened; stir once.
4. Add vinegar to mixture in casserole; stir. Add chopped spinach and mix well. Cover with waxed paper. Cook in microwave oven 2 minutes at HIGH, or until spinach is heated.

4 servings

MEAT-STUFFED ACORN SQUASH

2 medium acorn squash
1 pound ground beef
¼ cup chopped onion
1 tablespoon butter
1 teaspoon salt
¼ cup packed brown sugar
⅛ teaspoon nutmeg
8 teaspoons butter
Salt and pepper to taste
Nutmeg (optional)

1. Cook squash following directions in Fresh Vegetable Cooking Chart. Cut squash in half; scoop out seeds. Cover with plastic wrap.
2. Put ground beef into a 1-quart glass casserole. Cover with waxed paper. Cook in microwave oven 4 minutes at HIGH, or until meat is no longer pink; stir occasionally. Drain and set aside.
3. Cook onion and butter in a 1-cup glass measuring cup in microwave oven (2 minutes at HIGH). Add to ground beef along with salt, brown sugar and nutmeg.
4. Scoop out some of the cooked squash from each half, leaving a ¼-inch rim; add to beef mixture and mix with a fork. Set squash halves on a microwave-safe platter.
5. Put 1 teaspoon butter into each squash half and sprinkle with salt and pepper. Spoon one quarter of meat-and-squash mixture into each squash shell. Top with 1 teaspoon butter and sprinkle with nutmeg, if desired. Cover with plastic wrap. Cook in microwave oven 2 minutes at HIGH.
6. Allow to stand covered 5 minutes.

4 servings

DILLY SQUASH

2 tablespoons butter
1 pound yellow summer squash (2 small), sliced
1 tablespoon dried parsley flakes
¼ teaspoon dried dill weed
¼ teaspoon salt
Dash onion powder

1. Melt butter in a 1½-quart glass casserole in microwave oven (30 seconds at HIGH). Add remaining ingredients; stir well. Cover with an all-glass lid or plastic wrap.
2. Cook in microwave oven 4 to 5 minutes at HIGH, or until tender; stir after 2 minutes. Allow to stand 2 minutes before serving.

4 servings

ZUCCHINI BOATS

6 medium zucchini, 6 to 7 inches in length, washed and ends removed
1 medium tomato, cut in small pieces
¼ cup chopped salted almonds
1 tablespoon chopped parsley
1 teaspoon finely chopped onion
½ teaspoon seasoned salt
2 tablespoons butter
¼ cup cracker crumbs

1. Cook zucchini following directions in Fresh Vegetable Cooking Chart. Let cool until easy to handle.
2. Remove top third of each zucchini and chop coarsely. Scoop out and discard centers. Set zucchini aside in a 2-quart glass baking dish or on a microwave-safe serving platter. Put chopped zucchini and tomato into a bowl. Add almonds, parsley, onion and seasoned salt; mix well.
3. Melt butter in a small glass dish in microwave oven (about 15 seconds at HIGH). Brush zucchini with half of melted butter. Spoon filling into zucchini shells. Mix remaining melted butter and cracker crumbs. Sprinkle over filling.
4. Heat uncovered in microwave oven to serving temperature (2 to 3 minutes at HIGH).

6 servings

ZUCCHINI PROVENÇALE

2 cans (6 ounces each)
  tomato paste
3 ounces (½ can) water
1 clove garlic, minced
1 teaspoon salt
⅛ teaspoon pepper
8 to 10 small zucchini,
  sliced
⅔ cup coarsely chopped
  onion
½ pound fresh mushrooms,
  cleaned and sliced
  lengthwise
3 tablespoons olive oil
⅔ cup grated Parmesan
  cheese

1. Combine tomato paste, water, garlic, salt and pepper in a bowl; set aside.
2. Combine zucchini, onion, mushrooms and oil in a 2-quart glass casserole. Cover with an all-glass lid or plastic wrap. Cook in microwave oven 6 to 7 minutes at HIGH, or until zucchini is just tender; stir twice.
3. Stir half of cheese into zucchini mixture. Pour tomato mixture over zucchini and top with remaining cheese. Cook covered in microwave oven 3 minutes at BAKE.

About 8 servings

CANDIED SWEET POTATOES

4 medium sweet potatoes
¼ cup (½ stick) butter
½ cup firmly packed brown
  sugar
1½ teaspoons lemon juice

1. Cook sweet potatoes following directions in Fresh Vegetable Cooking Chart. Peel cooked potatoes and cut into 1-inch slices.
2. Melt butter and brown sugar in a 1½-quart glass casserole in microwave oven (about 45 seconds at HIGH). Stir in lemon juice.
3. Add potatoes to sugar mixture and toss lightly to coat.
4. Cover with an all-glass lid or waxed paper. Heat in microwave oven 6 minutes at HIGH; stir occasionally.

6 servings

STUFFED TOMATOES

4 firm ripe tomatoes
2 tablespoons butter or
  margarine
2 tablespoons finely
  chopped green onion
1 cup soft bread crumbs
⅛ teaspoon poultry
  seasoning, or pinch sage
½ teaspoon salt
½ teaspoon sugar
  Few grains pepper
  Paprika

1. Wash tomatoes and cut.out stems; scoop out and reserve a small amount of pulp.
2. Put butter and onion into a 1-quart glass casserole. Cook uncovered in microwave oven 3 to 4 minutes at HIGH, or until tender; stir after 1 minute.
3. Add bread crumbs, poultry seasoning, salt, sugar, pepper and tomato pulp to cooked onion; toss lightly. Fill tomatoes with stuffing and put into an 8-inch round glass cake dish. Sprinkle with paprika. Cover with waxed paper.
4. Cook in microwave oven 3 to 4 minutes at HIGH, or until tomatoes are tender.

4 servings

STEWED TOMATOES

2 **large tomatoes**
2 **tablespoons sugar**
½ **teaspoon seasoned salt**
 Dash pepper
1 **tablespoon butter**
1 **tablespoon cornstarch**
¼ **cup water**
¼ **cup snipped parsley**

1. Peel and quarter tomatoes. Put into a 1-quart glass casserole. Add sugar, seasoned salt, pepper and butter. Cover with all-glass lid or plastic wrap. Cook in microwave oven 5 minutes at HIGH, or until tender; stir halfway through cooking time.
2. Blend cornstarch and water. Gradually add to the cooked tomatoes; stirring constantly. Cook covered in microwave oven 1 minute at HIGH.
3. Stir parsley into tomatoes before serving.

4 servings

TOMATO CASSEROLE

3 **tablespoons butter**
2 **tablespoons chopped green pepper**
2 **tablespoons chopped onion**
1 **can (16 ounces) tomatoes (undrained)**
1 **tablespoon flour**
1 **teaspoon sugar**
½ **teaspoon salt**
1 **cup seasoned croutons**

1. Put butter, green pepper and onion into a 1-quart glass casserole. Cook uncovered in microwave oven 3 to 4 minutes at HIGH, or until tender; stir after 1 minute.
2. Add tomatoes and liquid to casserole; mix well. Cover with an all-glass lid or plastic wrap. Bring to boiling in microwave oven (2½ to 3½ minutes at HIGH); stir occasionally.
3. Add flour, sugar and salt to tomatoes; mix. Cook uncovered in microwave oven 2 to 3 minutes at HIGH; stir several times.
4. Top with croutons.

4 servings

RATATOUILLE

1 **cup sliced onion**
2 **tablespoons butter**
1 **medium eggplant, pared and cut in ½-inch pieces (about 2 cups cubes)**
2 **medium zucchini, cut lengthwise, then in ¼-inch pieces**
1 **medium green pepper, cut in strips**
½ **teaspoon salt**
½ **teaspoon marjoram**
¼ **teaspoon oregano**
¼ **teaspoon garlic salt**
⅛ **teaspoon pepper**
2 **large tomatoes, peeled and cut in wedges**

1. Put onion and butter into a 2-quart glass casserole. Cook uncovered in microwave oven 1½ minutes at HIGH; stir after 1 minute.
2. Add eggplant, zucchini and green pepper to onion butter. Cover with an all-glass lid or plastic wrap. Cook in microwave oven 3 minutes at HIGH.
3. Add seasonings to vegetables and stir well. Cook covered in microwave oven 2 minutes at HIGH.
4. Add tomatoes and mix well. Cook covered in microwave oven 5 to 6 minutes at HIGH, or until vegetables are tender.

6 to 8 servings

HINT: To remove peel from tomatoes, cook tomatoes uncovered in microwave oven 30 to 45 seconds at HIGH. Allow to stand 2 minutes, then peel.

Index